MW01406036

PREP IT
FREEZE IT
COOK IT!

ABEYGALE BURNE

PREP IT FREEZE IT COOK IT!
THE GRAB BAG SLOW COOKER BOOK

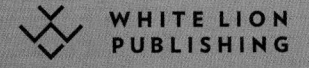

WHITE LION PUBLISHING

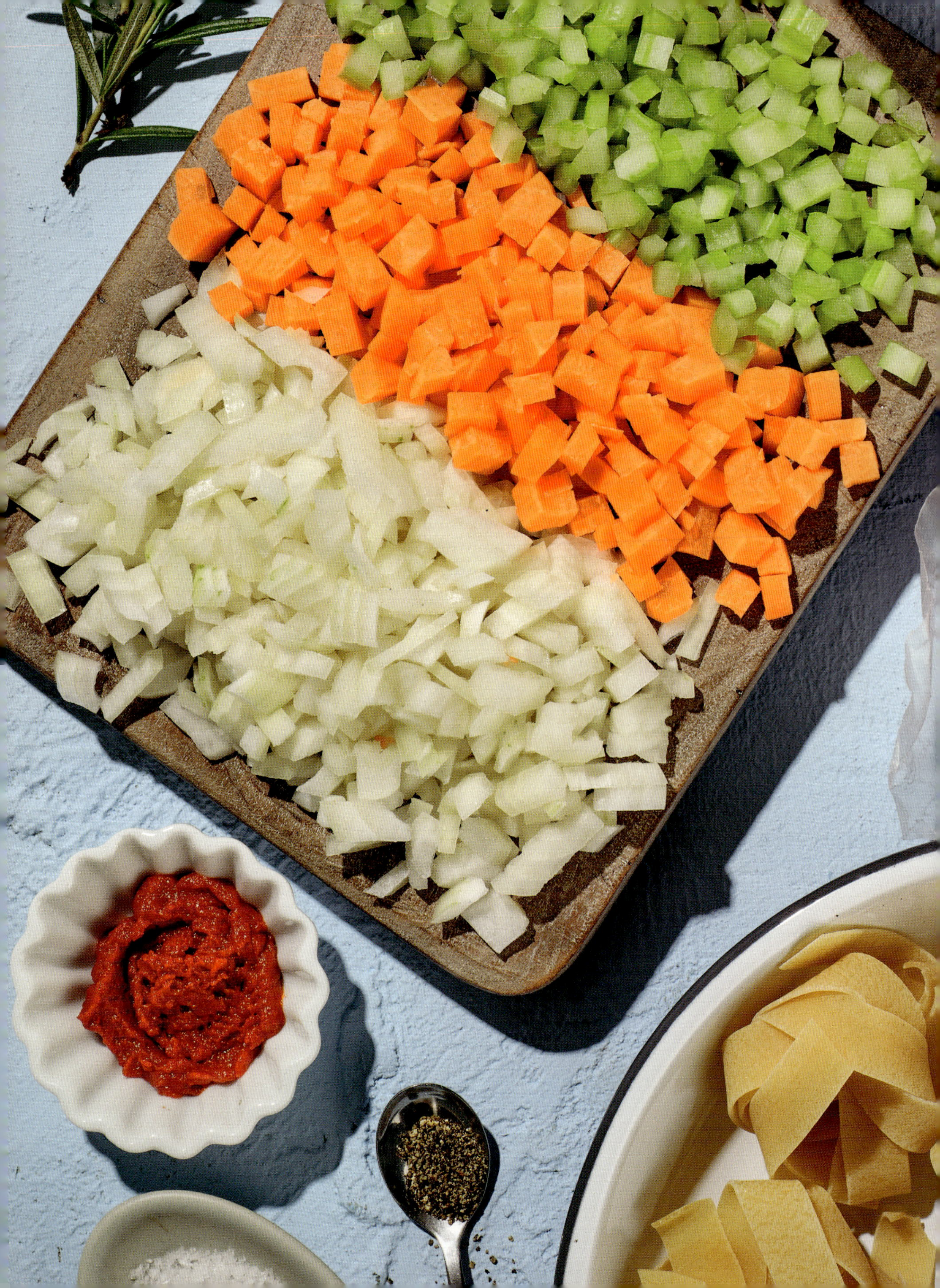

CONTENTS

Introduction 6

Family Classics 26
Winter Warmers 64
Comforting Curries 96
Hearty Soups 128
Vegetarian & Vegan 156
Something Sweet 182

Index 196
Supplier Information 202
About the Author 204
Thank You & Acknowledgements 206

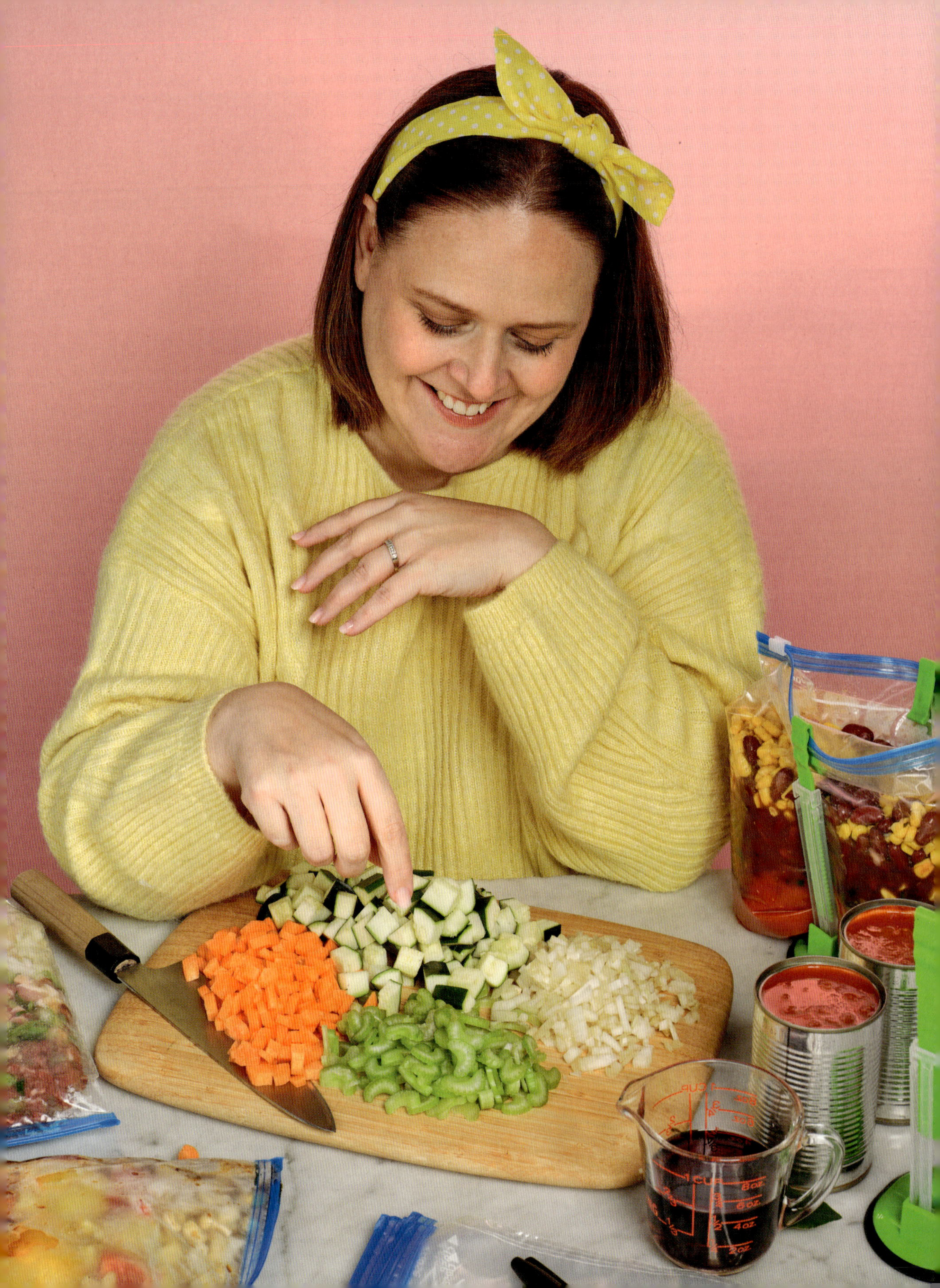

Introduction

Time is such a precious commodity. We spend our lives rushing from one thing to another, whether it be the school run, work, taking the kids to clubs, rushing to appointments or meetings... the list goes on. Finding handy shortcuts can be life changing.

Using the slow cooker is a fantastic way to save time, but preparing the ingredients in the morning isn't always possible. Using a slow cooker grab bag will not only save the prep time but the cooking time too. Setting the slow cooker before you start your day and coming home to the amazing aroma filling the house – and just digging in – is a feeling like no other.

You can also use the grab bags as a way to budget and save money. If I see meat on offer or reduced in the supermarket, I'll pick it up and straight away it gets made into a grab bag and frozen. Using up fresh ingredients by adding them to bags means you'll have less waste in your fridge at the end of the week from things you haven't got around to using, or had an plan for but ended up getting a takeaway that night instead. By spending a couple of hours prepping the bags, you'll have zero waste.

Putting together these recipes for you has been such a joy. I have rediscovered recipes from when the kids were small, and created new ones that I know will soon become family favourites. I hope these dishes become part of your family life, too, and that you enjoy the time saved on what matters to you.

How to Use This Book

The grab bag concept has been around for a long time; it is also known by a few other names such as dump bags or Go! cooking bags.

The idea is simple: you prepare your ingredients, place them into a freezer bag and pop them into the freezer. When you're ready to cook, just grab a bag, defrost it the day before, then empty the contents into a slow cooker, and you're all set!

By preparing meals this way, you can quickly build up a stock of grab bags in your freezer for busy days when you don't have time to cook, for workdays when you need a hassle-free dinner, or simply to have on hand because the recipes are so delicious.

All the recipes in this book can of course be made fresh and cooked straight away in the slow cooker, but the beauty of the grab bag system is having a supply ready to go when you need it, with the prep already done.

Each bag takes just a few minutes to prepare. You can make multiple bags of the same dish or mix and match recipes from this book to batch-prepare several meals at once. I like to set aside some time on Sundays to restock the freezer for the week ahead.

You'll find this book has been divided into six sections, family classics, winter warmers, comforting curries, hearty soups, vegetarian/vegan and something sweet.

Each recipe has 'at a glance' symbols along the bottom of the page, these show you: how long you can freeze the dish for, how long it takes to defrost, how long to cook (on low or high) and how many people the recipe serves. The cooking time represents the initial cooking time, some recipes will require further cooking.

HOW LONG YOU CAN FREEZE THE DISH FOR

HOW LONG IT TAKES TO DEFROST

HOW LONG TO COOK (ON LOW OR HIGH)

HOW MANY PEOPLE THE RECIPE SERVES

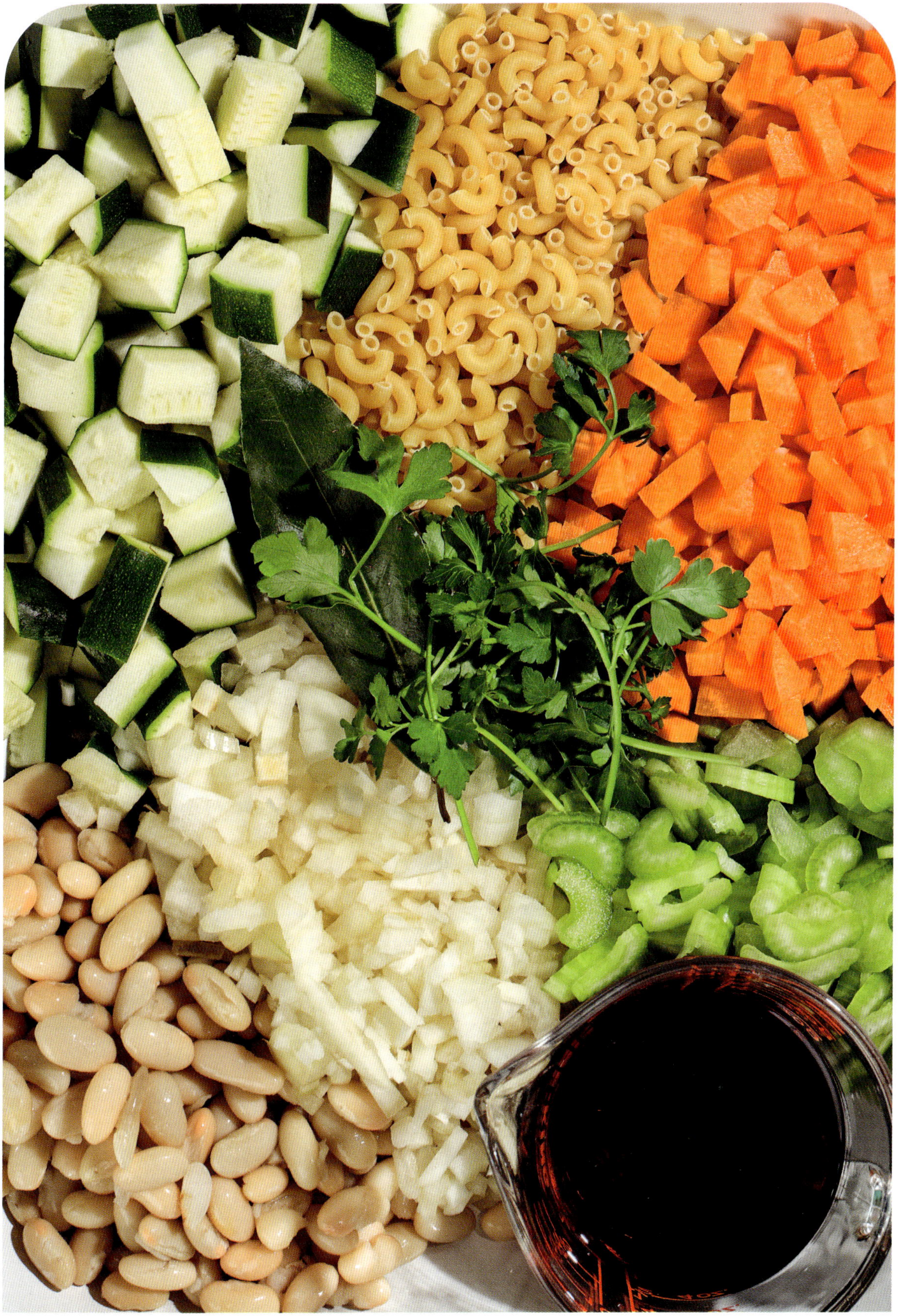

Equipment

One of the reasons why slow cooker grab bags are so great is that you don't need any fancy equipment to prepare them – just a few basics that can be easily picked up at the supermarket and you'll be good to go. Here are some staples that I use to make my life easier.

Slow cooker
For the recipes in this book, I used a 6.5 litre (about 7 quart) slow cooker, but the ingredients will comfortably fit in any slow cooker above 4 litres (4¼ quarts).

Find yourself a slow cooker that has a 'keep warm' function; once cooking is completed, it will switch to keep warm mode, meaning you can leave the meal for longer if necessary. Some have a delay start function too, which can be handy, but I'd be cautious about delaying the start for more than one hour so the food isn't sitting at room temperature for too long.

Freezer bags
These can be picked up from most supermarkets in a variety of sizes. For the recipes in this book, I recommend using bags measuring about 30 x 40cm (12 x 16 inches) and smaller bags are useful for recipes that require items to be frozen separately. Remember, they are for freezing only; we don't cook in the bag.

Grab bag holders
I really recommend getting some grab bag holders. These clip onto the bags and hold them up and open, making preparation easy and mess-free.

Measuring spoons
Available online or in supermarkets, get yourself a set of these spoons so that your measuring is accurate and consistent throughout. They range in size from ¼ teaspoon (1.25ml) to 1 tablespoon (15ml) and I highly recommend using them. Small quantities in this book have all been measured using these standardized spoons rather than those from the cutlery drawer.

Good knives and a knife sharpener
There is nothing that will make the process more enjoyable than a sharp knife. Use a sharpener each time you prepare the ingredients for your bags and you'll glide through all the chopping.

Bag labelling
It's very useful to have a permanent marker pen, which should remain visible after freezing, and a roll of masking tape to help with labelling.

Slow cooker liners
If you prefer, you could use a slow cooker liner. These are disposable liners that you remove after the meal has been dished up and go straight in the bin. You don't need to scrub the bowl and, once cooled, it can be packed away for the next time. You can also get silicon reusable liners, all of which can be found online.

Tips & Tricks

- Completely clear your working area before you get started: tidy space, tidy mind!

- When you are writing your shopping list, pre-write items on your freezer bags so you remember what recipes you've bought the ingredients for.

- If there are any additional steps to the recipe, find the relevant page in this book and keep it open, next to the slow cooker, while the meal is cooking so that you can reference it quickly and easily.

- If you live in a two-person household, make the recipe up in a bowl with the ingredients listed, then spilt it between two bags. It'll save you having to work out how much of everything you need and you'll get double dinners, which will keep in the freezer for months.

- Conversely, intentionally preparing double the amount of ingredients, or even triple, and making multiple bags at a time is such a great way to batch prepare several meals at one time. This is for freezing only, as you will only have space in the slow cooker to cook one meal bag at a time.

- To prevent your potatoes from browning while freezing, you can par-boil them and allow to completely cool before adding to the bag.

- Buy good-quality stock pots or cubes, you'll really notice the difference. Store them in an airtight container.

- You can create a spice collection fairly cheaply by adding one or two jars to your shopping basket each week – before you know it, you'll have a full spice rack!

How to Prepare your Grab Bags

Once you've decided which recipe you would like to cook, gather all the ingredients and prepare each one according to the instructions in the recipe. Add the ingredients to the bag in the order stated in the recipe.

Using a grab bag holder will make the process easier and cleaner. They hold the bags open and steady when filling and help prevent spillages from unevenly filled bags on the counter.

Clean up as you go. All peel and packaging can go in the correct bins as you prep. Utilize your space as best you can, moving prepared items onto the kitchen table or another area as you go so that you are not overwhelmed with containers and limiting your working area.

Grab a permanent marker and label each bag with the recipe name, the date it was prepared, and the page number of the recipe if additional steps are needed when you come to cook.

For disposable bags, you can write directly on them. But if you do intend to wash and reuse the bags, just make sure you don't write the first recipe title too big in the label box. You can then simply cross this out and write the next one underneath. If you're using reusable silicon bags, take a roll of masking tape, tear off a small strip and write the recipe name on it. Stick this to the bag and then just peel off once it's been tipped into the slow cooker.

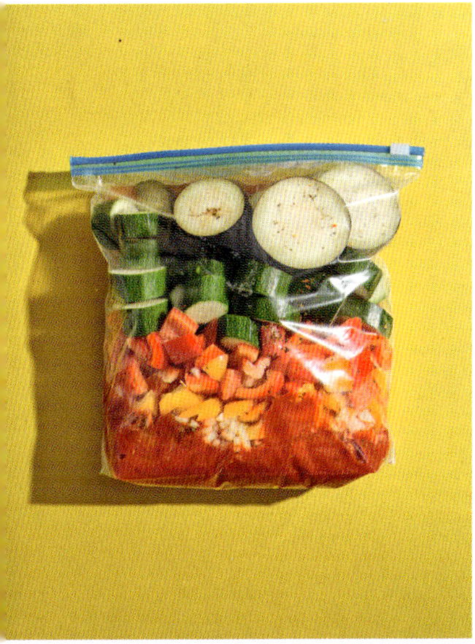
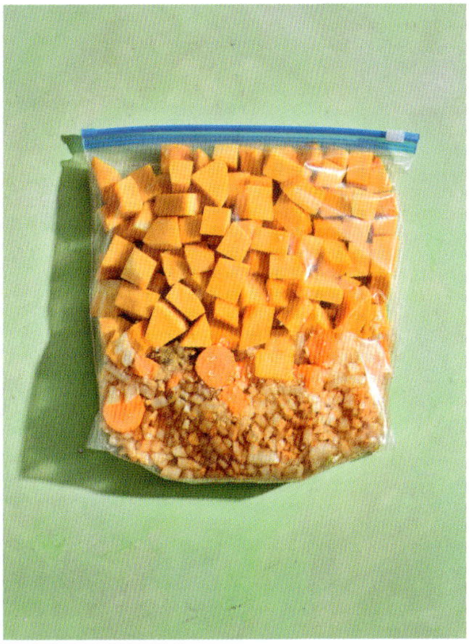
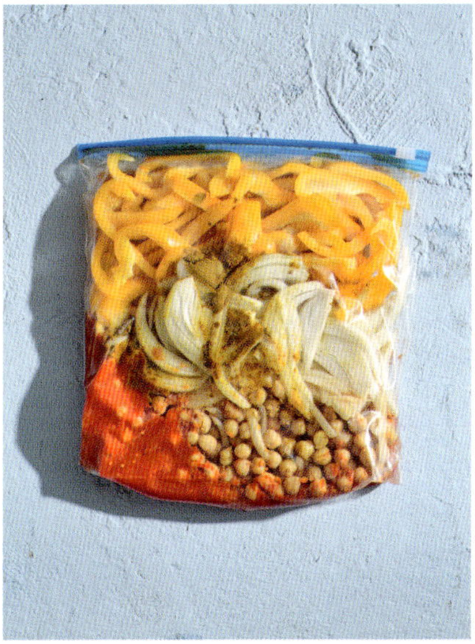
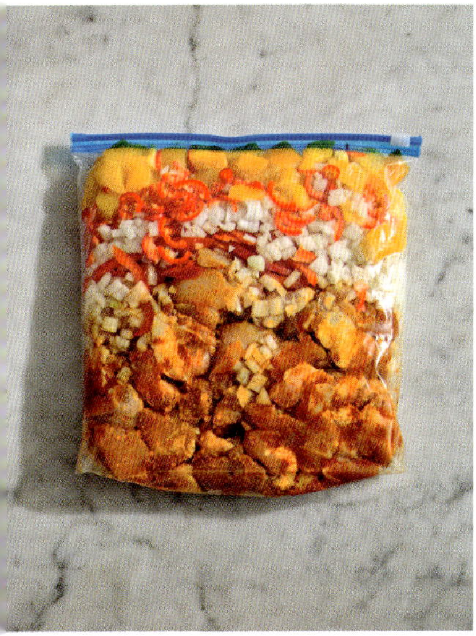
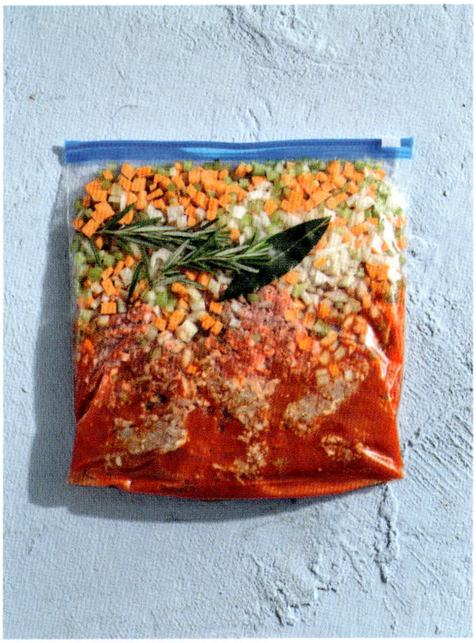
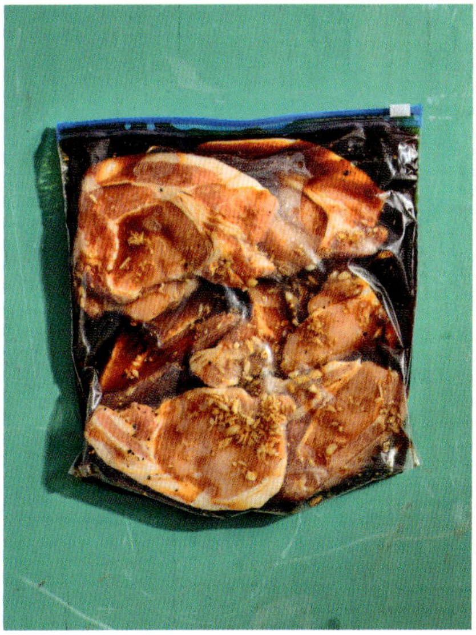
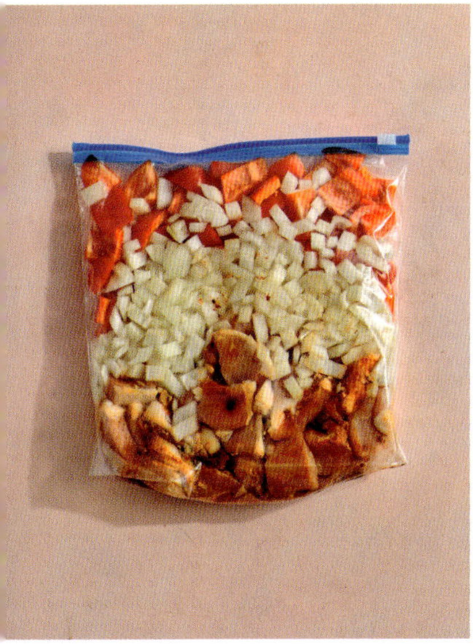
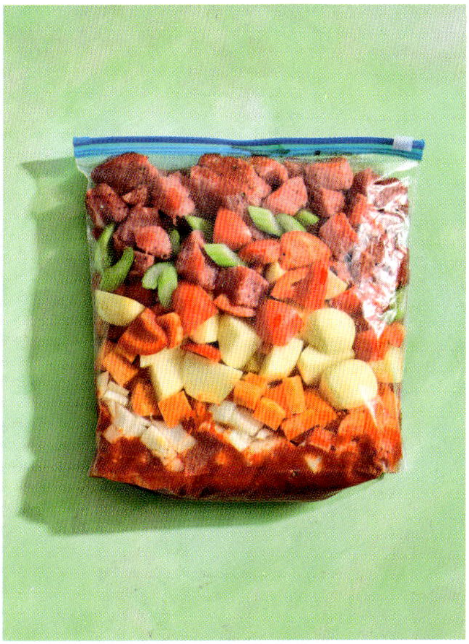
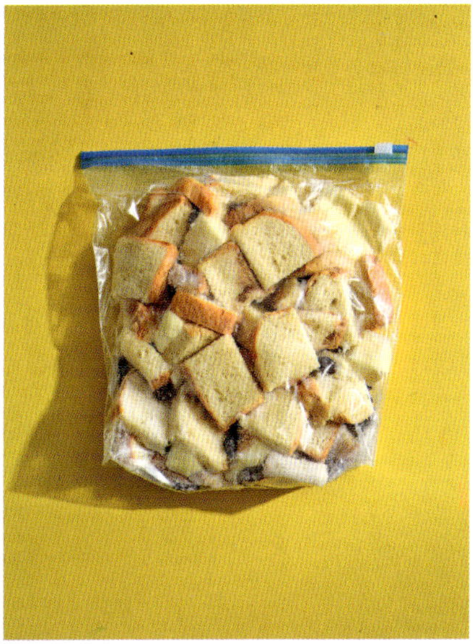

How to Freeze

Once you've filled your freezer bag with your recipe of choice, try to remove as much air as possible from the bag. This will help prevent your food getting freezer burn. There are a few ways to achieve this:

- Fill your sink with cold water and submerge the open bag in the water as deep as you can without water entering the bag. Seal the bag while still in the water. The pressure of the water removes a lot of air from the bag.

- You could also lay the bag on your work surface, with the top open, and press the bag as flat as possible, removing air as you get to the top, then seal.

- Or you could vacuum seal your bags using a special machine and appropriate bags.

I place the bags on a flat shelf in my freezer to freeze, then once they are completely frozen, I move the bag to a drawer with my other bags. If you are freezing more than one bag at a time, I highly recommend placing a sheet of baking paper between the bags to prevent them from freezing together.

How to Defrost

When defrosting, make sure to leave the grab bags in the fridge so that the food remains at a safe temperature once defrosted, and allow enough time for defrosting (as stated in the recipe). Remove the bag from the freezer and place it on the bottom shelf of your fridge. If there is any ice sitting on the outside of the bag, this will defrost, so by placing the bag on the lowest shelf you are preventing this from dripping onto your other food. You can also place the bag in a baking tray to defrost to avoid any drips. I particularly recommend this for recipes with more liquid, just in case of any leaks.

Make sure the food is completely defrosted before emptying the food into the slow cooker and cook according to the recipe instructions. The bags are not to be put in the slow cooker, they are for freezing only, not cooking.

The bags can be cleaned out and reused, just make sure to relabel with the new contents. To clean, fill the bag with warm water and washing up liquid, then seal it and shake it for a minute. Empty out the water, then thoroughly scrub with fresh warm water and washing up liquid. This is really important to remove any trace of previous raw ingredients.

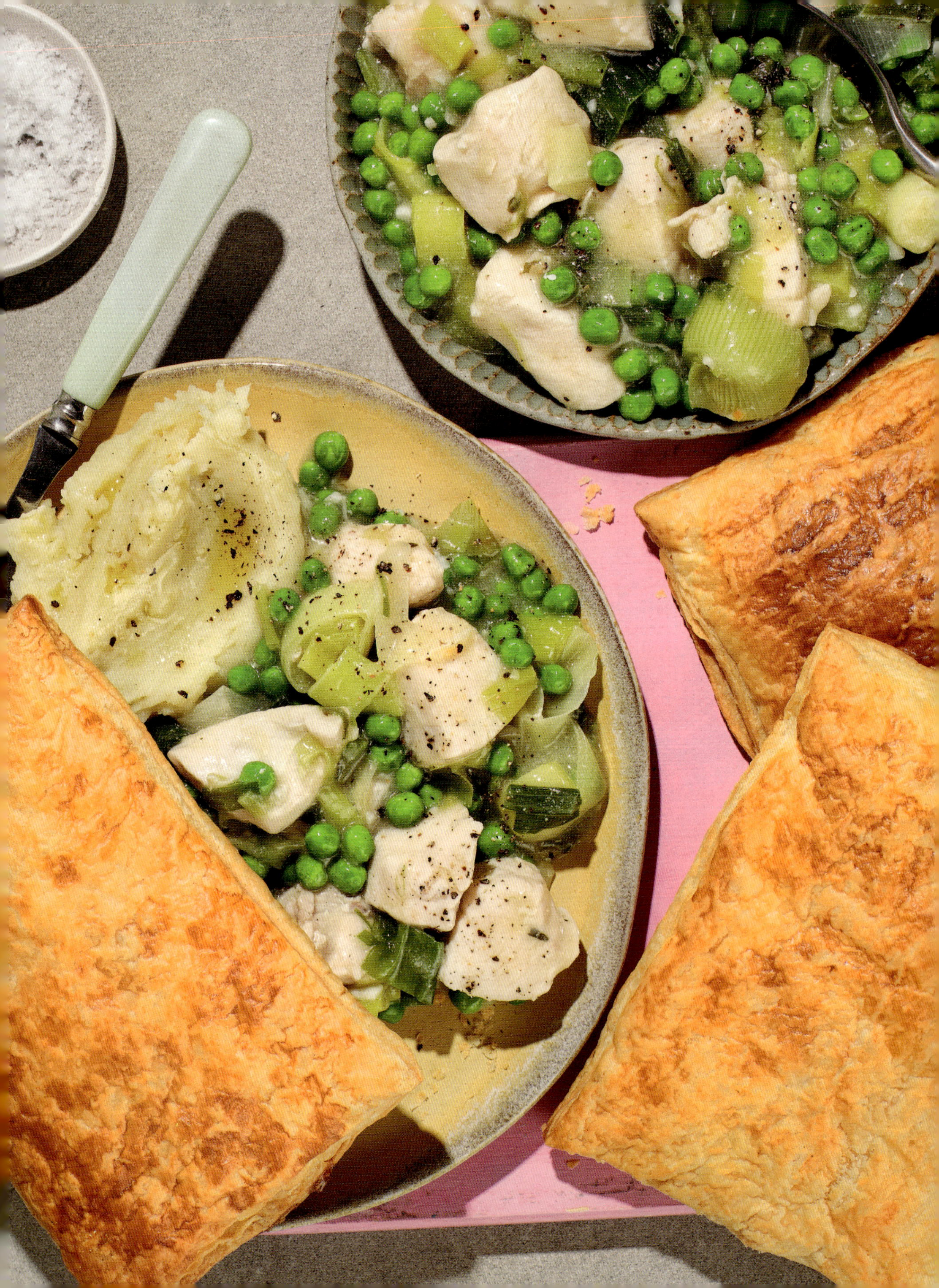

How to Cook

Your slow cooker should be placed on your worktop, but not directly under any cupboards as the steam may damage your woodwork and any downward facing light fittings. If it's safe to do so – for example, it's away from kids being able to reach up and pull it over – place the cooker towards the edge of your counter. I place a chopping board on my hob and then pop my slow cooker on top so it's safely out of the reach of little hands and also has nothing above apart from the extractor fan (which remains off until I remove the lid).

To cook your grab bag meals, empty the contents of the bag into your slow cooker. Set the time and temperature according to the recipe and leave it to do its thing.

It's really important to keep the lid on until directed to remove it in each recipe. The steam created in the slow cooker is the majority of liquid we need and it will take a good 10–15 minutes for the steam to build up again once the lid is removed. By keeping the lid in place, you are also keeping the heat in and won't be slowing down the cooking time. I know it can be tempting to peek but trust the process. When you do remove the lid, lift it straight up and take it to your sink. Tip the lid on its side and allow any extra liquid to pour away.

If you find your meals are getting too watery from the steam, you can try the tea towel trick. I recommend using this only if your slow cooker has a ceramic bowl and is not metal.

Place a tea towel over the underside of your lid and pull the sides up over the top of the lid. Place the lid on the slow cooker and keep the tea towel folded up over the lid – we don't want it touching the hot sides of the slow cooker. The fabric will soak up a lot of the steam and can be popped in the wash after use. Only try this if you will be home while the meal is cooking and can supervise the cooking process.

Store any leftovers, once completely cool, in an airtight container in the fridge. You must make sure you heat through thoroughly and ensure all food is piping hot. If using a microwave, stir halfway through cooking on High, to ensure the food is hot throughout. Food should only be reheated once.

Grab Bag Batch Shopping Lists

A great way to save time and money is to batch-prep multiple bags so you have a number of meals ready to cook at any time. Most of the recipes in this book serve 4–6 people, so a simple way to batch prep is by doubling or tripling the ingredients and then making a number of separate bags. This method is quick and efficient – just set aside 30 minutes after shopping to prep, pack and freeze, giving you 12–18 meals set aside in their grab bags.

Also, you might sometimes want to batch prep across a number of recipes, using largely similar ingredients, to create a variety of dishes ready to cook. This is a great way to use up a glut of vegetables or fruit you might have or allow you to take advantage of any bulk buys or offers that are on at the grocery stores.

These shopping lists combine a selection of my favourite and classic recipes from the book, making it easy to see everything you need in one go to make these dishes.

Once you have got the hang of grab bag batch prepping, and found your own favourites from the book, you can take a few minutes to create your own lists that make your shopping and prepping easier and more economical.

GENERAL PANTRY INGREDIENTS

- [ ] Salt (Both sea salt and cooking salt)
- [ ] Black pepper
- [ ] Olive oil
- [ ] Vegetable oil
- [ ] Non-stick cooking spray
- [ ] Chopped tomatoes (canned)
- [ ] Paprika
- [ ] Ground cumin
- [ ] Dried chilli (including powder, flakes and paste)
- [ ] Garlic powder
- [ ] Stock (Both cubes and jellied pots. Available flavours include beef, vegetable, chicken-flavoured and red wine)
- [ ] Coconut milk (canned)
- [ ] Tomato purée (paste)
- [ ] Rice

MY FAVOURITE CHICKEN RECIPES

Corn Chicken Chilli (Page 68)
Mango Chicken Curry (Page 103)
Chicken Balti (Page 122)

- [ ] 4 chicken breasts (about 700g/1lb 9oz)
- [ ] 18 skinless, boneless chicken thighs
- [ ] 2 onions
- [ ] 2 red bell peppers
- [ ] 2 red chillies
- [ ] 2 green chillies
- [ ] 2.5cm (1 inch) piece of root ginger
- [ ] 7 garlic cloves
- [ ] 350g (12oz) frozen sweetcorn
- [ ] 200g (7oz) frozen mango cubes
- [ ] garlic powder
- [ ] chilli powder
- [ ] ground turmeric
- [ ] paprika
- [ ] garam masala
- [ ] ground cumin
- [ ] ground coriander
- [ ] 2 x 300g (10½oz) jars mild salsa
- [ ] 1 x 400g (14oz) can kidney beans
- [ ] 1 x 400ml (14oz) can coconut milk
- [ ] 2 x 400g (14oz) cans chopped tomatoes
- [ ] red curry paste

TO SERVE
Rice or naan bread

BRAISING BEEF RECIPES

Beef & coconut curry (Page 126)
Spicy Beef (Page 69)
Mongolian-Style Beef (Page 66)

- [ ] 3.2kg (7lb) braising beef/steak
- [ ] 3 onions
- [ ] 2 red bell peppers
- [ ] 7 garlic cloves
- [ ] 3 tsp finely grated root ginger
- [ ] 1 jalapeño chilli
- [ ] 2 tbsp cornflour (cornstarch)
- [ ] 3 tbsp brown sugar
- [ ] 2 tbsp tomato purée (paste)
- [ ] 2 tsp sugar
- [ ] 1 tbsp runny honey
- [ ] 200ml (7fl oz/scant 1 cup) light soy sauce
- [ ] 1 tbsp olive oil
- [ ] 1 tsp ground cumin
- [ ] 1 tbsp mild chilli powder
- [ ] A pinch of chilli flakes
- [ ] 2 x 400g (14oz) cans chopped tomatoes
- [ ] 1 x 400ml (14oz) can coconut milk
- [ ] 1 tbsp jarred chipotle paste
- [ ] 1 beef stock cube
- [ ] 1 beef jelly stock pot
- [ ] 2 tbsp curry paste

TO SERVE:
Rice or naan bread

MINCE BEEF CLASSICS

Mexican Beef Taco Shells (Page 56)
Spaghetti Bolognese (Page 50)
Lily's Cottage Pie (Page 92)

- ☐ 2.25kg (5lb) beef mince (5% fat)
- ☐ 3 onions
- ☐ 3 celery stalks
- ☐ 3 carrots
- ☐ 6 garlic cloves
- ☐ 3 x 400g (14oz) cans chopped tomatoes
- ☐ 1 x 400g (14oz) can pinto beans
- ☐ 150g (5½oz) frozen sweetcorn
- ☐ 1 chicken jelly stock pot
- ☐ 1 beef jelly stock pot
- ☐ 1 red wine stock pot (or beef stock pot as an alternative)
- ☐ 3 tbsp tomato purée (paste)
- ☐ 1 x 30g (1oz) packet taco seasoning
- ☐ 2 tbsp plain (all-purpose) flour
- ☐ 2 bay leaves
- ☐ 1 tsp dried oregano
- ☐ 5 tbsp Worcestershire sauce
- ☐ 80g (2¾oz) Cheddar cheese
- ☐ Grated Parmesan cheese

TO SERVE:
8 tortillas or hard-shelled tacos / 800g (1lb 12oz) mashed potatoes /
Spaghetti / Avocado / Sour cream / Salsa / Green beans

MY FAVOURITE MINCE BEEF RECIPES

Lasagna Soup (Page 149)
Taco Soup (Page 134)
Roy's Mince & Beans (Page 30)

- ☐ 1.35kg (3lb) lean minced beef (5% fat)
- ☐ 3 onions
- ☐ 2 carrots
- ☐ 4 garlic cloves
- ☐ 2 green chillies
- ☐ 200g (7oz) mushrooms
- ☐ Handful of coarsely chopped fresh spinach
- ☐ 250g (9oz) shredded mozzarella cheese
- ☐ 300g (10½oz) frozen sweetcorn
- ☐ 6 dried lasagna sheets
- ☐ 1 x 25g (1oz) packet of taco seasoning
- ☐ 1½ tsp onion powder
- ☐ 1 tsp garlic powder
- ☐ 2 tsp Italian seasoning
- ☐ 4 x 400g (14oz) cans chopped tomatoes
- ☐ 1 x 400g (14oz) can kidney beans
- ☐ 1 x 400g (14oz) can black beans
- ☐ 1 x 200g (7oz) can baked beans
- ☐ 3 beef stock cubes
- ☐ 4 tbsp tomato purée (paste)

TO SERVE:
Crusty bread / Mashed potatoes

PORK FAVOURITES

Smoky Pork Loins (Page 45)
Teriyaki Pork Loins (Page 52)
Slow-cooked Pork & Cider Hotpot (Page 90)

- [ ] 14 pork loins (total 1.6kg / 3lb 8oz)
- [ ] 1kg (2lb 4oz) pork shoulder
- [ ] 2 onions
- [ ] 2 red bell peppers
- [ ] 2 leeks
- [ ] 6 garlic cloves
- [ ] 1 tsp peeled and grated fresh root ginger
- [ ] 500g (1lb 2oz) potatoes
- [ ] 2 tbsp plain (all-purpose) flour
- [ ] 2 tsp smoked paprika

- [ ] 1 tbsp light brown sugar
- [ ] 2 bay leaves
- [ ] 2 tbsp Worcestershire sauce
- [ ] 300ml (10fl oz/1¼ cups) light soy sauce
- [ ] 60ml (2fl oz/¼ cup) rice wine vinegar
- [ ] 1 tbsp sesame oil
- [ ] 250ml (9fl oz/1 cup) dry (hard) cider
- [ ] 1 chicken stock cube
- [ ] 1 chicken jelly stock pot

TO SERVE:
Mashed potatoes / Sweet potato mash / Long-stem broccoli

VEGETARIAN CLASSICS

Veggie Lasagna (Page 170)
Vegetable Fajitas (Page 178)
Vegetarian Chilli (Page 166)

- [ ] 7 carrots
- [ ] 2 courgettes (zucchini)
- [ ] 5 red bell peppers
- [ ] 2 green bell peppers
- [ ] 1 yellow bell pepper
- [ ] 2 celery stalks
- [ ] 2 red onions
- [ ] 1 onion
- [ ] 4 garlic cloves
- [ ] 250g (9oz) baby spinach
- [ ] 400g (14oz) closed cup mushrooms
- [ ] 480g (1lb 1oz) chestnut (cremini) mushrooms

- [ ] 300g (10½oz) cherry tomatoes
- [ ] 4 x 400g (14oz) cans chopped tomatoes
- [ ] 1 x 400g (14oz) can cannellini bean
- [ ] 250g (9oz) ricotta cheese
- [ ] 100g (3½oz) mozzarella cheese
- [ ] 1 large egg
- [ ] 8 dried whole-wheat lasagna sheets
- [ ] 1 x 30g (1oz) packet fajita spice mix
- [ ] 2 tsp ground cumin
- [ ] 3 tsp paprika
- [ ] 1 tsp ground coriander

TO SERVE:
Tortilla wraps / Guacamole / Salsa / Bread /
Side salad (lettuce, cucumber, tomatoes) / Sour cream (optional)

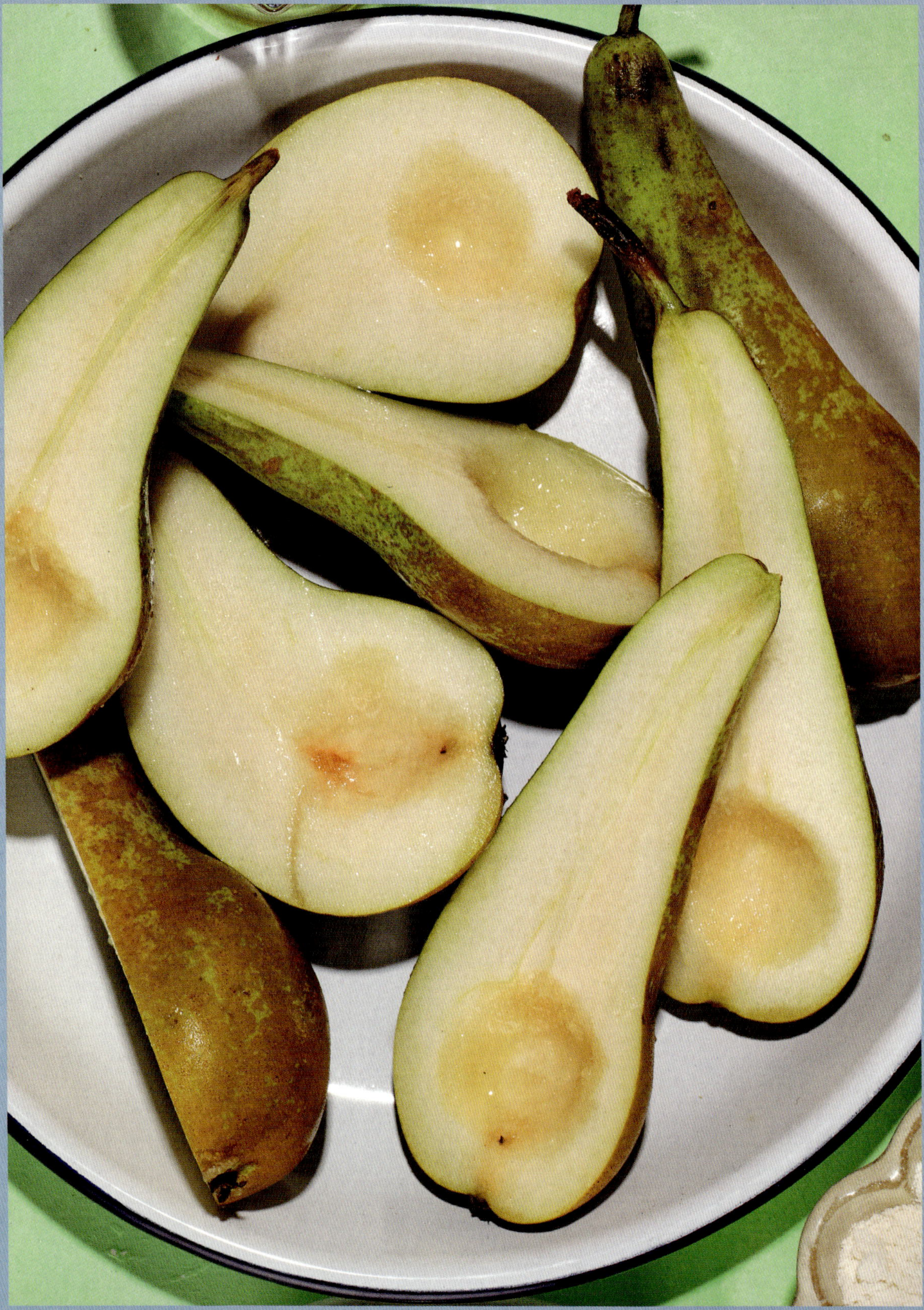

VEGETARIAN – BUTTERNUT SQUASH AND/ SWEET POTATO

Sweet Potato Curry (Page 158)
Butternut Squash & Courgette Casserole (Page 180)
Vegetable Korma (Page 167)

- [ ] 700g (1lb 9oz) butternut squash
- [ ] 400g (14oz) sweet potatoes
- [ ] 2 onions
- [ ] 2 carrots
- [ ] 4 courgettes (zucchini)
- [ ] 1 red bell pepper
- [ ] 2 red chillies
- [ ] 4 garlic cloves
- [ ] 1 tbsp freshly grated ginger
- [ ] 300g (10½oz) cauliflower
- [ ] 200g (7oz) canned chickpeas
- [ ] 1 x 400g (14oz) can chopped tomatoes
- [ ] 1 x 400ml (14oz) can coconut milk
- [ ] 2 tbsp tomato purée (paste)
- [ ] 1 tsp garlic powder
- [ ] 1 tsp dried mixed herbs
- [ ] ½ tsp ground cumin
- [ ] 1 tsp paprika
- [ ] 1 tsp mild curry powder
- [ ] 3 tsp garam masala
- [ ] 1 tsp ground turmeric
- [ ] 2 heaped tbsp ground almonds
- [ ] 2 tbsp cornflour (cornstarch)
- [ ] 1 vegetable jelly stock pot
- [ ] 1 meat-free chicken-flavour stock cube
- [ ] 25g (1oz) butter
- [ ] 150g (5½oz) Parmesan cheese

TO SERVE:
Roti / Crusty bread and/or mashed potatoes / White rice and/or naan bread / Mango chutney

APPLES

Apple Crumble (Page 187)
Caramel Apple Crispy (Page 190)
Cinnamon Baked Apples (Page 191)

- [ ] 700g (1lb 9oz) Bramley apples
- [ ] 12 Granny Smith or Golden Delicious apples
- [ ] Juice of 2 lemons
- [ ] 3 tbsp golden caster (granulated) sugar
- [ ] 2½ tsp ground cinnamon
- [ ] 1 tbsp cornflour (cornstarch)
- [ ] 120g (4¼oz/1 cup less 1½ tbsp) plain (all-purpose) flour
- [ ] 50g (1¾oz/½ cup) porridge oats
- [ ] 50g (1¾oz/¼ cup) dark brown sugar
- [ ] 2 tbsp sultanas (golden raisins)
- [ ] 80g (2¾oz) unsalted butter
- [ ] 150g (5½oz) caramel (shop-bought jar)
- [ ] 300ml (10½fl oz/1¼ cups) apple juice

TO SERVE:
Custard, cream, or ice cream

BLUEBERRIES

Blueberry Jam (Page 184)
Mixed Berry Cobbler (Page 192)

- [ ] 750g (1lb 10oz) blueberries
- [ ] 250g (9oz) raspberries
- [ ] 125g caster (granulated) sugar
- [ ] 2 tbsp granulated sugar
- [ ] ½ tsp ground cinnamon
- [ ] Juice of 1 lemon

TO SERVE:
Custard

One-month meal plan

There are so many combinations of bags that can be prepped, ready to be defrosted and cooked later. I hope you'll enjoy going through the book, picking out your favourite recipes and working out your plan for what you'll make and when you'll serve them. Below is an example of a one-month plan I like to follow so I have a good variety of dishes ready to go for various meals.

DAYS 1–7

Monday	Defrost Chicken Fajitas (Page 28)
Tuesday	Cook Chicken Fajitas
Wednesday	Defrost Spanish Beef (Page 62)
Thursday	Cook Spanish Beef
Friday	Defrost Slow-cooked Pork & Cider Hotpot (Page 90)
Saturday	Cook Slow-cooked Pork & Cider Hotpot + Defrost Maple Pear Crumble (Page 188)
Sunday	Cook Maple Pear Crumble

DAYS 8–14

Monday	Defrost Lily's Cottage Pie (Page 92)
Tuesday	Cook Lily's Cottage Pie
Wednesday	Defrost Kung Pao Chicken (Page 114)
Thursday	Cook Kung Pao Chicken
Friday	Defrost Cheese & Broccoli Soup (Page 138)
Saturday	Cook Cheese & Broccoli soup + Defrost Mixed Berry Cobbler (Page 192)
Sunday	Cook Mixed Berry Cobbler

DAYS 15–21

Monday	Defrost Vegetable Tagine (Page 164)
Tuesday	Cook Vegetable Tagine
Wednesday	Defrost Lasagna Soup (Page 149)
Thursday	Cook Lasagna Soup
Friday	Defrost Chicken Tikka Masala (Page 120)
Saturday	Cook Chicken Tikka Masala Defrost Bread & Butter Pudding (Page 194)
Sunday	Cook Bread & Butter Pudding

DAYS 22–28

Monday	Defrost Beef Ragu (Page 80)
Tuesday	Cook Beef Ragu
Wednesday	Defrost Buffalo Chicken Pasta (Page 72)
Thursday	Cook Buffalo Chicken Pasta
Friday	Defrost Vegetarian Chilli (Page 166)
Saturday	Cook Vegetarian Chilli Defrost Apple Crumble (Page 187)
Sunday	Cook Apple Crumble

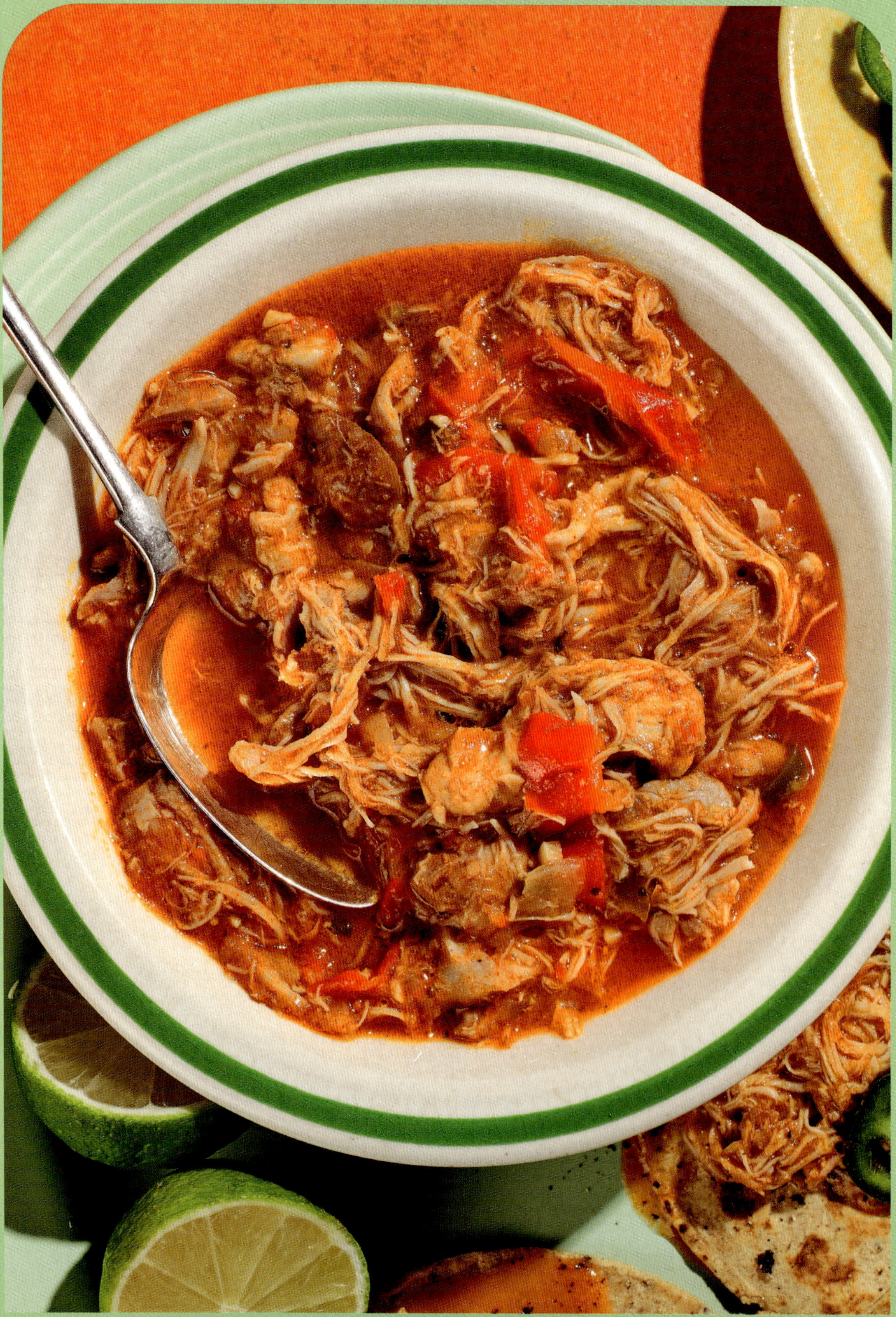

FAMILY

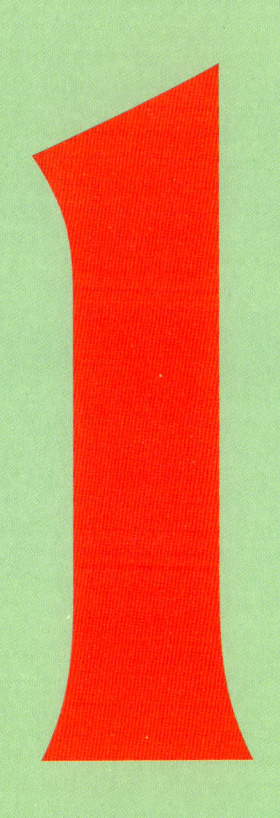

1

CLASSICS

FAMILY CLASSICS

Chicken Fajitas

I love to make a batch of this, laying out everything on the table so that everyone can just dig in whenever they get in from school, college or work. It's a definite family favourite!

- 10 skinless, boneless chicken thighs, sliced into strips
- 1 x 30g (1oz) packet fajita seasoning
- 1 green (bell) pepper, deseeded and sliced into strips
- 1 yellow (bell) pepper, deseeded and sliced into strips
- 1 red (bell) pepper, deseeded and sliced into strips
- 1 large onion, sliced

TO SERVE:
Tortilla wraps
Salsa
Guacamole
Sour cream
Limes
Coriander (cilantro) leaves

1. Put the chicken in your grab bag, followed by the fajita seasoning. Close the bag and shake to coat the chicken in seasoning.

2. Open the bag and add the peppers and onion, and shake again.

3. Remove as much air as you can from the bag before sealing. Label the bag with the contents and the date you prepared it, then place it in the freezer, making sure it lies as flat as possible.

4. Defrost the bag thoroughly in the fridge for approximately 8–10 hours before cooking.

5. To cook, empty the contents of the bag into the slow cooker. (You can wash the bag and reuse, but don't forget to re-label.) Cook on low for 8 hours or on high for 4 hours.

6. Serve the fajitas with tortilla wraps, salsa, guacamole, sour cream, limes and coriander.

3 MONTHS | **8–10 HOURS** | **LOW** 8 hours / **HIGH** 4 hours | **SERVES 4**

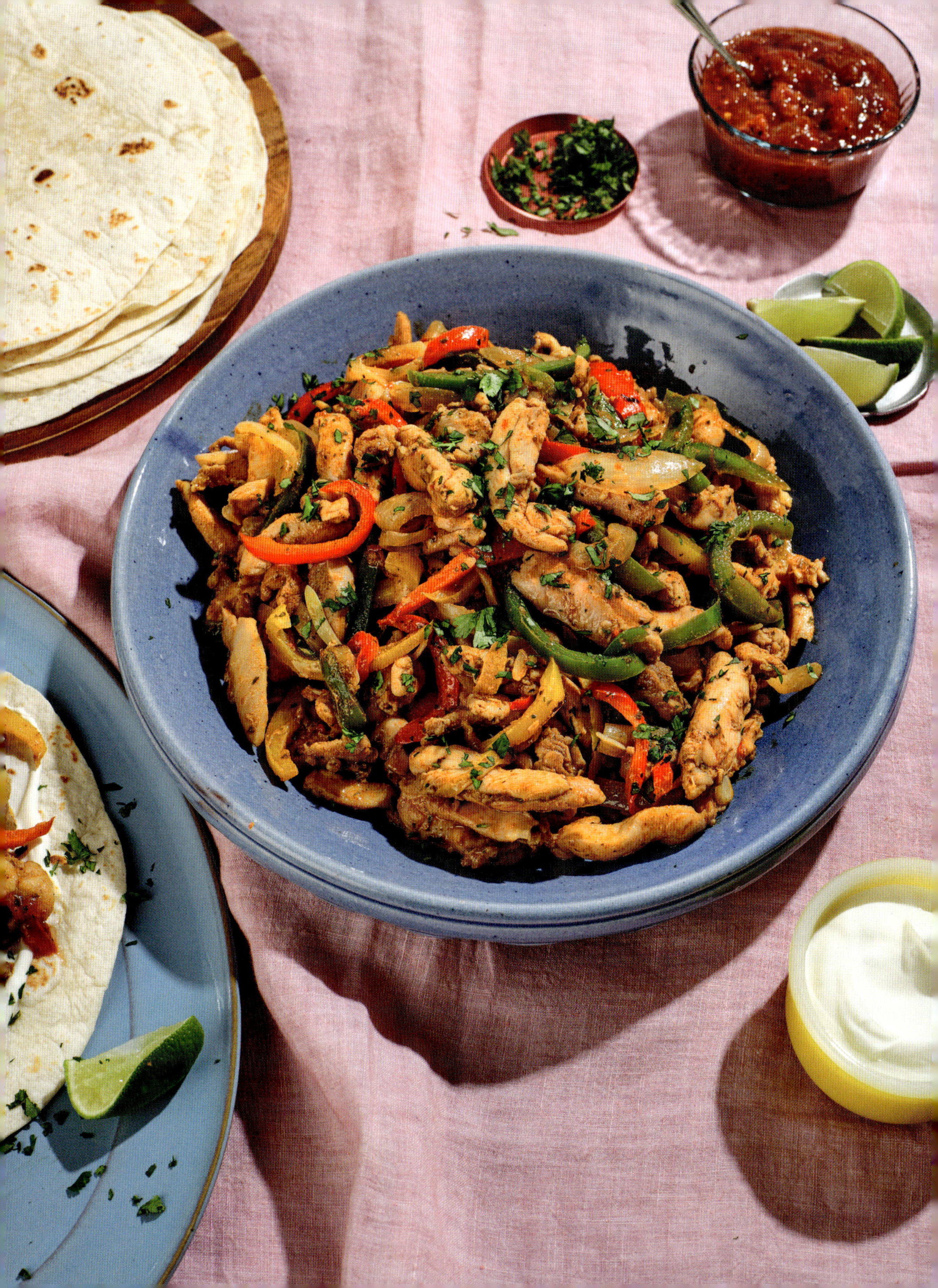

FAMILY CLASSICS

Roy's Mince & Beans

Every time we went for dinner at my grandparents' house when we were kids, my grandad would whip up his signature mince and beans for my sister and me. He made it with a cold joint of pork that he'd shred in the food processor and then add into a pot with beans and gravy. Over the years I've changed it to minced beef as my kids prefer the texture.

- 500g (1lb 2oz) minced beef (5% fat)
- 1 x 200g (7oz) can baked beans
- 1 garlic clove, crushed
- 1 beef stock cube, dissolved in 100ml (3½fl oz/scant ½ cup) hot water
- 1 onion, peeled and chopped
- 2 tbsp tomato purée
- Salt and pepper
- Mashed potatoes, to serve

1. Put all the ingredients in the grab bag and mix well. Season with salt and pepper.

2. Remove as much air as you can from the bag before sealing. Label the bag with the contents and the date you prepared it, then place it in the freezer, making sure it lies as flat as possible.

3. Defrost the bag thoroughly in the fridge for approximately 8–10 hours before cooking.

4. To cook, empty the contents of the bag into your slow cooker. (You can wash the bag and reuse, but don't forget to re-label.) Cook on low for 8 hours or on high for 4 hours.

5. Serve with mashed potatoes.

3 MONTHS | **8–10 HOURS** | **LOW 8 hours / HIGH 4 hours** | **SERVES 4**

FAMILY CLASSICS

Chicken Casserole

A hearty meal after a long day at work, this recipe is a staple in our home, especially on cold winter days.

1kg (2lb 4oz) boneless, skinless chicken thighs, chopped into chunks
40g (1½oz/¼ cup) plain (all-purpose) flour
2 onions, peeled and chopped
2 celery stalks, chopped
3 carrots, peeled and chopped
1 chicken jelly stock pot
1 tsp dried thyme
2 tbsp wholegrain mustard
250ml (9fl oz/1 cup) boiling water
4 tbsp crème fraîche
Salt and black pepper
Mashed potato, to serve

1. Combine the chicken and flour in a grab bag and shake to coat the chicken. This is going to help thicken the sauce. Next, add the onions, celery, carrots, stock pot, dried thyme, mustard and a sprinkle of salt and pepper. Mix everything together.

2. Remove as much air as you can from the bag before sealing. Label the bag with the contents and the date you prepared it. Write on the front that you need to add the relevant quantities of boiling water and crème fraîche at the time of cooking (or a note to refer to this page number). Place the bag in the freezer, making sure it lies as flat as possible.

3. Defrost the bag thoroughly in the fridge for approximately 8–10 hours before cooking.

4. To cook, empty the contents of the bag into your slow cooker, add the boiling water and stir everything together. Cook on low for 8 hours or on high for 4 hours.

5. When the casserole has finished cooking, add the crème fraîche and stir well.

6. Serve the chicken casserole with mashed potato.

3 MONTHS | **8–10 HOURS** | **LOW 8 hours** | **HIGH 4 hours** | **SERVES 4**

FAMILY CLASSICS

Beef Casserole with Dumplings

I always find beef casserole so moreish! I like to make dumplings, which cook on top of the stew during the last hour of cooking.

900g (2lb) braising beef, chopped into chunks
2 tsp cornflour (cornstarch)
1 onion, chopped
3 celery stalks, chopped
3 carrots, peeled, halved and chopped into chunks
2 bay leaves
1 tsp dried thyme
2 tbsp tomato purée
2 tbsp Worcestershire sauce
2 beef jelly stock pots
200ml (7fl oz/scant 1 cup) boiling water

FOR THE DUMPLINGS:
150g (5½oz/ 1 cup plus 2 tbsp) self-raising flour
70g (2½oz/¾ cup) suet
½ tsp salt

1. Put the beef in the grab bag and add the cornflour. Shake well in the closed bag to coat the beef. Reopen the bag and add the onion, celery, carrots, bay leaves, thyme, tomato purée, Worcestershire sauce and stock pots. Remove as much air as you can from the bag before sealing. Label the bag with the contents and preparation date. Note on the front to add measured boiling water at the time of cooking (or note this page number). Place the bag in the freezer, making sure it lies as flat as possible.

2. Defrost the bag thoroughly in the fridge for approximately 8–10 hours before cooking.

3. To cook, empty the contents of the bag into your slow cooker, add the boiling water and stir. Cook on low for 8 hours or on high for 4 hours.

4. Towards the end of cooking time, prepare the dumplings (they will need to cook for the final 30 minutes). In a mixing bowl, stir together the salt, flour and suet. Make a well in the middle and add 1 tablespoon of ice-cold water. Stir together until it forms a firm dough. You may need to add a little more water. Roll the dough into eight balls.

5. Thirty minutes before the end of the cooking time, add the dumplings to the top of the casserole and cook for the remaining time until the dumplings are risen and fluffy.

3 MONTHS | 8–10 HOURS | LOW 8 hours | HIGH 4 hours | SERVES 4

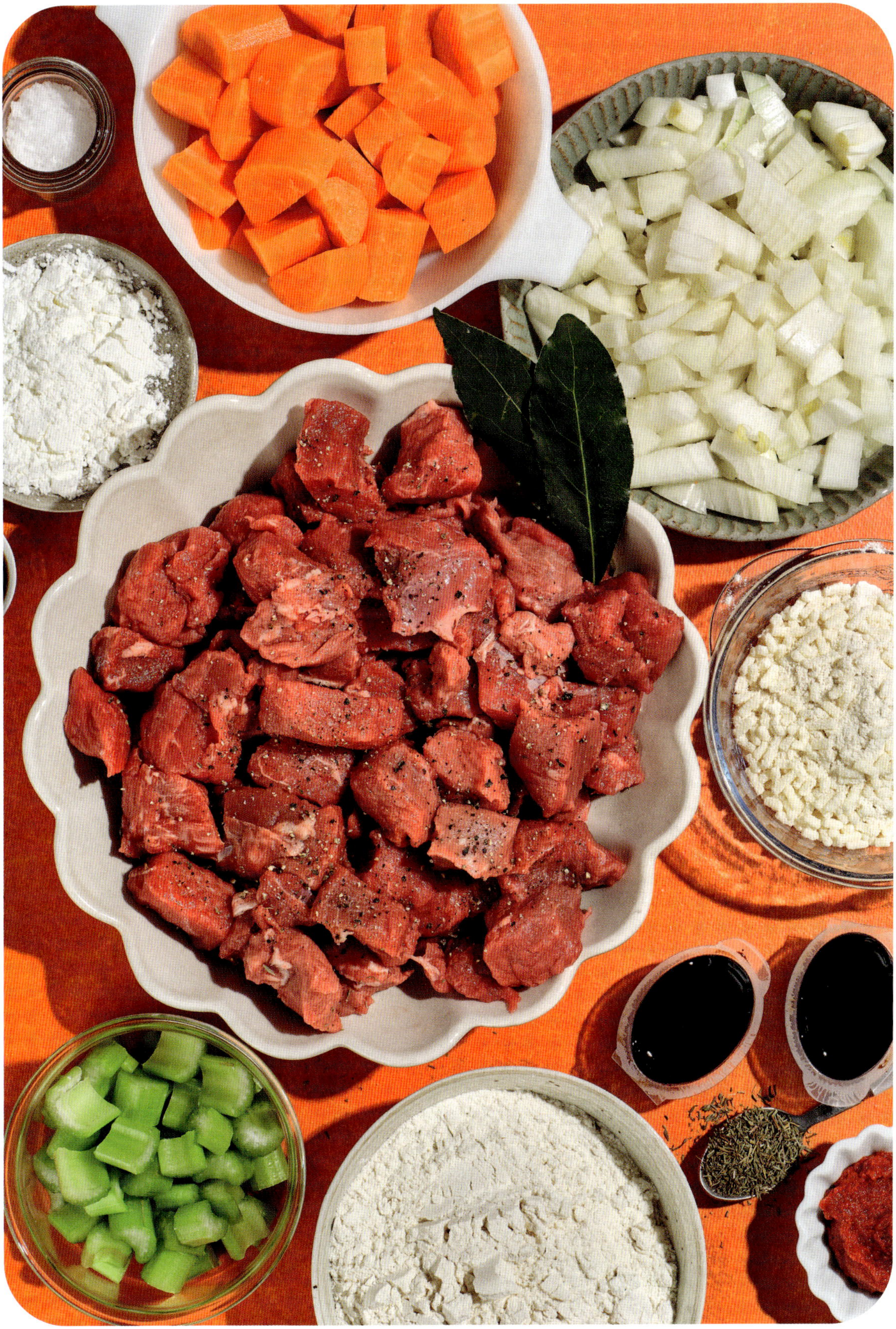

FAMILY CLASSICS

Meatballs with Herby Tomato Sauce

My husband groans whenever I say it's meatballs for dinner. Not because he doesn't like them, but because he's sick to death of them! The kids absolutely love this meal and if anyone's ever ill (which is often with three kids in the house), I like to make these as I know they'll be sure to fill up by eating the lot. I buy ready-made meatballs, but you can make your own if you prefer.

2 x 400g (14oz) cans chopped tomatoes
1 tsp garlic powder
1 tsp dried oregano
1 tsp dried thyme
1 tbsp tomato purée (paste)
24 pork meatballs
2 red (bell) peppers, deseeded and chopped
1 onion, diced
Salt and black pepper

TO SERVE:
Tagliatelle
Parmesam cheese, grated
Basil leaves, to garnish

1. Open both cans of chopped tomatoes and into one of the cans add the garlic powder, oregano, thyme and a good pinch of salt and pepper. Stir well.

2. Add the tomato purée to the other can and stir well.

3. Put the meatballs in your grab bag and add the two cans of chopped tomatoes, along with the peppers and onion.

4. Remove as much air as you can from the bag before sealing. Label the bag with the contents and the date you prepared it, then place it in the freezer, making sure it lies as flat as possible.

5. Defrost the bag thoroughly in the fridge for approximately 8–10 hours before cooking.

6. Empty the contents of the bag into the slow cooker. (You can wash the bag and reuse, but don't forget to re-label.) Cook on low for 8 hours or on high for 4 hours.

7. Serve the meatballs and their sauce with tagliatelle, grated Parmesan and garnish with basil leaves.

3 MONTHS | **8–10 HOURS** | **LOW 8 hours / HIGH 4 hours** | **SERVES 4**

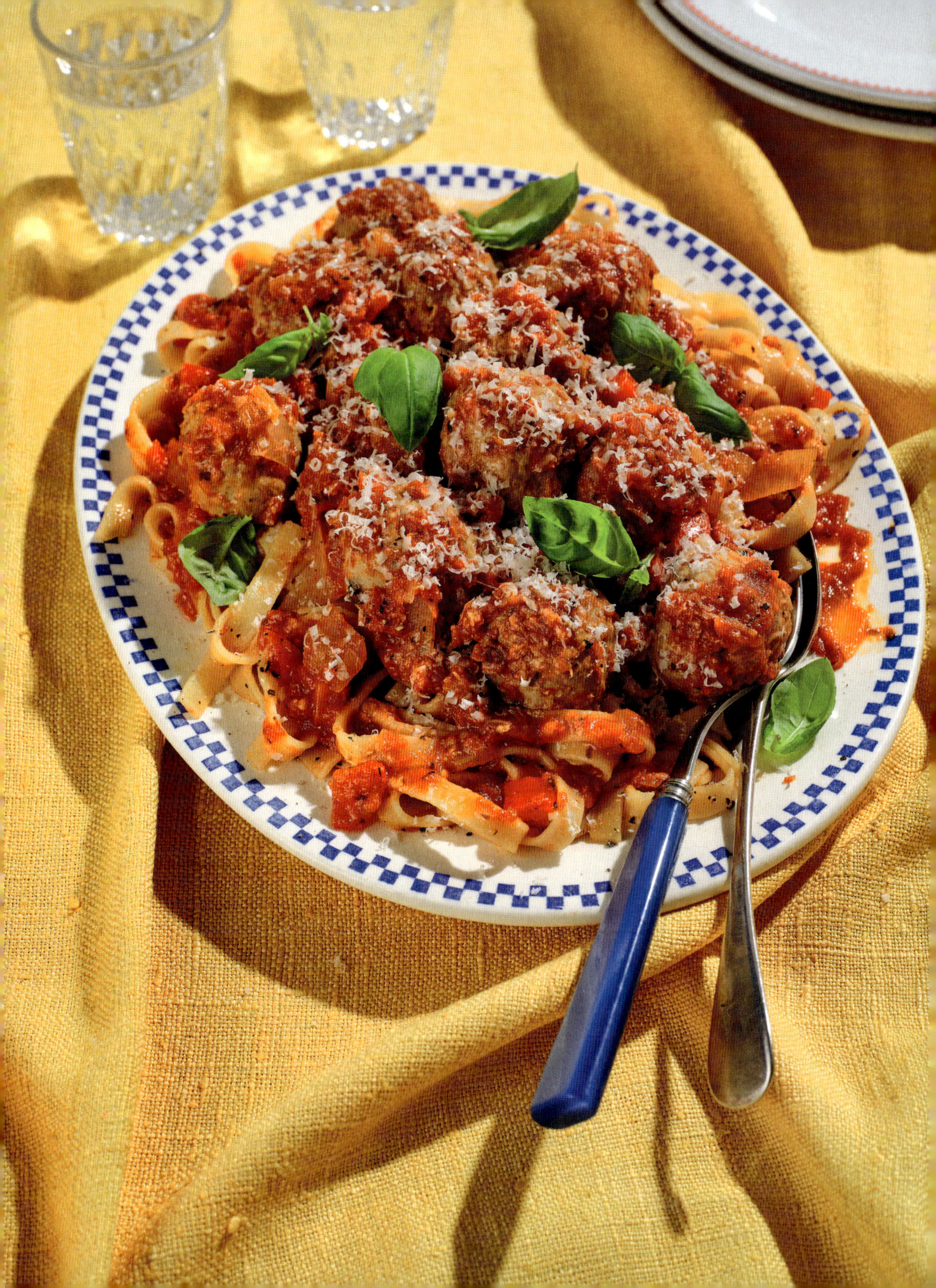

FAMILY CLASSICS

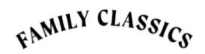

Chicken Burritos

Serve this in a big bowl with tortilla wraps and cheese and you have yourself a winner!

- 4 chicken breasts (about 700g/1lb 9oz)
- 1 large onion, chopped
- 2 green (bell) peppers, deseeded and chopped into chunks
- 1 x 300g (10½oz) jar mild salsa
- 1 x 400g (14oz) can mixed beans in spicy sauce
- ¼ tsp sea salt
- ¼ tsp black pepper
- Tortilla wraps and grated Cheddar cheese, to serve

1. Put the chicken, onion, green peppers, salsa and mixed beans in a grab bag and season with the salt and pepper. Close the bag and mix everything together.

2. Remove as much air as you can from the bag before sealing. Label the bag with the contents and the date you prepared it, then place it in the freezer, making sure it lies as flat as possible.

3. Defrost the bag thoroughly in the fridge for approximately 8–10 hours before cooking.

4. Empty the contents of the bag into the slow cooker and cook on low for 8 hours or on high for 4 hours.

5. Once cooked, use two forks to shred the chicken. Tip the chicken back into the slow cooker and mix everything together.

6. Serve the chicken in tortilla wraps with a sprinkle of grated cheese.

3 MONTHS | 8–10 HOURS | LOW 8 hours | HIGH 4 hours | SERVES 4

TIP:
Ramp up the heat and add some fresh jalapenos thirty minutes before serving!

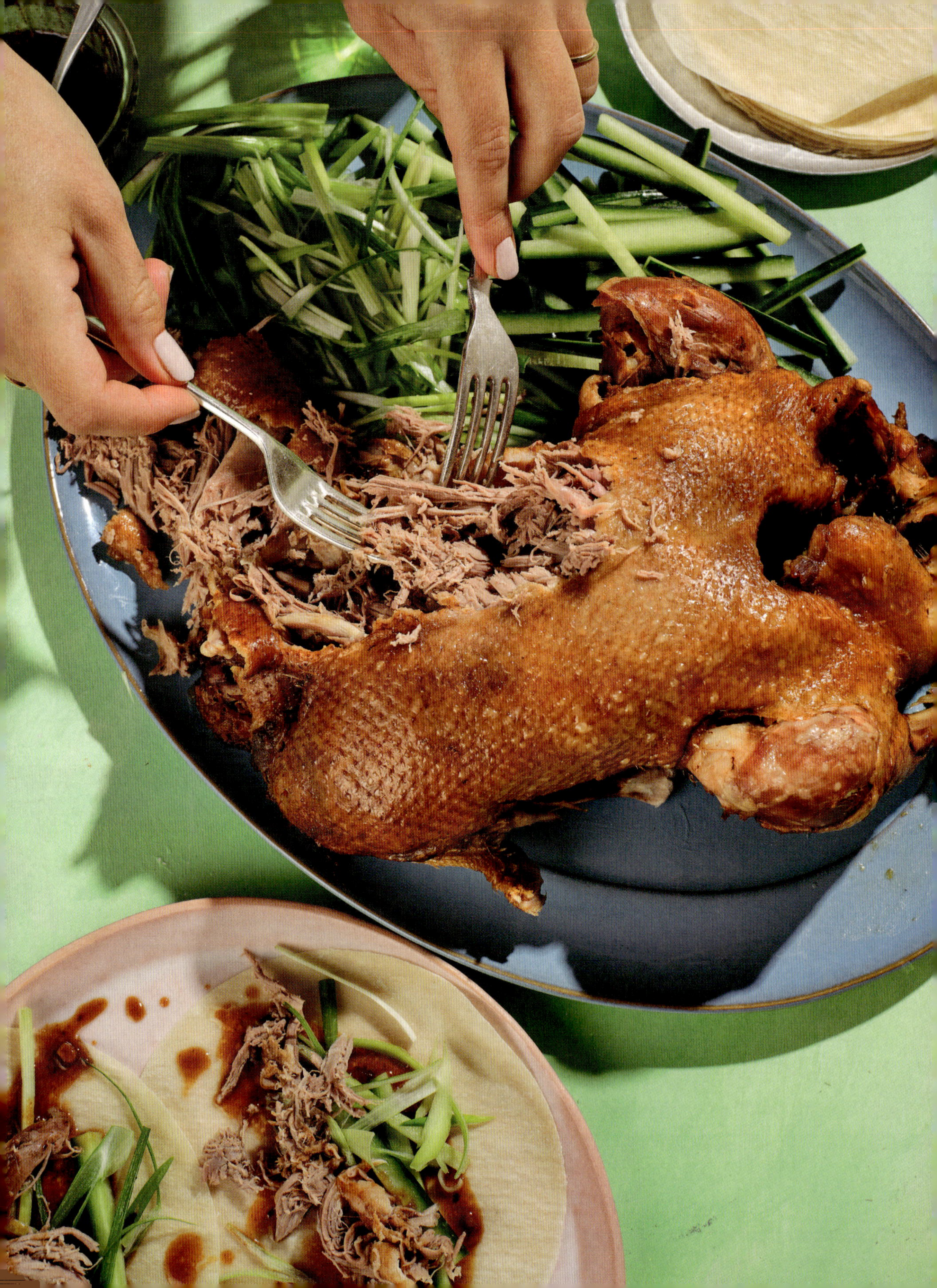

FAMILY CLASSICS

Shredded Hoisin Duck

This recipe was featured in one of my first videos to go viral, and it's still a staple meal in our house to this day. If you don't like a lot of fat in your sauce, oven cook the duck for ten minutes first, then allow to cool and drain away the fat that has been rendered. For crispy skin, remove the duck from the slow cooker and drain any juices back into the pot. Place the duck on a roasting tray and roast for 20 minutes at 170°C fan/375°F/Gas 5.

200ml (7fl oz/scant 1 cup) hoisin sauce
150ml (5fl oz/scant ⅔ cup) chicken stock
4 tbsp runny honey
2 tbsp light soy sauce
3 garlic cloves, grated
1 tbsp peeled and thinly sliced root ginger
2kg (4lb 8oz) whole duck

TO SERVE:
16 Chinese pancakes
1 cucumber, thinly sliced into strips
4 spring onions (scallions), thinly sliced into strips

1. Put the hoisin sauce, chicken stock, honey, soy sauce, garlic and ginger in a bowl. Whisk to combine.

2. Add the whole duck to a grab bag and pour the sauce over the duck. Seal the bag and leave in the fridge to marinate for 3–4 hours.

3. Once marinated, remove as much air as you can from the bag before sealing. Label the bag with the contents and the date you prepared it, then place it in the freezer, making sure it lies as flat as possible.

4. Defrost the bag thoroughly in the fridge for 24–48 hours before cooking.

5. To cook, empty the contents of the bag into the slow cooker. (You can wash the bag and reuse, but don't forget to re-label.) Cook on low for 8 hours or on high for 4 hours.

6. Once cooked, shred the duck with 2 forks and serve the with the pancakes, cucumber and spring onions.

3 MONTHS | **24–48 HOURS** | **LOW 8 hours / HIGH 4 hours** | **SERVES 4**

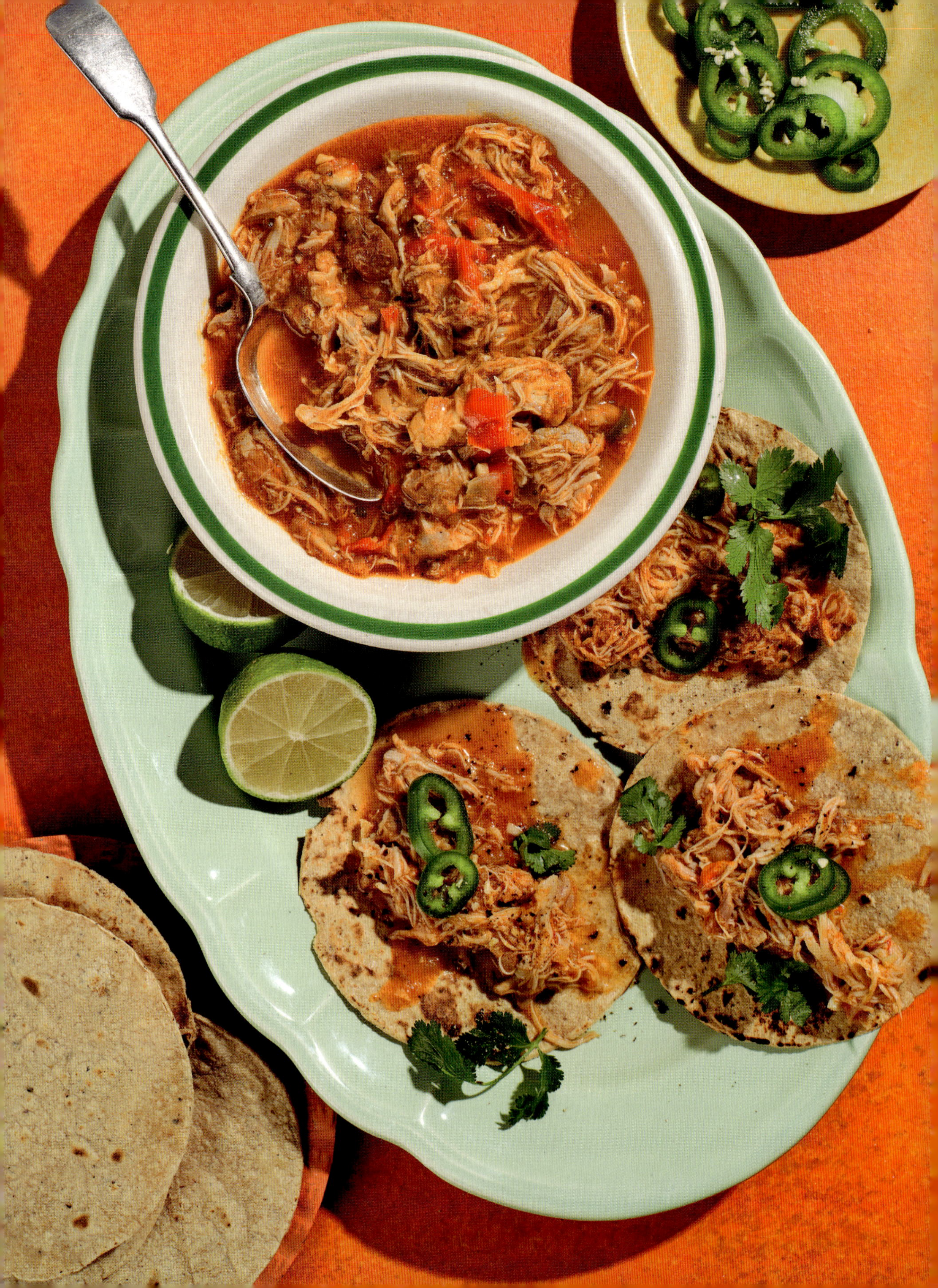

FAMILY CLASSICS

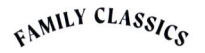

Chicken Enchiladas

This is a meal I'll prepare on days when the family are all coming home at different times. I'll cook it and leave it on the 'keep warm' function, then everyone can help themselves throughout the evening. It saves my sanity and me from making several dinners!

- 12 chicken thighs (about 1.2kg/2lb 11oz)
- 1½ tsp paprika
- 1 tsp ground cumin
- ½ tsp salt
- 1½ tsp chilli powder
- 3 garlic cloves, peeled and minced
- 1 red (bell) pepper, deseeded and chopped into strips
- 1 red onion, peeled and sliced
- 1 jalapeño, chopped into thin slices
- 1x 300g (10½oz) jar mild salsa
- 300g (10½oz) Cheddar cheese, grated
- 8 corn tortillas

1. Combine all the ingredients, apart from the cheese and tortillas, in your grab bag. Mix together.

2. Remove as much air as you can from the bag before sealing. Label the bag with the contents and the date you prepared it, then place it in the freezer, making sure it lies as flat as possible.

3. Defrost the bag thoroughly in the fridge for approximately 8–10 hours before cooking.

4. To cook, empty the contents of the bag into the slow cooker. (You can wash the bag and reuse, but don't forget to re-label.) Cook on low for 8 hours or on high for 4 hours.

5. Thirty minutes before the cooking time is up, shred the chicken, add the grated cheese and stir in. Allow to cook for the final 30 minutes, then add the coriander and green chillies. Stir and serve.

3 MONTHS | **8–10 HOURS** | **LOW 8 hours** | **HIGH 4 hours** | **SERVES 4**

FAMILY CLASSICS

Shepherd's Pie

This is a total family classic, but done my way. I use pre-made mashed potato; I'll either buy it freshly made from the supermarket chilled section or get a frozen packet that I'll just keep with the Shepherd's pie bag in the freezer.

- 1 onion, chopped
- 3 fresh thyme sprigs
- 4 carrots, peeled and diced
- 500g (1lb 2oz) lean minced lamb (5% fat)
- 2 tbsp tomato purée (paste)
- 1 x 400g (14oz) can haricot beans, drained and rinsed
- 1 tbsp Worcestershire sauce
- 2 tbsp cornflour (cornstarch)
- 900g (2lb) frozen ready-made mashed potato

1. Put the onion, thyme, carrots and lamb in a grab bag, then add the tomato purée, beans and Worcestershire sauce. Remove as much air as you can from the bag before sealing. Label the bag with the contents and the date you prepared it. Write on the front that you need to add the relevant quantities of cornflour and mashed potato at the time of cooking. Place the bag in the freezer, making sure it lies as flat as possible.

2. Defrost the bag thoroughly in the fridge for approximately 8–10 hours before cooking.

3. To cook, empty the contents of the bag into your slow cooker. Cook on high for 4 hours or on low for 8 hours.

4. Half an hour before the meal has finished cooking, mix the cornflour with 2 tablespoons of cold water in a jug and add to the slow cooker. This will help to thicken the sauce. Continue cooking for the remaining time.

5. Towards the end of the cooking time, cook the frozen mash according to the packet instructions. If your slow cooker pot is oven safe, top the mince with the mashed potatoes and cook, uncovered, in the oven preheated to 180°C/160°C fan/350°F/Gas 4 for 20 minutes. If your slow cooker pot is not oven safe, continue cooking the meal for a further 30 minutes in the slow cooker, then top with the cooked mashed potatoes before serving. Brown under the grill if liked.

| 3 MONTHS | 8–10 HOURS | LOW 8 hours / HIGH 4 hours | SERVES 4 |

TIP
The pepper will go very soft during cooking, so if you prefer a crisper texture, you can add the pepper to the slow cooker half an hour before its finished cooking. I would freeze this in a separate smaller bag and clip to the pork bag as this keeps everything together for cooking.

FAMILY CLASSICS

Smoky Pork Loins

You can serve this with a load of steamed vegetables, it's so filling and yummy. You could use pork chops instead and serve them whole, but I do love the cheaper option of loin.

- 8 pork loin steaks (about 600g/1lb 5oz), chopped into chunks
- 2 onions, peeled and chopped
- 2 red (bell) peppers, deseeded and chopped
- 2 tbsp Worcestershire sauce
- 2 garlic cloves, finely chopped
- 1 chicken stock cube
- 2 tsp smoked paprika
- Salt and black pepper

1. Put the pork loins in a grab bag and add the onions and peppers.

2. Next, add the Worcestershire sauce, garlic, stock cube and smoked paprika and season with salt and pepper. Mix to combine.

3. Remove as much air as you can from the bag before sealing. Label the bag with the contents and the date you prepared it, then place it in the freezer, making sure it lies as flat as possible.

4. Defrost the bag thoroughly in the fridge for approximately 8–10 hours before cooking.

5. To cook, empty the contents of the bag into your slow cooker. (You can wash the bag and reuse, but don't forget to re-label.) Cook on low for 6 hours or on high for 3 hours.

3 MONTHS | **8–10 HOURS** | **LOW 6 hours | HIGH 3 hours** | **SERVES 4**

FAMILY CLASSICS

Sausage Stew

I love to serve this with a smooth cheesy mash: to make this I just mash my potatoes, add a dash of milk and knob of butter and stir it all together, then add a good handful of grated mature Cheddar cheese and stir again. Yummy!

A splash of oil
12 pork sausages (about 700g/1lb 9oz)
1 x 400g (14oz) can chopped tomatoes
1 tsp salt
1 tsp black pepper
1 tsp paprika
1 tsp dried thyme
2 onions, peeled and chopped into chunks
2 carrots, peeled and sliced
2 celery stalks, sliced
1 x 400g (14oz) can cannellini beans, drained and rinsed
1 x 400g (14oz) can butter beans, drained and rinsed
2 garlic cloves, minced
2 tbsp tomato purée (paste)
1 vegetable jelly stock pot

1. Heat the oil in a frying pan over medium-high heat and sear the sausages on all sides until browned all over – you may need to do this in batches. Remove from the pan and allow to cool completely.

2. Open the can of chopped tomatoes and add the salt, pepper, paprika and thyme. Mix well. Now add all the remaining ingredients to your grab bag along with the canned tomatoes and mix well.

3. Remove as much air as you can from the bag before sealing. Label the bag with the contents and the date you prepared it, then place it in the freezer, making sure it lies as flat as possible.

4. Defrost the bag thoroughly in the fridge for approximately 8–10 hours before cooking.

5. To cook, empty the contents of the bag into your slow cooker. (You can wash the bag and reuse, but don't forget to re-label.) Cook on low for 8 hours or on high for 4 hours.

3 MONTHS | **8–10 HOURS** | **LOW** 8 hours / **HIGH** 4 hours | **SERVES 4**

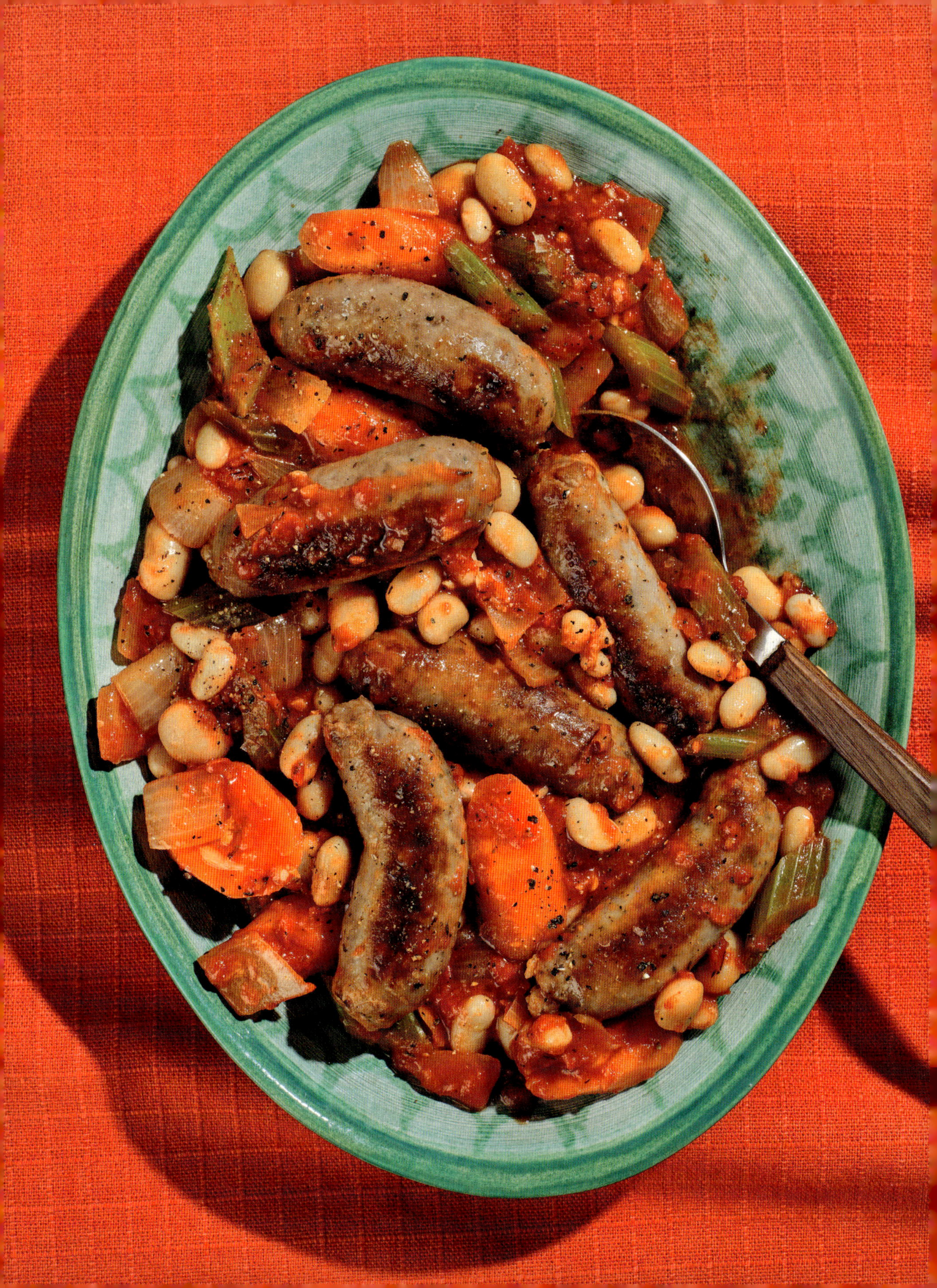

FAMILY CLASSICS

Beef Goulash

This is a hearty and filling dish that I like to serve in big pasta bowls with a side of fresh crusty bread for dunking!

1x 400g (14oz) can chopped tomatoes
1 tsp garlic powder
2 tsp smoked paprika
500g (1lb 2oz) stewing beef, chopped into chunks
400g (14oz) potatoes, peeled and diced
2 carrots, peeled and diced
2 celery stalks, chopped
1 onion, chopped
2 red (bell) peppers, deseeded and chopped
2 tbsp tomato purée (paste)
1 beef jelly stock pot
300ml (10½fl oz/1¼ cups) boiling water
Salt and black pepper
Crusty bread, to serve

1. Open the canned tomatoes and add the garlic powder and smoked paprika and season with salt and pepper. Stir well.

2. Into the bag, put the beef, potatoes, carrots, celery, onion, peppers, tomato purée and beef stock pot. Pour in the canned tomatoes and stir well.

3. Remove as much air as you can from the bag before sealing. Label the bag with the contents and the date you prepared it. Write on the front that you need to add the relevant quantity of boiling water at the time of cooking (or a note to refer to this page number). Place the bag in the freezer, making sure it lies as flat as possible.

4. Defrost the bag thoroughly in the fridge for approximately 8–10 hours before cooking.

5. To cook, empty the contents of the bag into your slow cooker, add the boiling water and stir. (You can wash the bag and reuse, but don't forget to re-label.) Cook on low for 6 hours or on high for 3 hours.

6. Serve with crusty bread.

3 MONTHS | 8–10 HOURS | LOW 6 hours / HIGH 3 hours | SERVES 4

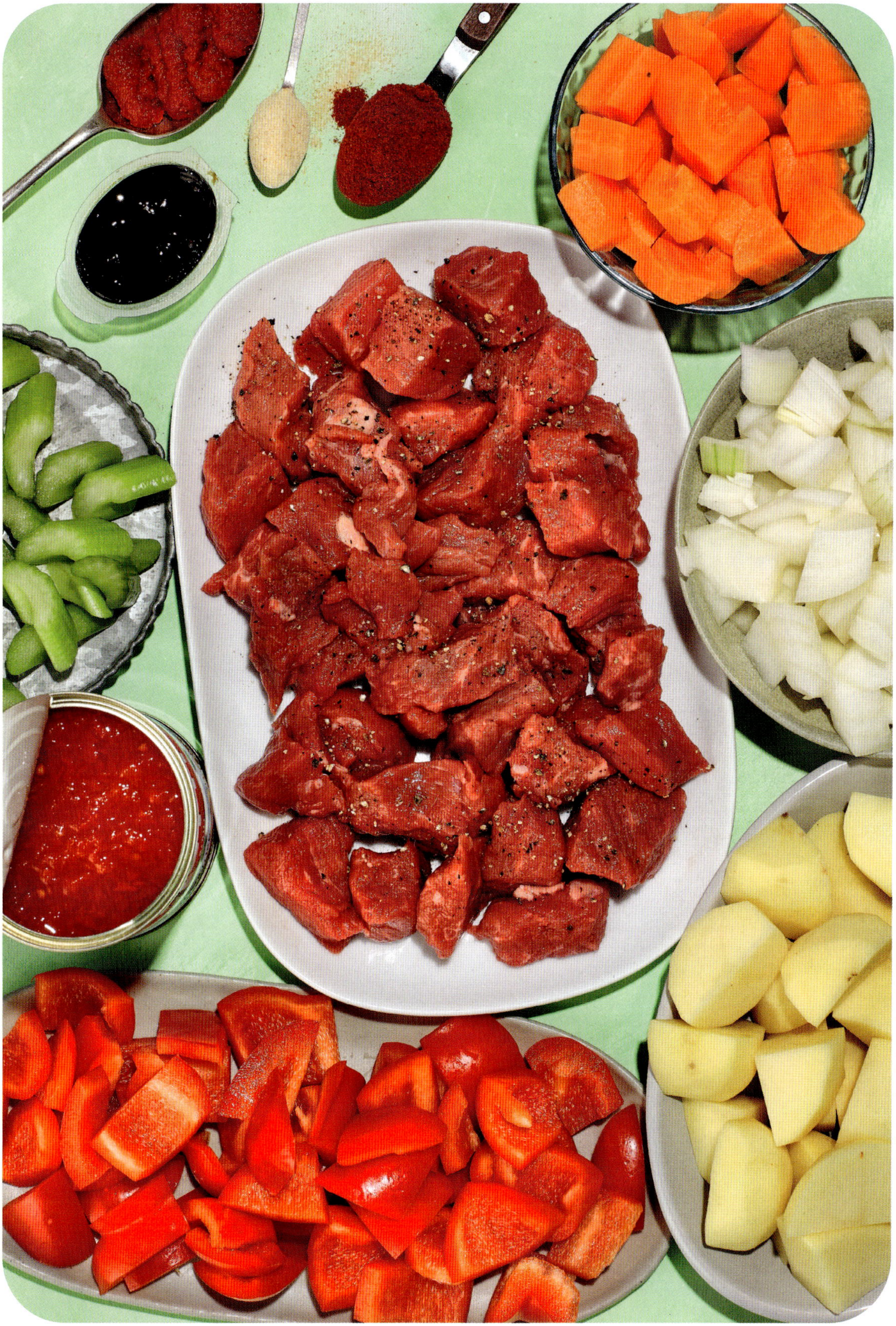

FAMILY CLASSICS

Spaghetti Bolognese

This is my version of a 'Spag Bol'. I try and keep the ingredients to as few as possible while still packing it full of flavour. Having recently discovered red wine stock pots, I now make sure I keep quite a large stash as they are so easy to use and packed with flavour.

- 2 x 400g (14oz) cans chopped tomatoes
- 2 garlic cloves, minced
- 1 tsp dried oregano
- 2 tbsp Worcestershire sauce
- 2 tbsp tomato purée (paste)
- 1 large onion, diced
- 1 red wine stock pot (or a beef stock pot is a great alternative for kids)
- 750g (1lb 10oz) beef mince (5% fat)
- 2 bay leaves
- Salt and black pepper
- Spaghetti and grated Parmesan cheese, to serve

1. Open one can of chopped tomatoes and add the garlic, oregano, Worcestershire sauce and a pinch of salt and pepper. Stir to combine.

2. Add the tomato purée to the second can of tomatoes and stir to combine.

3. Open the grab bag and add the onion, stock pot, beef and bay leaves. Pour in the two cans of chopped tomatoes. Close the bag, keeping some air in, and give everything a good mix up.

4. Remove as much air as you can from the bag before sealing. Label the bag with the contents and the date you prepared it, then place it in the freezer, making sure it lies as flat as possible.

5. Defrost the bag thoroughly in the fridge for approximately 8–10 hours before cooking.

6. To cook, empty the contents of the bag into your slow cooker. (You can wash the bag and reuse, but don't forget to re-label.) Cook on high for 4 hours or on low for 8 hours.

7. Serve the Bolognese with spaghetti and a good sprinkle of Parmesan.

3 MONTHS | **8–10 HOURS** | **LOW 8 hours | HIGH 4 hours** | **SERVES 4**

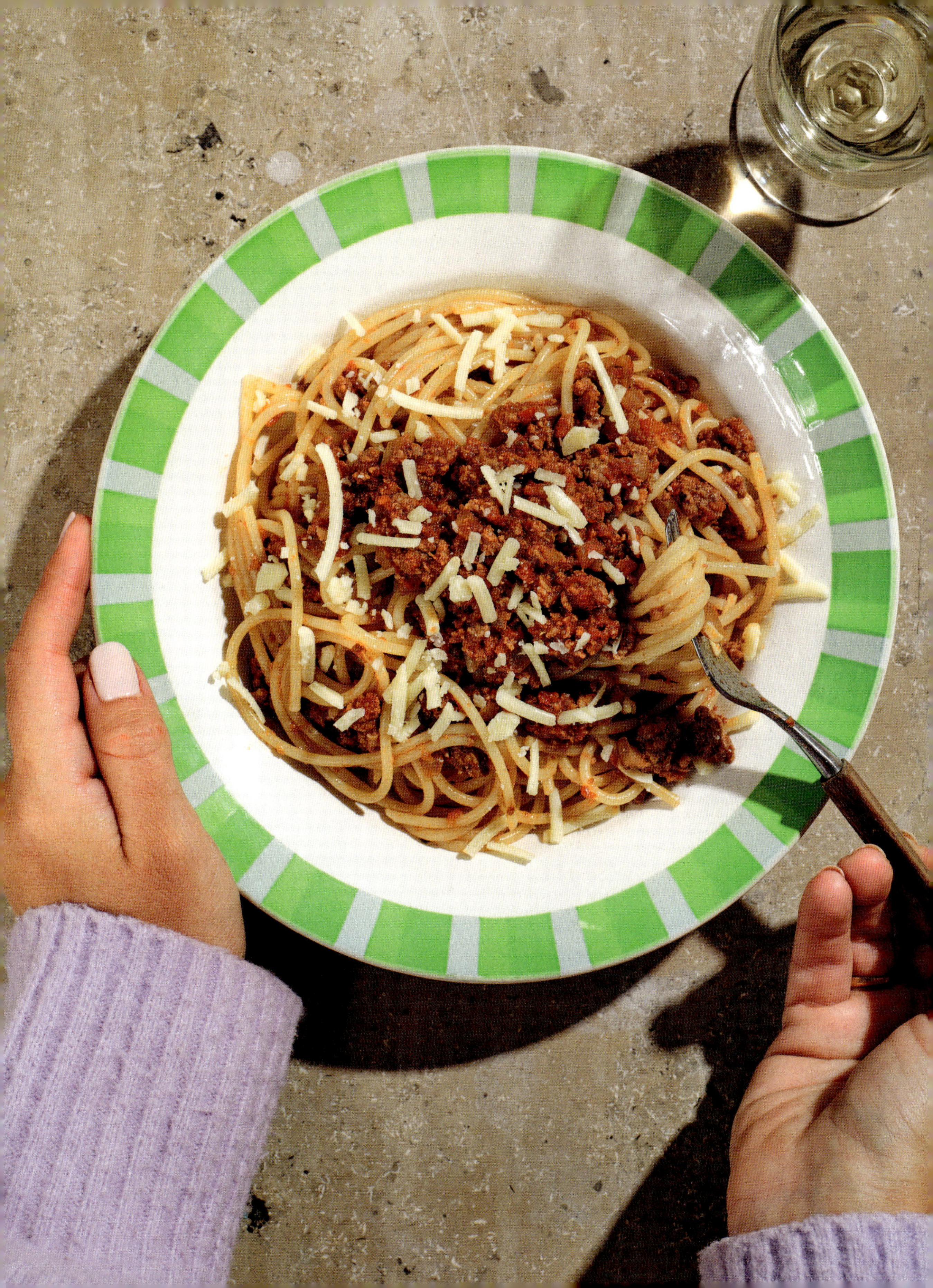

FAMILY CLASSICS

Teriyaki Pork Loins

Pork can so easily be overcooked but cooking it in the slow cooker pretty much solves that problem for you. Teamed with the sweet and salty sauce, this is going to be a recipe you come back to time and time again.

- 300ml (10fl oz/1¼ cups) light soy sauce
- 60ml (2fl oz/¼ cup) rice wine vinegar
- 1 tbsp sesame oil
- 1 tbsp light brown sugar
- 3 garlic cloves, minced
- 1 tsp peeled and grated fresh root ginger
- 8 pork loin steaks (about 1kg / 1lb 2oz), sliced into 1cm (½ inch) wide pieces
- Long-stem broccoli and mashed potatoes, to serve

1. Put the soy sauce, rice wine vinegar, sesame oil, brown sugar, garlic and ginger in a bowl. Whisk together until combined.

2. Add the pork to the grab bag and pour the sauce over. Make sure the pork is well coated. Seal the bag. This can be left in the fridge for a day to marinate if you'd like some extra flavour in the pork.

3. Once marinated, remove as much air as you can from the bag before sealing. Label the bag with the contents and the date you prepared it, then place it in the freezer, making sure it lies as flat as possible.

4. Defrost the bag thoroughly in the fridge for approximately 8–10 hours before cooking.

5. To cook, empty the contents of the bag into your slow cooker. (You can wash the bag and reuse, but don't forget to re-label.) Cook on low for 8 hours or on high for 4 hours.

6. Serve the pork with long-stem broccoli and mashed potatoes. Drizzle the sauce over the mash – you won't regret it.

3 MONTHS | 8–10 HOURS | LOW 8 hours / HIGH 4 hours | SERVES 4

TIP
Grab some ready-made frozen mash and clip it to the bag so you don't use it for something else, and you won't have to worry about any extra cooking when you come to dish it up!

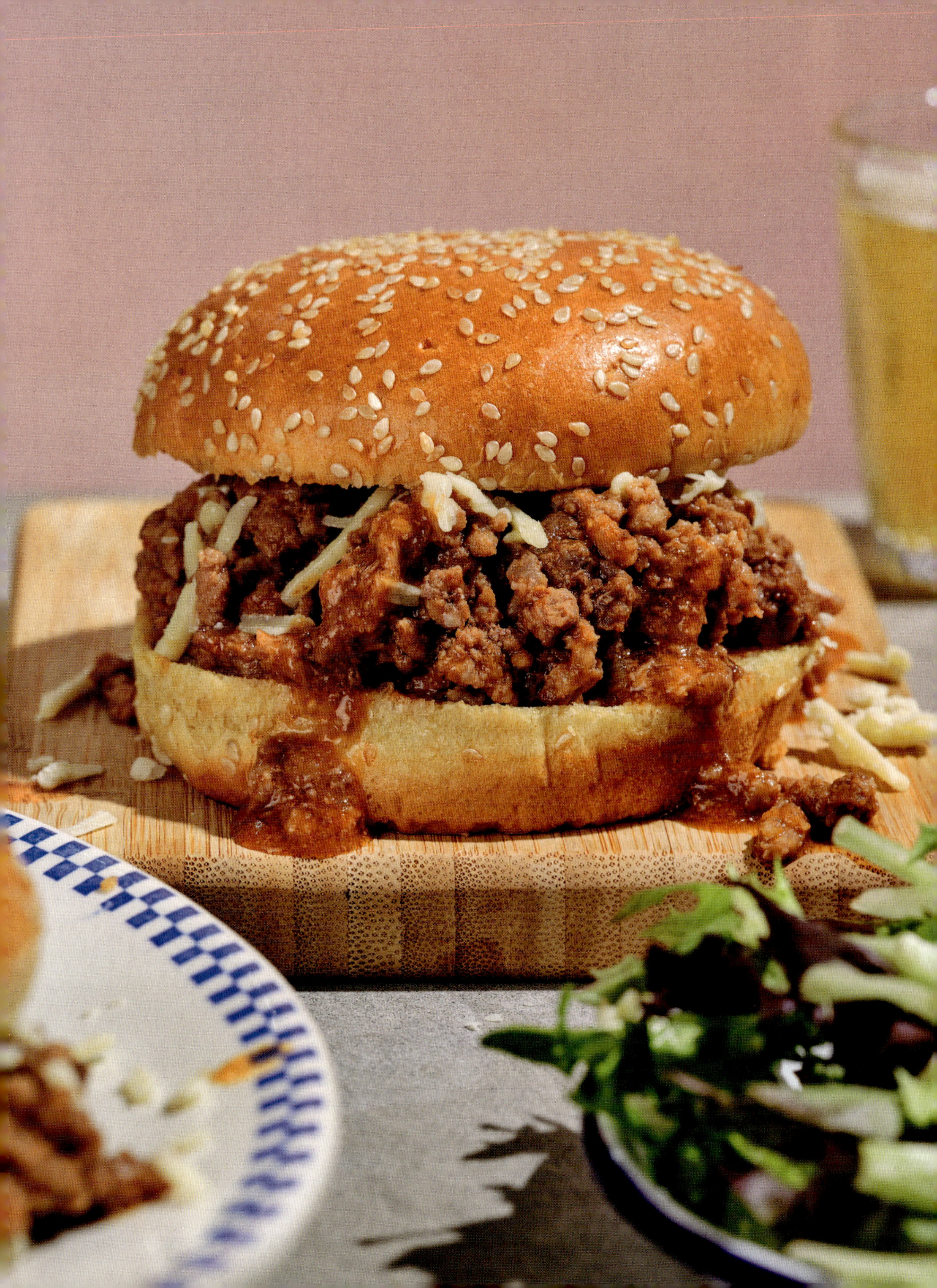

FAMILY CLASSICS

Sloppy Joes

This is a very American inspired dish. It's essentially just mince in a delicious sauce served on burger buns, but it's hearty and warming and ideal for the kids!

750g (1lb 10oz) minced beef (5% fat)
1 small onion, peeled and finely diced
1 tsp garlic powder
1 tbsp American-style mustard
200g (7oz/¾ cup) tomato ketchup
2 tbsp light brown sugar
8 burger buns
200g (7oz) mature Cheddar cheese, grated
Salt and black pepper
A side salad, to serve

1. In a bowl, combine the mince with the onion, garlic, mustard, ketchup and sugar. Stir well to combine. Transfer this into a grab bag.

2. Remove as much air as you can from the bag before sealing. Label the bag with the contents and the date you prepared it. Write on the front that you'll need eight burger buns and cheese for assembling (or a note to refer to this page number). Place the bag in the freezer, making sure it lies as flat as possible.

3. Defrost the bag thoroughly in the fridge for approximately 8–10 hours before cooking.

4. To cook, empty the contents of the bag into your slow cooker. (You can wash the bag and reuse, but don't forget to re-label.) Cook on low for 8 hours or on high for 4 hours.

5. Serve the meat sauce in burger buns with a sprinkle of cheese, along with a side salad.

3 MONTHS | **8–10 HOURS** | **LOW 8 hours** | **HIGH 4 hours** | **SERVES 4**

FAMILY CLASSICS

Mexican Beef Taco Shells

This is my version of tacos. I'm not sure sweetcorn is a usual ingredient here, but we love the added sweetness.

1 chicken jelly stock pot

200ml (7fl oz/generous ¾ cup) boiling water

80g (2¾oz) Cheddar cheese, grated

500g (1lb 2oz) beef mince (5% fat)

1 x 30g (1oz) packet of taco seasoning

½ tsp salt

½ tsp pepper

1 small onion, peeled and diced

2 garlic cloves, minced

2 tbsp tomato purée (paste)

1 x 400g (14oz) can pinto beans, rinsed and drained

150g (5½oz) frozen sweetcorn

8 taco shells, warmed

Avocado, sour cream, salsa and a salad, to serve

1. Put the chicken stock pot, boiling water and cheese into a bowl. Mix until the cheese has melted and the stock pot has dissolved. Leave to cool completely.

2. Put the beef mince in a bowl along with the taco seasoning, salt and pepper. Mix well until all combined and add to your grab bag.

3. Add all the remaining ingredients except the taco shells, and pour in the cheesy chicken stock.

4. Remove as much air as you can from the bag before sealing. Label the bag with the contents and the date you prepared it. Write on the front that you'll need eight corn tortillas for serving (or a note to refer to this page number). Place the bag in the freezer, making sure it lies as flat as possible.

5. Defrost the bag thoroughly in the fridge for approximately 8–10 hours before cooking.

6. To cook, empty the contents of the bag into your slow cooker. (You can wash the bag and reuse, but don't forget to re-label.) Cook on low for 8 hours or on high for 4 hours.

7. Serve the beef in the warmed taco shells, with avocado, sour cream and salsa.

3 MONTHS | **8–10 HOURS** | **LOW 8 hours | HIGH 4 hours** | **SERVES 4**

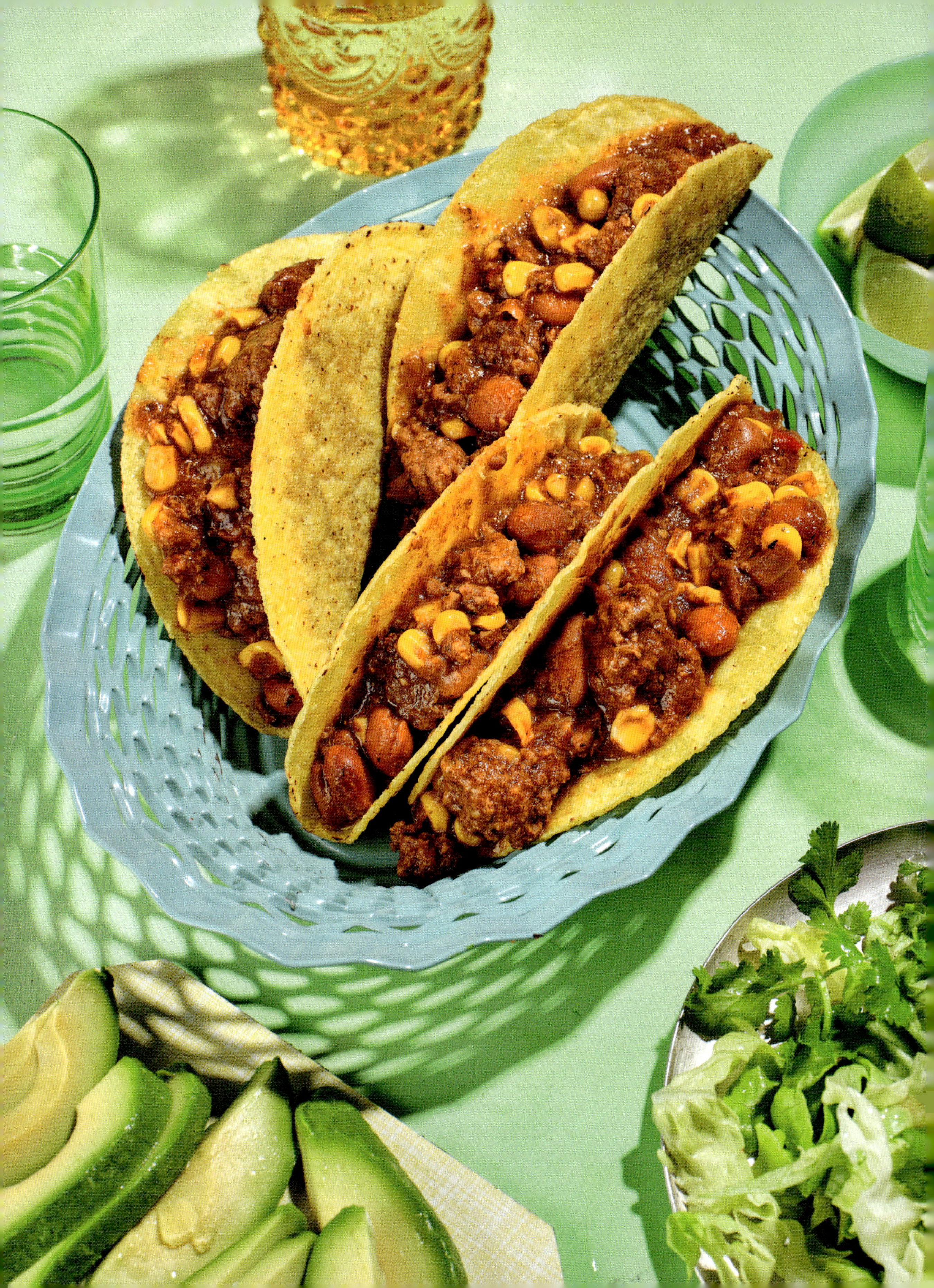

FAMILY CLASSICS

Spicy Shredded Beef

Beef can be a more expensive option for dinner, so I usually make this when I find good cuts of meat in the reduced section! It's so cost effective to grab the meat while it's on offer and whip up a grab bag, get it frozen and then enjoy.

500g (1lb 2oz) braising beef, sliced
1 onion, chopped
3 garlic cloves, minced
1 x 400g (14oz) can chopped tomatoes
1 tbsp chipotle paste
1 tbsp runny honey
2 tsp chilli powder
1 tsp ground cumin
1 beef jelly stock pot stock cube
300ml (10½fl oz/scant 1 cup) boiling water
Salt and black pepper
Rice, to serve

1. Put the beef into your grab bag and add the onion and garlic.

2. Open your can of tomatoes, add the chipotle paste and honey and stir well to combine. Next add the chilli powder and cumin and mix. Empty the can into the grab bag and add the beef stock pot. Close the bag and massage the beef through the bag to combine all the ingredients.

3. Remove as much air as you can from the bag before sealing. Label the bag with the contents and the date you prepared it. Write on the front that you need to add the relevant quantity of boiling water at the time of cooking, and freeze as flat as possible.

4. Defrost the bag thoroughly in the fridge for approximately 8–10 hours before cooking.

5. To cook, empty the contents into the slow cooker, add the boiling water and stir. Cook on low for 7 hours or on high for 3 hours.

6. Remove the beef from the slow cooker and shred it using two forks. Return the meat to the cooker, stir in and cook for another hour.

7. Taste and season with salt and pepper, then serve the spicy beef with rice.

---

3 MONTHS | **8–10 HOURS** | **LOW 7 hours** | **HIGH 3 hours** | **SERVES 4**

FAMILY CLASSICS

Apple & Honey Drumsticks

You might not think apple and chicken goes together but trust me, this is incredible. Make sure to drizzle the liquid left in the slow cooker over the whole meal – yum!

- 12 chicken drumsticks without skin (about 1.5kg/3¼lb)
- 4 Granny Smith apples (approx. 600g/1lb 5oz), peeled and chopped into chunks
- 1 tsp salt
- 2 tbsp runny honey
- Salad and chips, to serve

1. Put the chicken in the grab bag, along with the apples. Sprinkle over the salt, then pour over the honey. Close the bag and massage the chicken through the bag so that it is completely covered in honey.

2. Remove as much air as you can from the bag before sealing. Label the bag with the contents and the date you prepared it, then place it in the freezer, making sure it lies as flat as possible.

3. Defrost the bag thoroughly in the fridge for approximately 8–10 hours before cooking.

4. To cook, empty the contents of the bag into your slow cooker. (You can wash the bag and reuse, but don't forget to re-label.) Cook on low for 6 hours or on high for 3 hours.

5. Remove the chicken and apples from the slow cooker and drizzle some of the cooking liquid in the slow cooker over the chicken. Serve with a salad and chips.

3 MONTHS | **8–10 HOURS** | **LOW 6 hours | HIGH 3 hours** | **SERVES 4**

TIP
To add a bit of bite and remove some of the fat, you can fry off your bacon before adding to the bag. Just make sure to allow it to cool completely before adding it to the bag.

FAMILY CLASSICS

Chicken & Bacon Pot

This is such a comfort meal. Chicken and bacon is the ultimate combination to me. Any leftovers can be kept in the fridge until the next day and can be added to a sandwich for the most amazing lunch, or reheated for dinner.

- 6 skinless and boneless chicken breasts (about. 1kg/2lb 4oz)
- 6 thick-cut bacon rashers (about 300g/10½oz), chopped into small chunks
- 1 onion, peeled and diced
- 1 tsp garlic powder
- 1 tsp ground cumin
- 1 chicken jelly stock pot
- 500ml (17fl oz/2 cups) boiling water
- 2 tbsp balsamic vinegar
- Salt and black pepper
- Broccoli, sliced potatoes and cauliflower cheese, to serve

1. Put the chicken and bacon into the grab bag along with the onion. Sprinkle over the garlic powder and cumin. Close the bag and mix well.

2. Now add the stock pot and season with salt and pepper.

3. Remove as much air as you can from the bag before sealing. Label the bag with the contents and the date you prepared it. Write on the front that you need to add the relevant quantities of boiling water and vinegar at time of cooking. Place the bag in the freezer, making sure it lies as flat as possible.

4. Defrost the bag thoroughly in the fridge for approximately 8–10 hours before cooking.

5. To cook, empty the contents of the bag into your slow cooker, add the boiling water and balsamic vinegar and stir well. (You can wash the bag and reuse, but don't forget to re-label.) Cook on high for 3 hours, or on low for 6 hours.

6. Serve with broccoli, sliced potatoes and cauliflower cheese.

3 MONTHS | **8–10 HOURS** | **LOW** 6 hours | **HIGH** 3 hours | **SERVES 4**

FAMILY CLASSICS

Spanish Beef

This is my version of Spanish beef, which reminds me of childhood holidays in Majorca with my family. The smell of this cooking will be hard to resist.

- 2 x 400g (14oz) cans chopped tomatoes
- 1 tsp paprika
- 1 tsp cayenne pepper
- 450g (1lb) braising beef steak, chopped into 2.5cm (1 inch) chunks
- 400g (14oz) potatoes, peeled and chopped into chunks
- 1 onion, chopped into large dice
- 3 garlic cloves, peeled and minced
- 1 tbsp olive oil
- 170g (6oz) pitted green olives, sliced in half (optional)
- Salt and black pepper
- Lemon wedges, to serve
- Parsley sprigs, to garnish, optional

1. Open one of the cans of tomatoes, add the paprika and cayenne pepper and season with salt and pepper. Mix well.

2. Open the grab bag and add the braising steak, potatoes, onion, garlic, olive oil and olives, if using.

3. Pour in the canned tomatoes, seal the bag and shake well to combine all the ingredients.

4. Remove as much air as you can from the bag before sealing. Label the bag with the contents and the date you prepared it, then place it in the freezer, making sure it lies as flat as possible.

5. Defrost the bag thoroughly in the fridge for approximately 8–10 hours before cooking.

6. To cook, empty the contents of the bag into your slow cooker. (You can wash the bag and reuse, but don't forget to re-label.) Cook on low for 8 hours or on high for 3–4 hours.

7. Serve with the green beans (see Tip opposite) and lemon wedges, and garnish with parsley, if liked.

3 MONTHS | 8–10 HOURS | LOW 8 hours | HIGH 3–4 hours | SERVES 4

TIP:
I like to serve this with green beans sautéed with pine nuts. To make them, blanch 440g (15½oz) green beans in boiling water for 5 minutes, then drain. Heat 1 tbsp olive oil in a frying pan and add the drained beans and 50g (1¾oz) pine nuts. Cook for 3 minutes until soft.

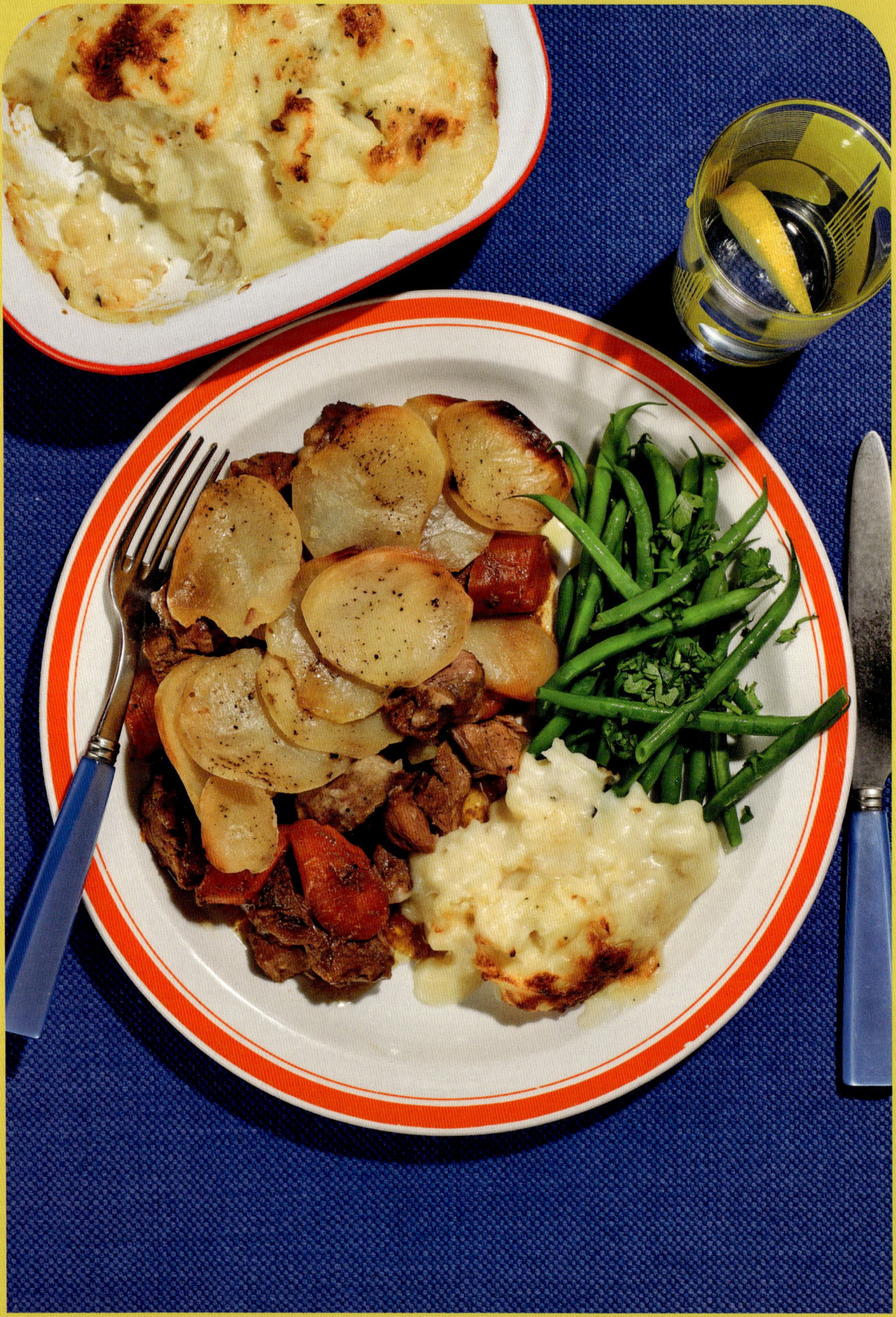

WINTER 2 WARMERS

WINTER WARMERS

Mongolian-Style Beef

What I love about this recipe is that, apart from the beef, it's all pretty much store cupboard ingredients so ideal to whip up when you find good cuts of meat for a good price. It's simple but packs a real punch!

500g (1lb 2oz) braising beef, chopped into chunks
2 tbsp cornflour (cornstarch)
3 tbsp brown sugar
1 tbsp grated root ginger
A pinch of chilli flakes
200ml (7fl oz/scant 1 cup) light soy sauce
2 garlic cloves, minced
200ml (7fl oz/scant 1 cup) boiling water
Rice, to serve

1. Put the beef in a grab bag, add the cornflour and close the bag. Shake to coat the beef chunks in the cornflour.

2. Open the bag and add the brown sugar, ginger, chilli flakes, soy sauce and garlic and make sure all the ingredients are mixed well.

3. Remove as much air as you can from the bag before sealing. Label the bag with the contents and the date you prepared it. Write on the front that you need to add the relevant quantity of boiling water at the time of cooking (or a note to refer to this page number). Place the bag in the freezer, making sure it lies as flat as possible.

4. Defrost the bag thoroughly in the fridge for approximately 8–10 hours before cooking.

5. To cook, empty the contents of the bag into your slow cooker, add the boiling water and stir. (You can wash the bag and reuse, but don't forget to re-label.) Cook on low for 7 hours or on high for 3 hours.

6. Serve the Mongolian beef with rice.

---

3 MONTHS | **8–10 HOURS** | **LOW 7 hours | HIGH 3 hours** | **SERVES 4**

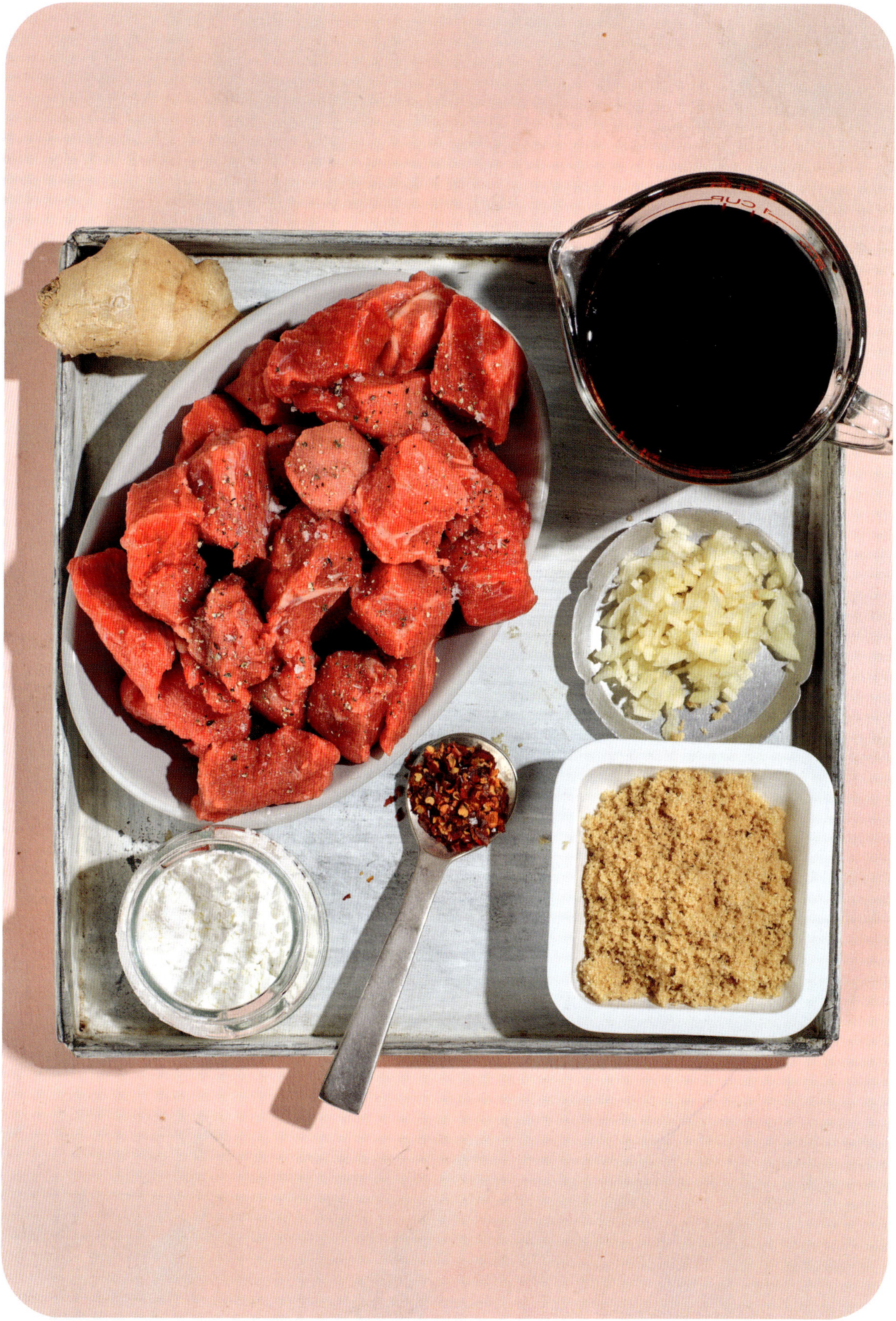

WINTER WARMERS

Corn Chicken Chilli

There is nothing more comforting than a big jacket potato covered in this delicious chilli. The smell of this filling your house will be hard to resist!

- 4 skinless chicken breasts (about 700g/1lb 9oz)
- 2 tsp garlic powder
- 2 tsp chilli powder
- 2 x 300g (10½oz) jars mild salsa
- 1x 400g (14oz) can kidney beans, drained and rinsed
- 350g (12oz) frozen sweetcorn
- Salt and black pepper
- Jacket potatoes, rice or pasta, to serve

1. Add the chicken to your grab bag and season with salt and pepper.

2. Next, add the garlic powder and chilli powder. Close the bag and rub the spices over the chicken.

3. Open the grab bag and add the salsa, kidney beans and sweetcorn. Close the bag and mix all the ingredients together.

4. Remove as much air as you can from the bag before sealing. Label the bag with the contents and the date you prepared it, then place it in the freezer, making sure it lies as flat as possible.

5. Defrost the bag thoroughly in the fridge for approximately 8–10 hours before cooking.

6. To cook, empty the contents of the bag into your slow cooker. (You can wash the bag and reuse, but don't forget to re-label.) Cook on low for 7½ hours or on high for 3½ hours.

7. After this initial cooking time, remove the chicken and shred it. Tip it back into the slow cooker, stir well and leave to cook for a further 30 minutes. (If you would like a thicker sauce, keep the lid off for this cooking time to evaporate some of the moisture.)

8. Serve the chilli over a jacket potato, rice or pasta.

3 MONTHS | **8–10 HOURS** | **LOW 7½ hours | HIGH 3½ hours** | **SERVES 4**

WINTER WARMERS

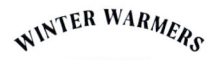

Spicy Beef

Don't be afraid to up the spice if you want it super spicy. We like this dish and the kids enjoy it too. I like to serve this over bowls of egg-fried rice.

- 1 x 400g (14oz) can chopped tomatoes
- 1 tsp ground cumin
- 1 tbsp mild chilli powder
- 1 tsp sea salt
- 1 tbsp jarred chipotle paste
- 1.2kg (2lb 11oz) braising steak, chopped
- 1 large onion, peeled and finely sliced
- 2 garlic cloves, minced
- 1 jalapeño chilli, finely diced
- 1 tbsp runny honey
- 1 beef jelly stock pot
- 400ml (14fl oz/1¾ cups) boiling water

1. Open the can of tomatoes and add the cumin, chilli powder, salt and chipotle paste. Mix well to combine.

2. Open the grab bag and add the steak, onion, garlic, jalapeños, honey and stock pot. Close the bag and shake to combine the ingredients. Now open the bag and pour in the can of tomatoes.

3. Remove as much air as you can before sealing. Label the bag with the contents and the date you prepared it. Write on the front that you need to add the relevant quantity of boiling water at the time of cooking (or a note to refer to this page number). Place the bag in the freezer, making sure it lies as flat as possible.

4. Defrost the bag thoroughly in the fridge for approximately 8–10 hours before cooking.

5. To cook, empty the contents of the bag into your slow cooker, then add the boiling water and stir well. (You can wash the bag and reuse, but don't forget to re-label.) Cook on low for 9 hours or on high for 4 hours.

3 MONTHS | **8–10 HOURS** | **LOW 9 hours** | **HIGH 4 hours** | **SERVES 4**

WINTER WARMERS

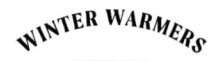

Pulled Pork

Whenever we go pumpkin picking, we always navigate to the pulled pork stand. It's my husband's ultimate chilly day food, but it can be pricey! So, make your own and enjoy with a soft roll, apple sauce and coleslaw.

- 2kg (4lb 8oz) pork shoulder joint
- 2 tsp ground cumin
- 1 tsp garlic powder
- 2 tsp cayenne pepper
- 3 tbsp wholegrain mustard
- 120ml (4fl oz/½ cup) apple cider vinegar
- Salt and black pepper
- Bread rolls, coleslaw and apple sauce, to serve

1. Remove any excess fat from the pork shoulder – you could cook this in the oven separately to make some delicious crackling. Leave a small amount of fat on the pork for flavour. Score into the top of the pork in a criss-cross formation and season with salt and pepper. Next, stir the cumin, garlic powder and cayenne pepper into the mustard, then rub this into the meat. Put the pork joint into a grab bag.

2. Remove as much air as you can from the bag before sealing. Label the bag with the contents and the date you prepared it. Write on the front that you need to add the apple cider vinegar at the time of cooking. Place the bag in the freezer, making sure it lies as flat as possible.

3. Defrost the bag thoroughly in the fridge for approximately 12 hours (time will vary depending on the thickness of your joint; if you prefer, you can slice the joint into two pieces when preparing the bag to speed up the defrosting process).

4. To cook, empty the contents of the bag into your slow cooker, add the vinegar and stir. Cook on low for 6½ hours or on high for 3 hours.

5. After the initial cooking time, remove the pork and shred. Return the meat to the slow cooker and mix well with all the juices. Leave to cook for a further 30 minutes. Serve in bread rolls with coleslaw and apple sauce.

| 3 MONTHS | 8–10 HOURS | LOW 6½ hours | HIGH 3 hours | SERVES 6 |

WINTER WARMERS

Buffalo Chicken Pasta

I like to use rigatoni for this, but you could use whatever dried pasta you fancy. The cayenne pepper in this gives it such a lovely warm kick, and with all the cheese? Well, you know it'll be delicious!

4 skinless, boneless chicken breasts
2 tsp cayenne pepper
2 tsp garlic powder
2 tablespoons buffalo sauce
½ salt
½ tsp black pepper
300g (10½oz) Cheddar cheese, grated
165g (5¾oz) cream cheese
1 chicken stock cube
300ml (10 ½floz/1¼ cups) boiling water
225g (8oz) dried rigatoni
Chopped chives, to garnish

1. Put the chicken breasts in a grab bag and add the cayenne pepper, garlic powder, buffalo sauce, salt and pepper. Close the bag and shake well to coat the chicken in the seasonings. Open the bag and add the grated cheese and cream cheese, and crumble in the stock cube.

2. Remove as much air as you can from the bag before sealing. Label the bag with the contents and the date you prepared it. Write on the front that you need to add the relevant quantity of boiling water and the pasta at the time of cooking (or a note to refer to this page number). Place the bag in the freezer, making sure it lies as flat as possible.

3. Defrost the bag thoroughly in the fridge for approximately 8–10 hours before cooking.

4. To cook, empty the contents of the bag into your slow cooker and add the boiling water. (You can wash the bag and reuse, but don't forget to re-label.) Mix everything well until the stock cube has dissolved. Cook on low for 7 hours or on high for 3 hours.

5. Once the cooking time is up, shred the chicken and add it back to the pot along with the dried rigatoni. Leave to cook for a further 30 minutes, or until the rigatoni is cooked through.

4 MONTHS | **8–10 HOURS** | **LOW 7 hours | HIGH 3 hours** | **SERVES 4**

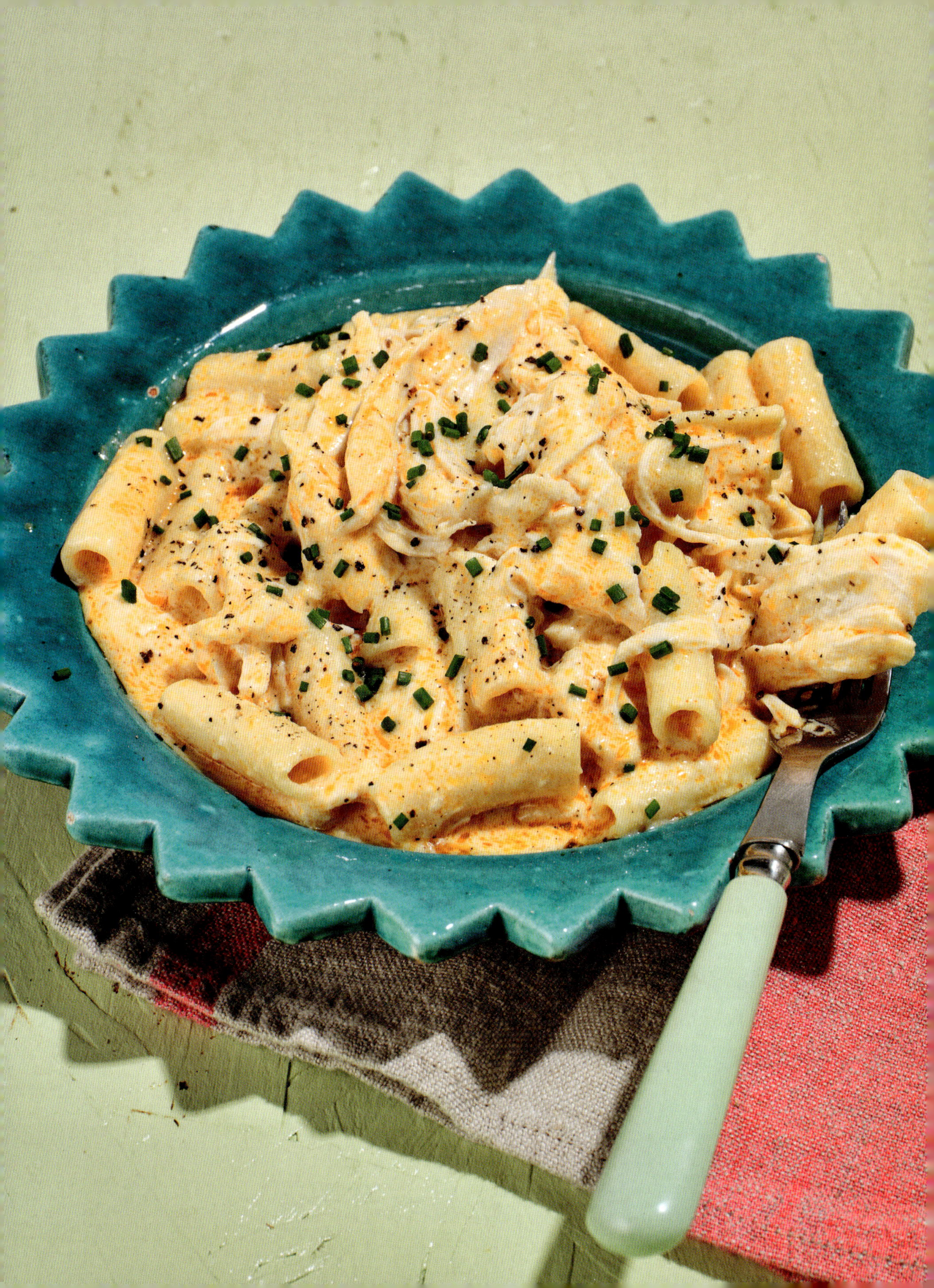

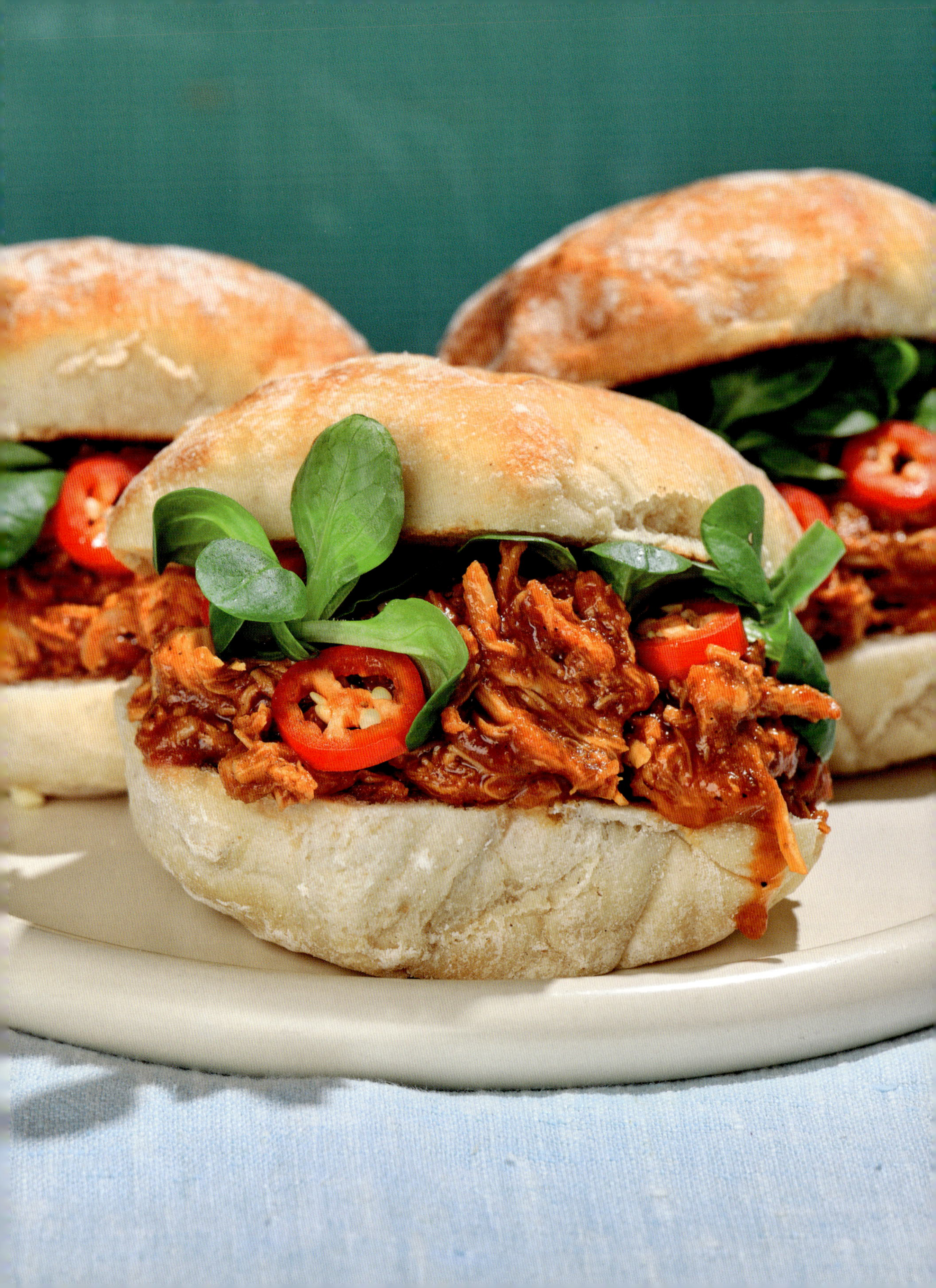

Winter Warmers

BBQ Chicken

This is a great dish to serve at a family get together or party; just pop the bowl on the table and let everyone dig in!

- 3 skinless, boneless chicken breasts (about 500g/1lb 2oz)
- 200g (7oz/¾ cup) tomato ketchup
- 100g (3½ oz/½ cup) dark brown sugar
- 2 tbsp apple cider vinegar
- 1 tsp chilli powder
- 1 tsp onion powder
- 1 tsp garlic powder
- ½ tsp chilli flakes
- Salt and black pepper
- Bread rolls, salad and coleslaw, optional, to serve
- Red chilli slices, to garnish, optional

1. Put the chicken in a grab bag and add all the remaining ingredients. Season with salt and pepper. Close the bag and shake well to combine.

2. Remove as much air as you can from the bag before sealing. Label the bag with the contents and the date you prepared it, then place it in the freezer, making sure it lies as flat as possible.

3. Defrost the bag thoroughly in the fridge for approximately 8–10 hours before cooking.

4. To cook, empty the contents of the bag into your slow cooker. (You can wash the bag and reuse, but don't forget to re-label.) Cook on low for 8 hours or on high for 4 hours.

5. Shred the chicken and stir back into the sauce in the cooker, then serve in bread rolls with salad and coleslaw. Garnish with red chilli slices, if liked.

3 MONTHS | **8–10 HOURS** | **LOW 8 hours | HIGH 4 hours** | **SERVES 4**

WINTER WARMERS

Chicken & Leek Faux Pie

This is more of a deconstructed pie, as you're preparing the filling and pastry separately. You can make homemade pastry, but for ease I buy ready-rolled and whack it in the freezer so it is always ready to go.

- 3 skinless, boneless chicken breasts, (about 500g/1lb 2oz), chopped
- 2 leeks, sliced
- 250g (9oz/2 cups) frozen peas
- 2 garlic cloves, finely chopped
- 1 chicken stock cube
- 300ml (10½fl oz/1¼ cups) boiling water
- 320g (11¼oz) frozen ready-rolled sheet of puff pastry
- 2 tbsp cornflour (cornstarch)
- Salt and black pepper
- Mashed potato or chips, to serve

1. Put the chicken in a grab bag, then add the leeks, peas, garlic and stock cube. Season. Remove as much air as you can from the bag before sealing. Label the bag with the contents and the date you prepared it. Write on the front that you need to add the relevant quantities of boiling water, cornflour and pastry at the time of cooking. Place the bag in the freezer, making sure it lies as flat as possible.

2. Defrost the bag and the pastry thoroughly in the fridge for approximately 8–10 hours before cooking.

3. To cook, empty the contents of the bag into the slow cooker and add the boiling water. Stir until the stock cube has dissolved. Cook on low for 8 hours or on high for 4 hours.

4. Half an hour before the filling has finished cooking, preheat the oven as per the pastry cooking instructions on the packet. Lay the sheet of pastry on a baking tray and cut into four pieces, then cook as per the packet instructions.

5. Once the pastry is in the oven, mix the cornflour with 2 tablespoons of cold water and add to the slow cooker. Mix well and continue cooking for the remaining 30 minutes – this will help to thicken the sauce.

6. Serve the filling with a square of the cooked pastry on top and with mashed potato on the side.

3 MONTHS | 8–10 HOURS | LOW 8 hours | HIGH 4 hours | SERVES 4

TIP:
Using packet rice will speed up the serving process or you could pre-cook rice and freeze in a freezer bag. Make sure to defrost thoroughly and reheat correctly.

WINTER WARMERS

Jerk Chicken

This is my version of jerk chicken; I love to serve this with a bowl of rice and beans and let everyone dig in. You could also use the sauce to marinate chicken wings and whack on your BBQ!

- 12 skinless, boneless chicken thighs (about 1.2kg/2lb 12oz), sliced into strips
- 200g (7oz/½ cup) black treacle
- 1½ tbsp dried thyme
- 2 tsp salt
- 2 tsp ground allspice
- ½ tsp ground cardamom
- 1 jalapeño chilli, chopped
- 3 garlic cloves, minced
- 1 tbsp finely chopped fresh root ginger
- 1 tsp coconut oil, melted
- Rice to serve

1. Put the chicken thighs in a grab bag, then add the black treacle. Close the bag and rub the treacle over the chicken until it is well coated.

2. Now add the dried thyme, salt, allspice and cardamon. Close the bag and shake so that the seasonings evenly coat the chicken.

3. Finally, add the jalapeño, garlic and ginger along with the coconut oil.

4. Mix well again, then seal the bag. I like to let this bag sit in my fridge for 2–3 hours before freezing to really marinate the chicken.

5. Once it's marinated, remove as much air as you can from the bag before sealing. Label the bag with the contents and the date you prepared it, then place it in the freezer, making sure it lies as flat as possible.

6. Defrost the bag thoroughly in the fridge for approximately 8–10 hours before cooking.

7. To cook, empty the contents of the bag into the slow cooker. Cook on low for 8 hours or on high for 4 hours, and serve with rice.

---

3 MONTHS | **8–10 HOURS** | **LOW 8 hours** | **HIGH 4 hours** | **SERVES 4**

WINTER WARMERS

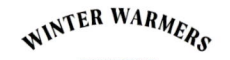

Beef Ragu

This is the perfect comfort food – fill a bowl and get some fresh bread for scooping up the last of the sauce. Utter perfection.

- 500g (1lb 2oz) minced beef (5% fat)
- 1 onion, chopped
- 1 carrot, peeled and chopped
- 1 celery, chopped
- 1 x 400g (14oz) can chopped tomatoes
- 2 tbsp Worcestershire sauce
- 2 tbsp tomato purée (paste)
- Bay leaf, optional
- Sprig of rosemary, optional
- 200g (7oz) dried linguine, pappardelle or tagliatelle
- 300ml (10½fl oz/1¼ cups) boiling water
- Salt and black pepper

1. Put the beef, onion, carrot, celery, chopped tomatoes, Worcestershire sauce and tomato purée in a grab bag. Season with salt and pepper.

2. Remove as much air as you can from the bag before sealing. Label the bag with the contents and the date you prepared it. Write on the front that you need to add the herbs if using, and the boiling water and pasta at the time of cooking (or a note to refer to this page number). Place the bag in the freezer, making sure it lies as flat as possible.

3. Defrost the bag thoroughly in the fridge for approximately 8–10 hours before cooking.

4. To cook, empty the contents of the bag into the slow cooker. Add the bay leaf and sprig of rosemary, if using. (You can wash the bag and reuse, but don't forget to re-label.) Cook on low for 6 hours or on high for 3 hours.

5. Once the cooking time is up, add the dried linguine to the slow cooker along with the boiling water and pop the lid back on. Leave for 30 minutes with the slow cooker on the keep warm setting, or until the linguine has cooked through. Stir well and serve, remove the bay leaf and rosemary before serving, if used.

---

3 MONTHS | **8–10 HOURS** | **LOW 6 hours** | **HIGH 3 hours** | **SERVES 4**

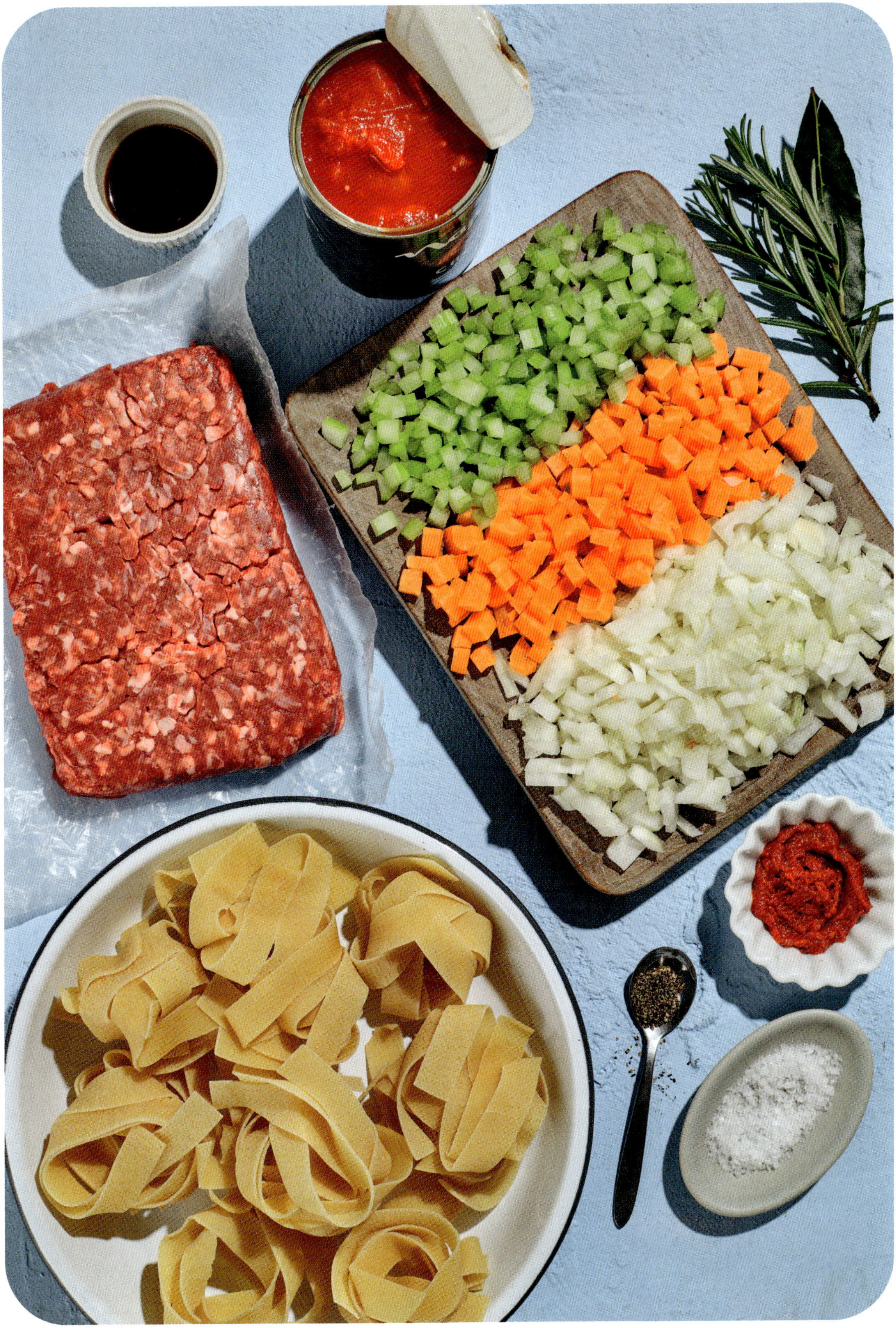

WINTER WARMERS

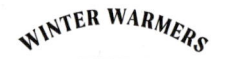

Maple Mustard Turkey

This was a bit controversial when I posted this online – so many people questioned if you can freeze the potatoes. The answer is yes! The potatoes are covered in the delicious maple mustard sauce and freeze beautifully.

1kg (2lb 4oz) new potatoes, skins on and chopped in half
40g wholegrain mustard
60g maple syrup
750g (1lb 10oz) turkey thigh joint
Salt and black pepper
1 tablespoon turkey gravy granules, optional
Vegetables of your choice, to serve

1. Put the potatoes in a grab bag and add the wholegrain mustard and maple syrup. Season with salt and pepper and close the bag. Give the contents a good mix to coat the potatoes.

2. Add the turkey joint to the bag; it's so big that I just sit it on top of the potatoes.

3. Remove as much air as you can from the bag before sealing. Label the bag with the contents and the date you prepared it, then place it in the freezer, making sure it lies as flat as possible.

4. Defrost thoroughly before cooking; the joint will be dense so this will need a longer defrosting time than most of my other recipes. I recommend a minimum of 24 hours in the fridge.

5. To cook, empty the contents of the bag into your slow cooker. (You can wash the bag and reuse, but don't forget to re-label.) Cook on low for 8 hours or on high for 4 hours. To test the turkey is cooked, insert a knife into the thickest part of the joint and the juices should run clear; cook for longer if needed. Add 1 tablespoon gravy granules to the sauce to thicken, if liked.

6. Serve the turkey with vegetables of your choice.

3 MONTHS | **24 HOURS** | **LOW 8 hours** | **HIGH 4 hours** | **SERVES 4**

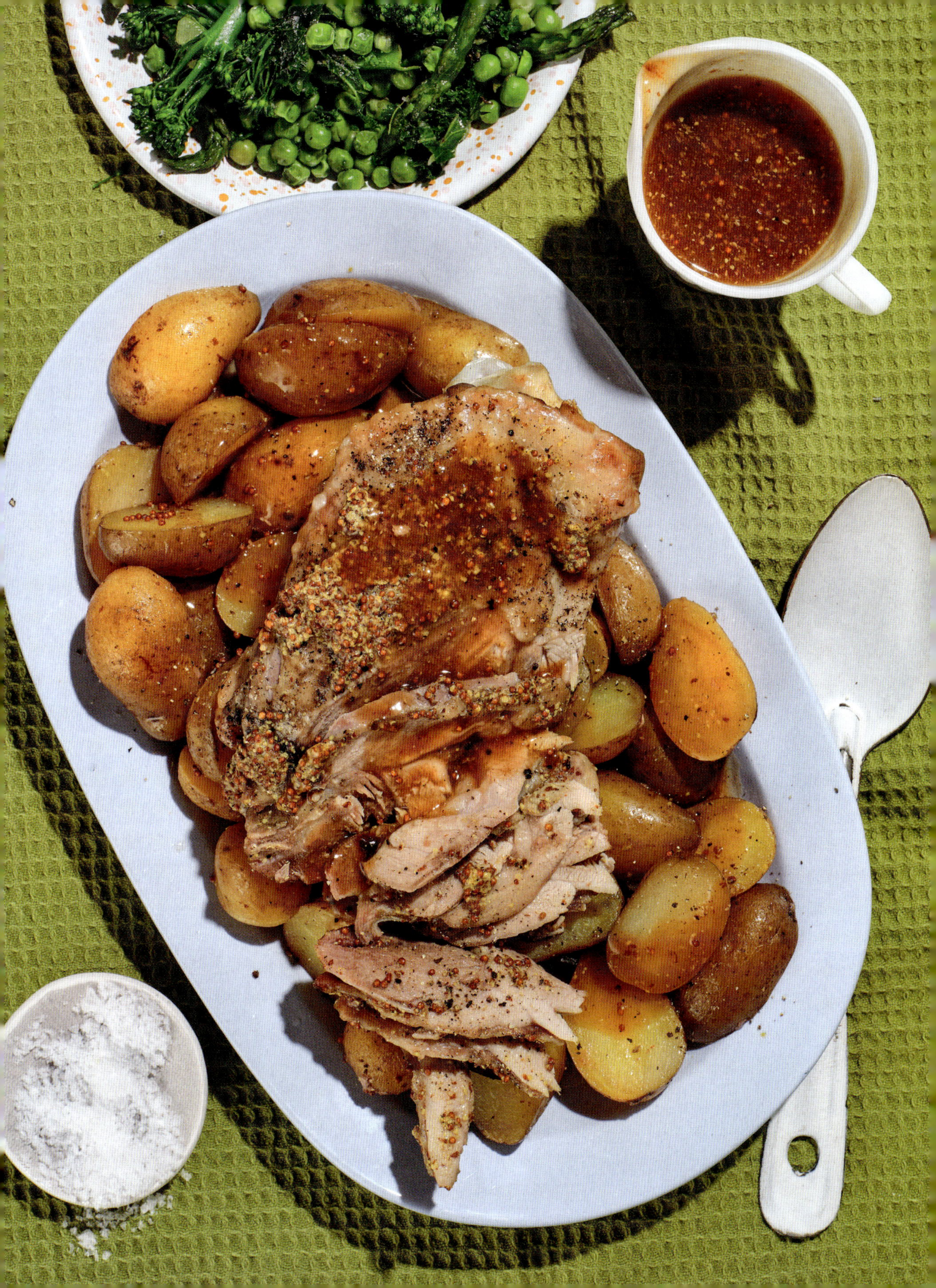

WINTER WARMERS

Chicken Chasseur

This is one for the adults, so we don't get to have this often, but the white wine is essential as it makes the meal so good!

- 1 tbsp olive oil
- 6 skinless and boneless chicken thighs
- 200g (7oz) mushrooms, chopped
- 1 onion, peeled and finely chopped
- 2 garlic cloves, crushed
- 1 x 400g (14oz) can chopped tomatoes
- 1 chicken jelly stock pot
- 150ml (5fl oz/scant ⅔ cup) white wine
- 2 bay leaves
- 200ml (7fl oz/scant 1 cup) boiling water
- Roast potatoes and long-stem broccoli, to serve
- Chopped parsley, to garnish (optional)

1. Heat the olive oil in a frying pan on medium heat. Add the chicken and fry until sealed on all sides. Leave to cool completely.

2. Put the cold chicken into a grab bag and add all the remaining ingredients except the boiling water.

3. Remove as much air as you can from the bag before sealing. Label the bag with the contents and the date you prepared it. Write on the front that you need to add the relevant quantity of boiling water at the time of cooking (or a note to refer to this page number). Place the bag in the freezer, making sure it lies as flat as possible.

4. Defrost the bag thoroughly in the fridge for approximately 8–10 hours before cooking.

5. To cook, empty the contents of the bag into your slow cooker, add the boiling water and stir everything together well. (You can wash the bag and reuse, but don't forget to re-label.) Cook on low for 8 hours or on high for 4 hours.

6. Serve the chicken chasseur with roast potatoes and broccoli and garnished with the herbs.

3 MONTHS | **8–10 HOURS** | **LOW 8 hours / HIGH 4 hours** | **SERVES 4**

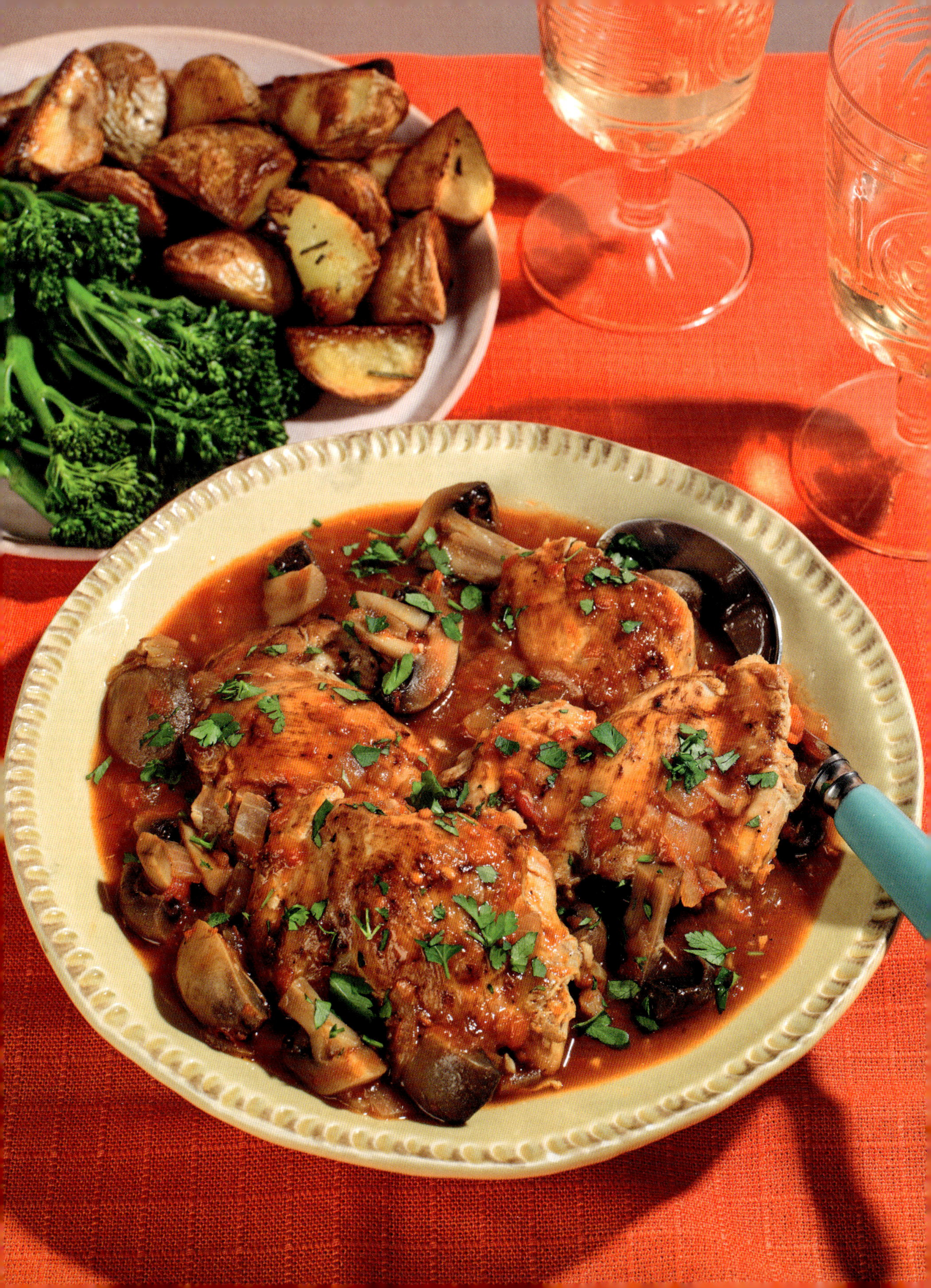

TIP:
If you buy duck legs with the skin on, remove this and then add to a deep fat frier with the temperature set at 200°C. Fry until golden, remove from the oil and season with salt and pepper. When you come to serve, sprinkle these on your curry for added flavour and crunch!

WINTER WARMERS

Pineapple & Duck Curry

Duck isn't the cheapest of meats, but if you see it on offer, get it and freeze it! I could eat this daily and I'd be happy. Duck is my favourite meat and pineapple my favourite fruit, so this is a match made in heaven for me.

- 1 x 227g (8oz) can pineapple chunks in juice
- 2 tbsp light brown sugar
- 4 tbsp Thai red curry paste
- 2 tbsp fish sauce
- 1 red chilli, deseeded and finely sliced
- 4 duck legs (about 900g/2lb), skin removed
- 1 x 400g (14oz) can coconut milk
- Salt and black pepper
- Sticky rice and Thai basil leaves (optional), to serve

1. In a bowl, combine the juice from the pineapple can with the sugar, curry paste, fish sauce and chilli. Mix well. Put your duck legs into a grab bag, then pour over the mixture from the bowl. Season with salt and pepper.

2. Put the pineapple chunks in a second smaller bag.

3. Remove as much air as you can from the bags before sealing. Label the bags with the contents and the date you prepared it. Clip the two bags together along the top edge. Write on the front that you need to add a can of coconut milk at the time of cooking (or a note to refer to this page number). Place the bags in the freezer, making sure they lie as flat as possible.

4. Defrost the bags thoroughly in the fridge for approximately 12-16 hours before cooking.

5. To cook, empty the contents of the duck bag into your slow cooker. Cook on low for 8 hours or on high for 4 hours. At the end of this cooking time, add the pineapple chunks and coconut milk. Mix well and leave to cook for a further 30 minutes.

6. Serve with sticky jasmine rice, garnished with Thai basil leaves, if using.

3 MONTHS | **12–16 HOURS** | **LOW 8 hours / HIGH 4 hours** | **SERVES 4**

WINTER WARMERS

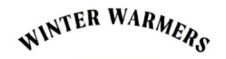

Chicken, Bacon & Potato Stew

This is one you need to make when you're heading out for the day and its chilly outside. Coming home when its cooked and getting warm with a full bowl or plate of this, and for the adults a glass of red, is perfection.

A splash of olive oil

12 smoked bacon rashers (slices), chopped

6 chicken thighs, bone in with skins removed

1 onion, peeled and chopped

2 carrots, peeled and chopped

400g (14oz) white potatoes, peeled and chopped into 2.5cm (1 inch) chunks

1 chicken jelly stock pot

300ml (10½fl oz/1¼ cups) boiling water

Salt and black pepper

Garden peas, to serve

Chives, to garnish (optional)

1. Add a splash of olive oil to a frying pan on a medium heat. Add the bacon pieces and fry for 2–3 minutes until crispy and golden. Leave to cool completely.

2. Put the bacon, chicken, onion, carrots, potatoes and stock pot into the grab bag. Close the bag and shake to combine.

3. Remove as much air as you can from the bag before sealing. Label the bag with the contents and the date you prepared it. Write on the front that you need to add the relevant quantity of boiling water at the time of cooking (or a note to refer to this page number). Place the bag in the freezer, making sure it lies as flat as possible.

4. Defrost the bag thoroughly in the fridge for approximately 8–10 hours before cooking.

5. To cook, empty the contents of the bag into your slow cooker and add the boiling water. Stir everything together well and season with salt and pepper. (You can wash the bag and reuse, but don't forget to re-label.) Cook on low for 6 hours or on high for 3 hours.

6. Serve in bowls with garden peas and chives.

3 MONTHS | 8–10 HOURS | LOW 6 hours | HIGH 3 hours | SERVES 4

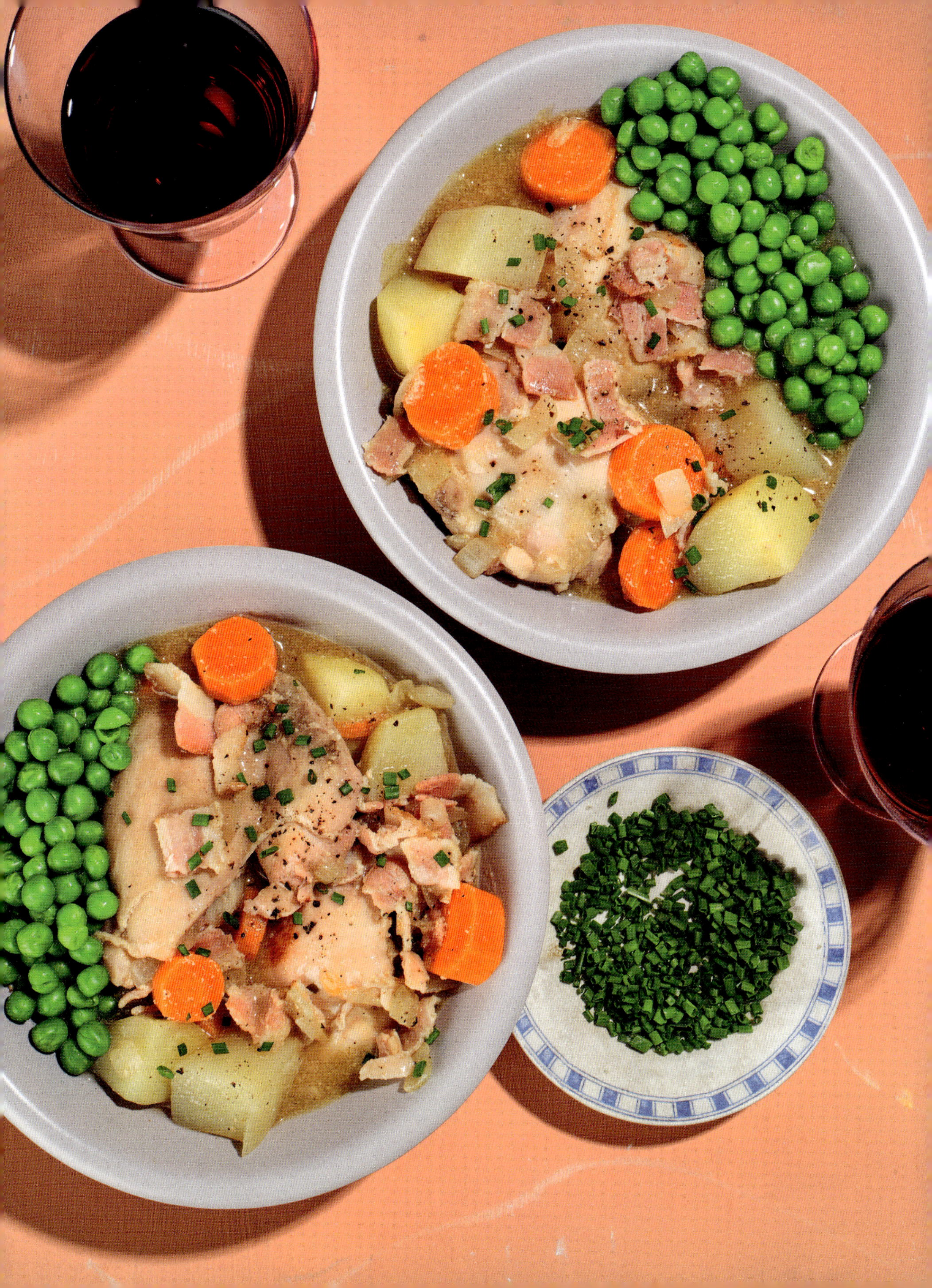

WINTER WARMERS

Slow-cooked Pork & Cider Hotpot

Pork and apple are the perfect combination, so let's ramp the apple up a gear and make it pork and cider! The cider makes the pork so soft and tender.

- 1kg (2lb 4oz) pork shoulder, fat removed and cut into chunks
- 2 leeks, sliced
- 3 garlic cloves, crushed
- 500g (1lb 2oz) potatoes, peeled and chopped into chunks
- 1 chicken jelly stock pot
- 200ml (7fl oz/scant 1 cup) boiling water
- 250ml (9fl oz/1 cup) dry (hard) cider
- 2 tbsp plain (all-purpose) flour
- 2 bay leaves
- Salt and black pepper
- Sweet potato mash, to serve

1. Put the pork chunks into a grab bag and add the leeks, garlic, potatoes and stock pot.

2. Remove as much air as you can from the bag before sealing. Label the bag with the contents and the date you prepared it. Write on the front that you need to add the relevant quantities of boiling water, cider, flour and bay leaves at time of cooking (or a note to refer to this page number). Place the bag in the freezer, making sure it lies as flat as possible.

3. Defrost the bag thoroughly in the fridge for approximately 8–10 hours before cooking.

4. Empty the contents of the bag into your slow cooker, add the boiling water and stir. (You can wash the bag and reuse, but don't forget to re-label.) Next add the cider, flour and the bay leaves, season with salt and pepper and stir again. Cook on low for 8 hours, or on high for 4 hours.

5. Serve with sweet potato mash.

3 MONTHS | **8–10 HOURS** | **LOW** 8 hours / **HIGH** 4 hours | **SERVES 4**

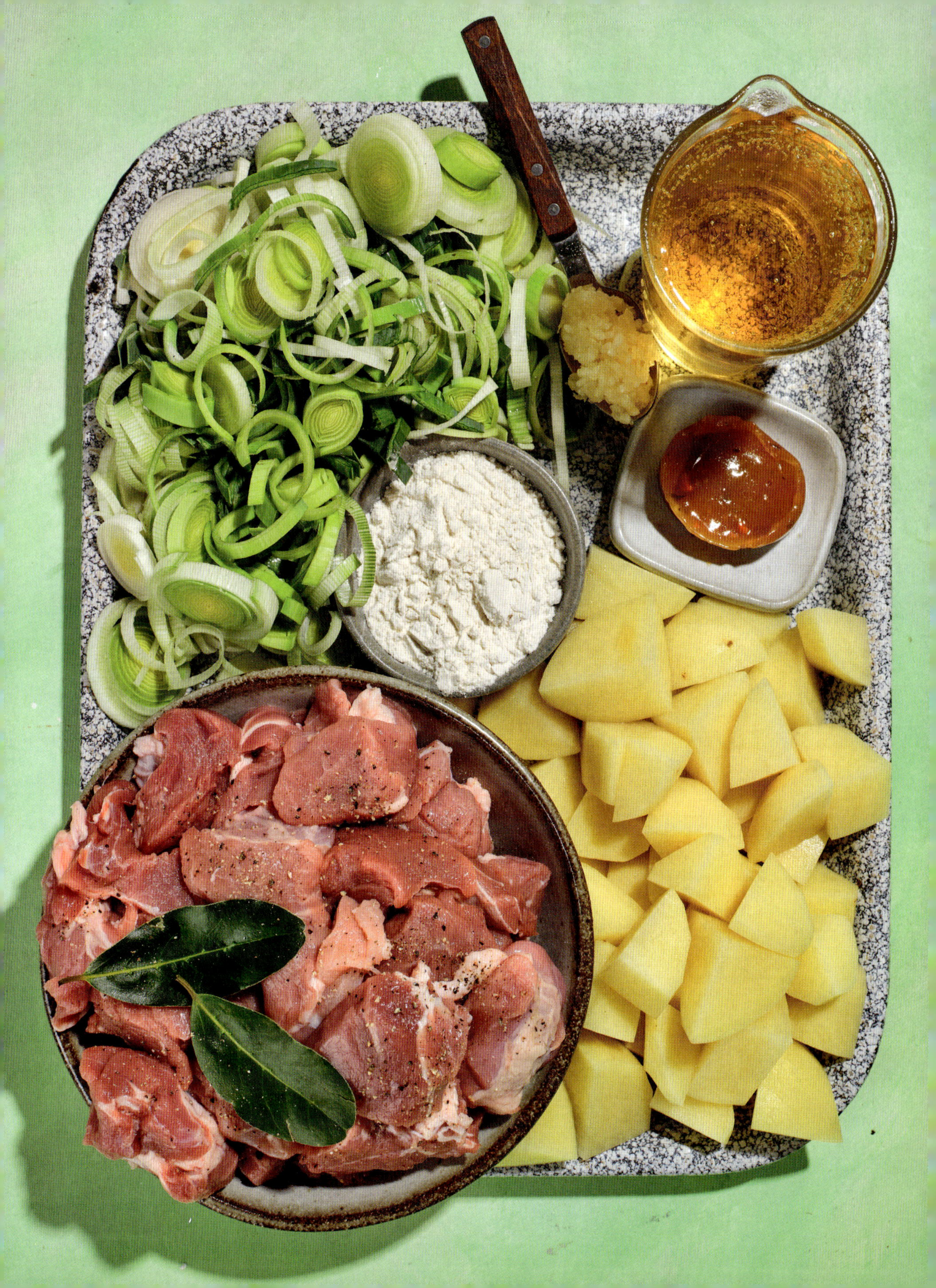

WINTER WARMERS

Lily's Cottage Pie

My daughter Lily says 'Ohhhh cottage pie' when this is cooking. It's her favourite! I like to make a double batch and freeze the leftovers in single-serving portions for her to have on other evenings.

- 1kg (2lb 4oz) beef mince (5% fat)
- 1 onion, peeled and finely chopped
- 3 celery stalks, chopped
- 3 carrots, chopped
- 2 garlic cloves, finely chopped
- 1 beef jelly stock pot
- 1 tbsp tomato purée (paste)
- 3 tbsp Worcestershire sauce
- 2 tbsp plain (all-purpose) flour
- 2 bay leaves
- 200ml (7fl oz/scant 1 cup) boiling water
- 800g (1lb 12oz) mashed potatoes
- Salt and black pepper
- Green beans, to serve

1. Break the beef up into small chunks. Add the beef to a grab bag and season with salt and pepper. Now add the onion, celery, carrots, garlic, stock pot, tomato purée and Worcestershire sauce.

2. Remove as much air as you can from the bag before sealing. Label the bag with the contents and the date you prepared it. Write on the front that you need to add the relevant quantities of flour, bay leaves, boiling water and mashed potatoes at the time of cooking (and a note to refer to this page number). Place the bag in the freezer, making sure it lies as flat as possible.

3. Defrost the bag thoroughly in the fridge for approximately 8–10 hours before cooking.

4. To cook, empty the contents of the bag into your slow cooker, add the flour, bay leaves and boiling water and mix everything together. (You can wash the bag and reuse, but don't forget to re-label.) Cook on low for 8 hours or on high for 4 hours.

5. Once cooked, top the mince filling with the mashed potatoes. Serve with green beans.

3 MONTHS | 8–10 HOURS | LOW 8 hours | HIGH 4 hours | SERVES 4

WINTER WARMERS

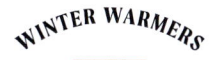

Campfire Stew

Gammon, delicious sauce and veggies – yes, yes and yes!
A scrumptious bowl of this and you'll be a bunch of happy campers!

- 2 carrots, peeled and chopped
- 2 celery stalks, chopped
- 2 onions, peeled and roughly chopped
- 2 red (bell) peppers, deseeded and chopped
- 2 garlic cloves, crushed
- 1 tbsp tomato purée (paste)
- 1½ tsp smoked paprika
- 1 tbsp Worcestershire sauce
- 2 x 400g (14oz) cans chopped tomatoes
- 1 x 400g (14oz) can haricot beans, drained and rinsed
- 750g (1lb 10oz) smoked gammon joint, boneless and skin removed
- Crusty bread, to serve

1. Put all the ingredients except the gammon in a grab bag, close the bag and shake to combine. Open the bag and place the gammon on top of the other ingredients.

2. Remove as much air as you can from the bag before sealing. Label the bag with the contents and the date you prepared it, then place it in the freezer, making sure it lies as flat as possible.

3. Defrost the bag thoroughly in the fridge for approximately 24–36 hours before cooking.

4. To cook, empty the contents of the bag into your slow cooker. (You can wash the bag and reuse, but don't forget to re-label.) Cook on low for 8 hours or on high for 4 hours. To check the gammon is cooked, insert a knife into the meat and the juices should run clear. Cook for longer if needed.

5. Once cooked, use two forks to shred the gammon, then return it to the pot and stir everything together.

6. Serve in bowls with crusty bread.

3 MONTHS | **24–36 HOURS** | **LOW 8 hours | HIGH 4 hours** | **SERVES 4**

WINTER WARMERS

Lamb Hotpot

I don't eat lamb, but the rest of the family love it so I try to make it for them occasionally! They go mad for this hotpot so it's something I make on days I'm not home for dinner.

- 1 tbsp olive oil
- 1 onion, peeled and chopped into chunks
- 3 carrots, peeled and chopped into chunks
- 700g (1lb 9oz) lamb leg steaks
- 1 x lamb jelly stock pot
- 8 potatoes (about 900g/2lb), peeled and sliced
- Salt and black pepper
- Cauliflower cheese (see below) and green beans, to serve

1. Heat the oil in a frying pan, then add the onion and carrots. Fry on a medium heat for 6 minutes. Add the lamb and fry for 3–4 minutes until browned. Allow to cool completely before adding to a grab bag, along with the stock pot, and season with salt and pepper.

2. Put the potato slices in a second bag and season with salt and pepper.

3. Remove as much air as you can from the bags before sealing. Label the bags with the contents and the date you prepared it, then clip the two bags together at the top.

4. Place the bags in the freezer, making sure they lie as flat as possible.

5. Defrost the bags thoroughly in the fridge for approximately 8–10 hours before cooking.

6. To cook, empty the contents of the lamb bag into your slow cooker. Arrange the potato slices on top of the lamb. (You can wash the bags and reuse, but don't forget to re-label.) Cover and cook on high for 4 hours or low for 8 hours.

7. Serve with cauliflower cheese and green beans.

3 MONTHS | **8–10 HOURS** | **LOW 8 hours** | **HIGH 4 hours** | **SERVES 4**

CAULIFLOWER CHEESE:

Preheat oven to 200°C/180°C fan/400°F/Gas 6. Chop cauliflower into florets, place in a lidded pan of boiling water and cook for 5-6 minutes until beginning to soften. Drain and place in a baking dish. Melt 30g (1oz/3 tbsp) butter in a pan on a low heat, add 4 tbsp plain (all-purpose) flour and stir well. Stir for 1 minute until the flour cooks off. Slowly add 500ml (17fl oz/2 cups) milk, whisking to avoid lumps. Add 100g (3oz) grated mature Cheddar cheese and whisk until combined. Remove from heat, pour over the cauliflower and bake for 25 minutes.

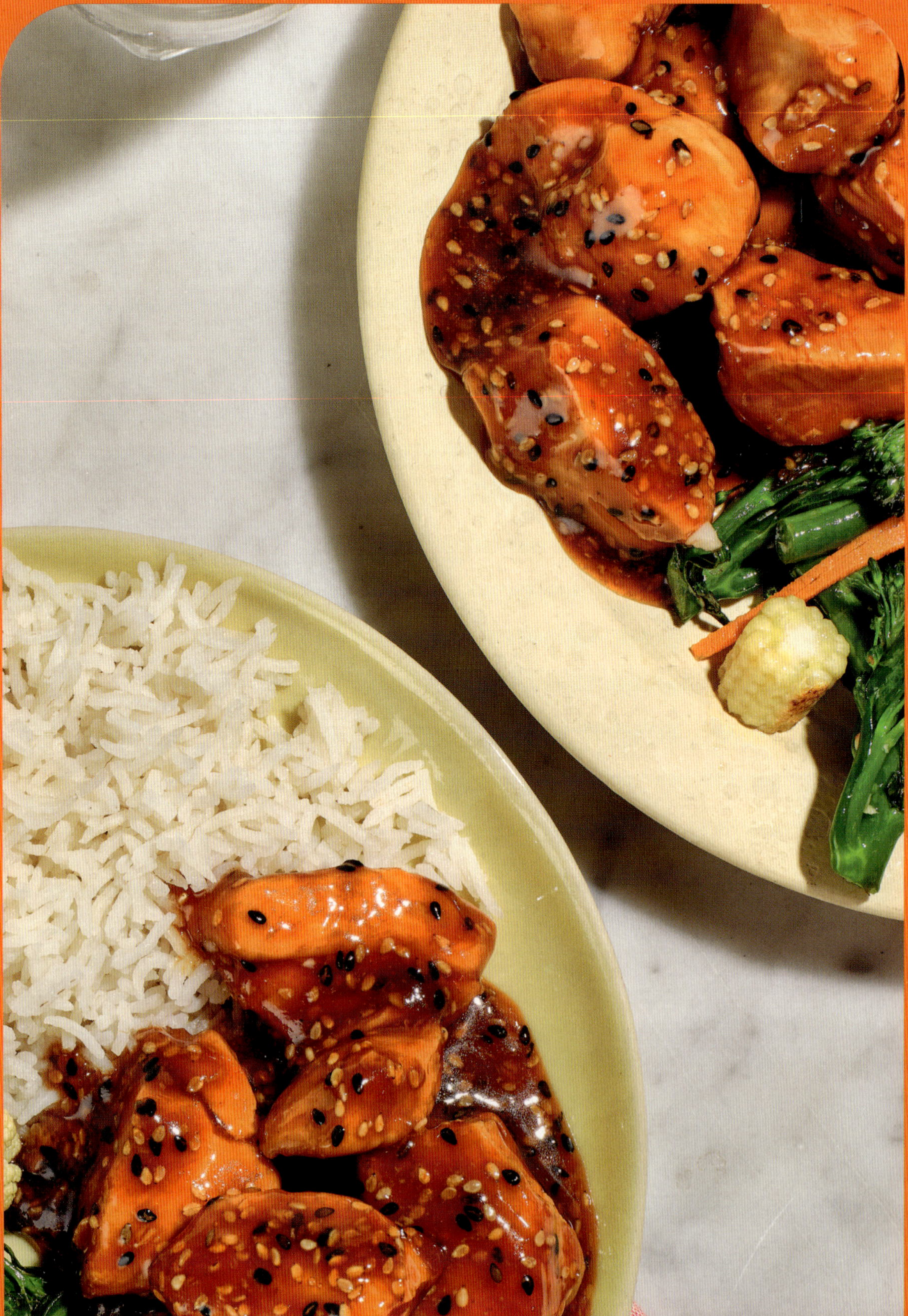

COMFORTING 3 CURRIES

COMFORTING CURRIES

Orange Chicken

I think orange chicken is more popular in the US than in the UK, but having seen so many recipes for it, I thought it was about time I made my own. And now I get asked by my eldest child to make this weekly!

- 4 skinless chicken breasts (about 700g/1lb 9oz), chopped into chunks
- 80g (2¾oz) cornflour (cornstarch)
- ½ tsp salt
- ½ tsp black pepper
- 100g (3½ oz) orange marmalade (with peel or without)
- 60ml (2fl oz/¼ cup) light soy sauce
- 1 tbsp rice wine vinegar
- 1 tsp sesame oil
- 1 tsp ground ginger
- 2 garlic cloves, finely chopped
- 2 tbsp olive oil
- 1 bay leaf
- 2 tbsp sesame seeds
- Basmati rice, to serve

1. Put the chicken, cornflour, salt and pepper into a grab bag, close the bag and shake so that the chicken is well coated.

2. Put the marmalade, soy sauce, rice wine vinegar, sesame oil, ginger, garlic and olive oil in a bowl and stir to combine. Pour this sauce over the chicken in the bag. Add the bay leaf.

3. Remove as much air as you can from the bag before sealing. Label the bag with the contents and the date you prepared it. Write on the front that you need to add the sesame seeds at the end of cooking (or a note to refer to this page number). Place the bag in the freezer, making sure it lies as flat as possible.

4. Defrost the bag thoroughly in the fridge for approximately 8–10 hours before cooking.

5. To cook, empty the contents of the bag into your slow cooker. (You can wash the bag and reuse, but don't forget to re-label.) Cook on low for 8 hours or on high for 4 hours.

6. When it's finished cooking, sprinkle the sesame seeds over, then serve with basmati rice.

3 MONTHS | **8–10 HOURS** | **LOW 8 hours | HIGH 4 hours** | **SERVES 4**

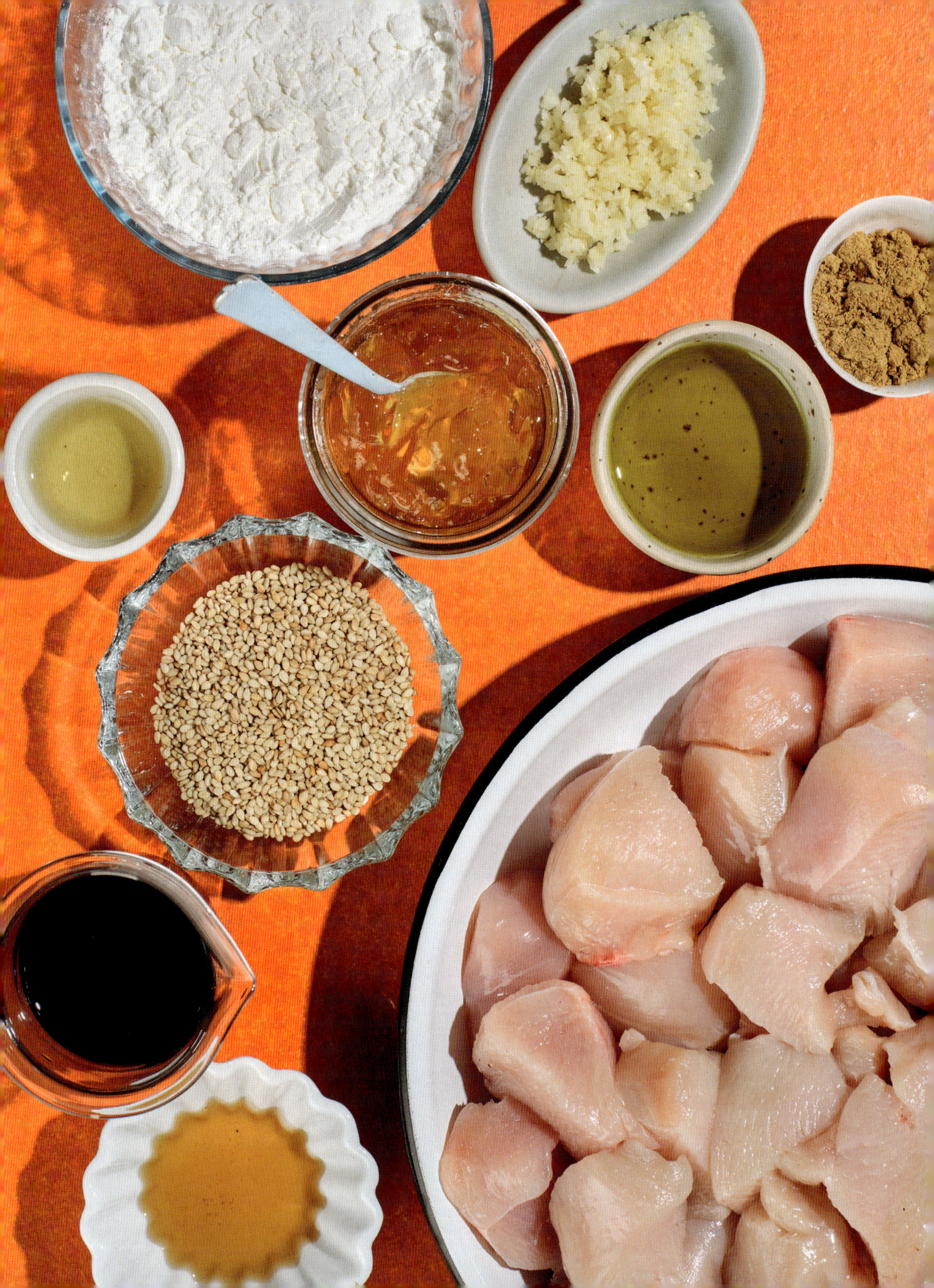

COMFORTING CURRIES

Butter Chicken

I love butter chicken and would live on it if I could. This is my version, and it gives a deep flavour with a wonderful smooth sauce.

- 1 x 400g (14oz) can chopped tomatoes
- ¼ tsp salt
- 2 tsp chilli powder
- 1½ tbsp garam masala
- 2 tbsp mild curry powder
- 4 skinless chicken breasts (about 700g/1lb 9oz), chopped into chunks,
- 1 onion, diced
- 3 garlic cloves, crushed
- 1 tbsp grated root ginger
- 2 tbsp butter
- 1 x 400ml (14oz) can coconut milk
- Rice and naan bread, to serve
- Coriander sprigs, to garnish, optional

1. In a bowl, combine the chopped tomatoes, salt, chilli powder, garam masala and curry powder. Mix well.

2. Open the grab bag and add the chicken chunks, then add the onion, garlic, ginger and butter. Pour in the chopped tomato mixture, close the bag and shake well to combine all the ingredients.

3. Remove as much air as you can from the bag before sealing. Label the bag with the contents and the date you prepared it. Write on the front that you need to add the coconut milk at the time of cooking. Place the bag in the freezer, making sure it lies as flat as possible.

4. Defrost the bag thoroughly in the fridge for approximately 8–10 hours before cooking.

5. To cook, empty the contents of the bag into your slow cooker. Cook for on high for 4 hours or on low for 8 hours.

6. Thirty minutes before the end of the cooking time, add the coconut milk and mix well. Leave the lid off the slow cooker so that the curry can thicken and continue cooking for the remaining time.

7. Serve with rice and naan bread and garnish with coriander, if liked.

3 MONTHS | **8–10 HOURS** | **LOW 8 hours** | **HIGH 4 hours** | **SERVES 4**

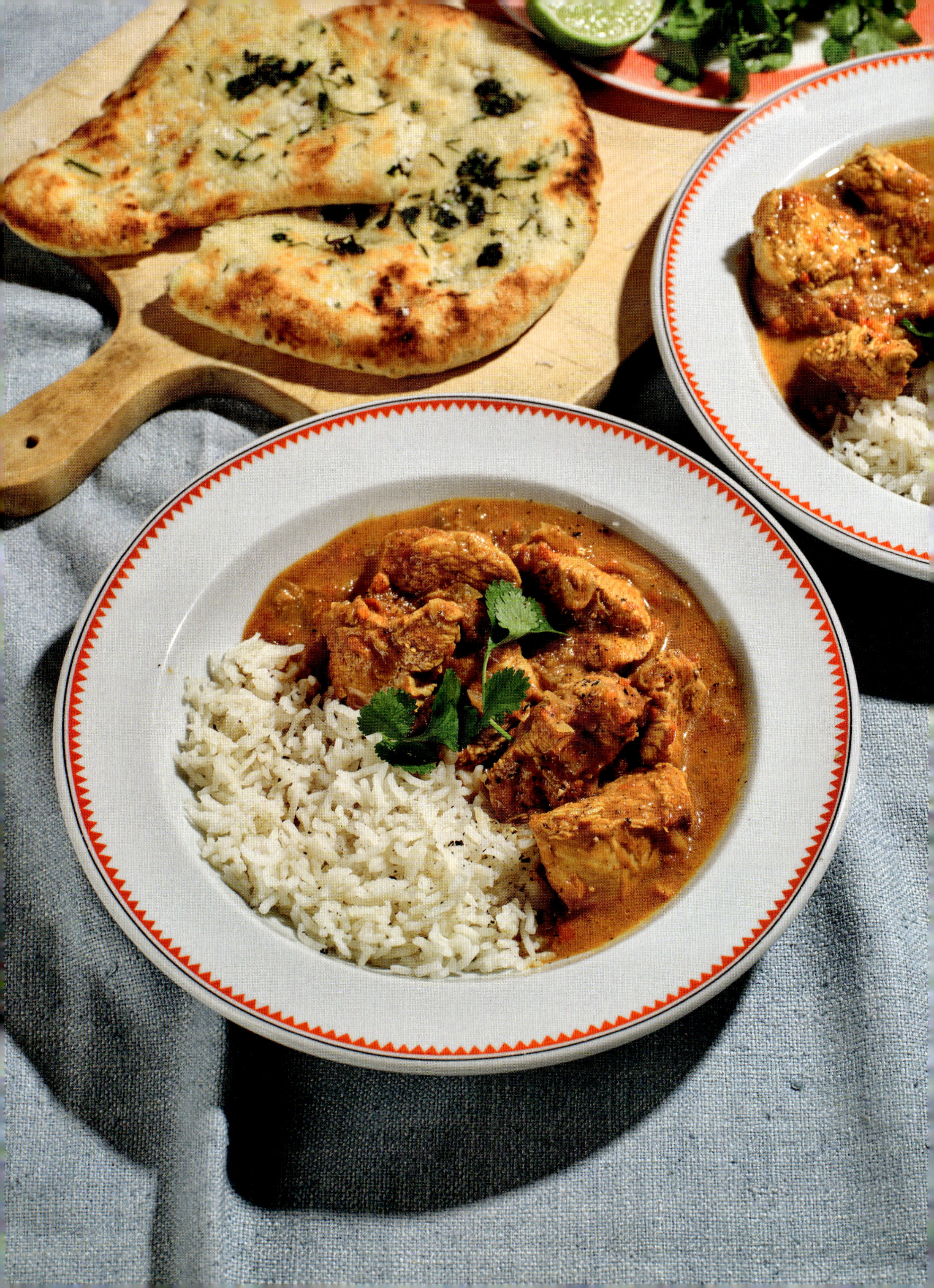

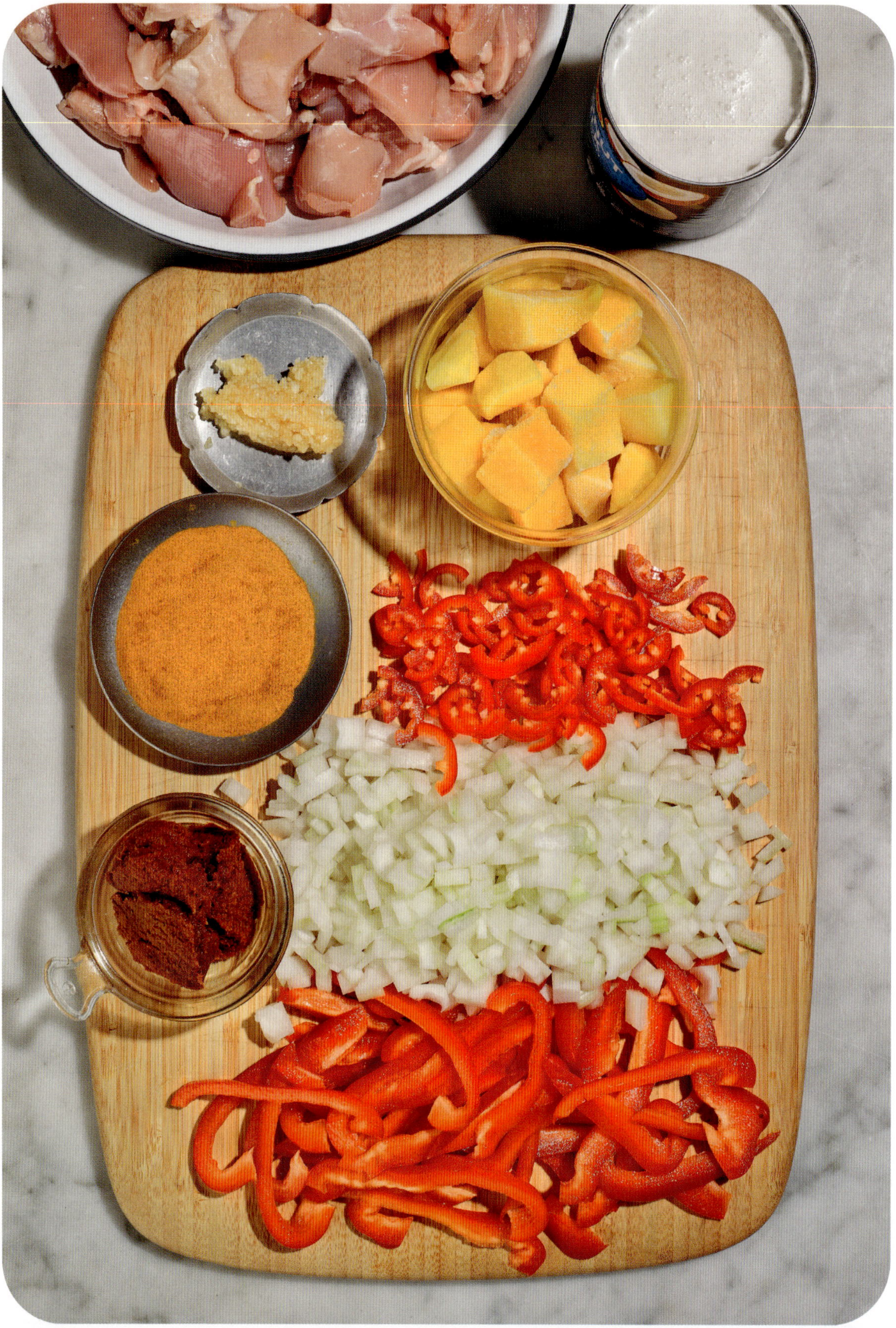

COMFORTING CURRIES

Mango Chicken Curry

This is without doubt my favourite recipe! It's a delicious curry with a sweetness from the mango that's so unique. If you're making this for kids and they aren't sure about the mango chunks, you can blitz them in the food processor and hide them in the sauce.

- 10 skinless boneless chicken thighs
- 2 tbsp red curry paste
- 1½ tsp ground turmeric
- 1 onion, chopped
- 1 red (bell) pepper, deseeded and chopped
- 3 garlic cloves, crushed
- 2 red chillies, deseeded and sliced
- 200g (7oz) frozen mango cubes
- 1 x 400ml (14oz) can coconut milk
- Rice, to serve

1. Chop the chicken thighs into bite-sized pieces and put them in your grab bag. Add the curry paste and turmeric, followed by the onion, pepper, garlic and chillies. Add the frozen mango to the bag. (You can blend the mango in a food processor before adding if you prefer.)

2. Remove as much air as you can from the bag before sealing. Label the bag with the contents and the date you prepared it. Write on the front that you need to add the coconut milk at the time of cooking (or a note to refer to this page number). Place the bag in the freezer, making sure it lies as flat as possible.

3. Defrost the bag thoroughly in the fridge for approximately 8–10 hours before cooking.

4. To cook, empty the contents of the bag into your slow cooker. (You can wash the bag and reuse, but don't forget to re-label.) Cook on high for 4 hours or on low for 8 hours.

5. Thirty minutes before the end of the cooking time, stir in the coconut milk and cook for the remaining time.

6. Serve the curry with rice.

3 MONTHS | **8–10 HOURS** | **LOW 8 hours** | **HIGH 4 hours** | **SERVES 4**

COMFORTING CURRIES

Pork Loin Curry

You can add so many different curry pastes to this recipe for a variety of meals – it's so versatile!

- 8 pork loin steaks (about 800g/1lb 12oz)
- 2 tbsp jalfrezi curry paste
- 1 onion, finely diced
- 2 garlic cloves, finely chopped
- 1 tbsp grated fresh root ginger
- 1 x 400g (14oz) can chopped tomatoes
- 4 tbsp low-fat natural yoghurt
- Salt and black pepper
- Rice, to serve

1. Combine all the ingredients, apart from the yoghurt, in the grab bag and season with salt and pepper. Mix together well

2. Remove as much air as you can from the bag before sealing. Label the bag with the contents and the date you prepared it. Write on the front that you need to add the relevant quantity of yoghurt at the time of cooking (or a note to refer to this page number). Place the bag in the freezer, making sure it lies as flat as possible.

3. Defrost the bag thoroughly in the fridge for approximately 8–10 hours before cooking.

4. To cook, empty the contents of the bag into your slow cooker. (You can wash the bag and reuse, but don't forget to re-label.) Cook on low for 8 hours or on high for 4 hours.

5. Before serving, add the yoghurt and mix well.

6. Serve the curry with rice.

3 MONTHS | **8–10 HOURS** | **LOW 8 hours | HIGH 4 hours** | **SERVES 4**

COMFORTING CURRIES

Beef & Red Pepper Curry

Casserole steak can be one of the cheapest cuts, but sometimes ends up a little tough when cooked on the hob. By using a slow cooker, your meat will be tender and melt in the mouth. Win–win!

- 750g (1lb 11oz) beef casserole steak, cut into chunks
- 1tbsp plain (all-purpose) flour
- 2 red (bell) peppers, deseeded and chopped
- 1 large onion, chopped
- 2 tsp ground cumin
- 1 tsp ground coriander
- 2 tsp chilli powder
- ½ tsp salt
- ½ tsp pepper
- 1 x 400g (14oz) can chopped tomatoes
- 1 beef jelly stock pot
- 2 tbsp mango chutney
- 1 tbsp tomato purée
- Rice, to serve

1. Put the casserole steak and flour into a grab bag. Close the bag and shake to coat the steak in the flour.

2. Now add the peppers, onion, cumin, coriander and chilli powder and season with the salt and pepper. Shake again to combine.

3. In a jug or bowl, combine the chopped tomatoes, beef stock pot, mango chutney and tomato purée. Whisk together, then pour into the bag and mix everything together.

4. Remove as much air as you can from the bag before sealing. Label the bag with the contents and the date you prepared it, then place it in the freezer, making sure it lies as flat as possible.

5. Defrost the bag thoroughly in the fridge for approximately 8–10 hours before cooking.

6. To cook, empty the contents of the bag into your slow cooker. (You can wash the bag and reuse, but don't forget to re-label.) Cook on high for 4 hours or on low for 8 hours.

7. Serve the curry with rice.

3 MONTHS | **8–10 HOURS** | **LOW 8 hours | HIGH 4 hours** | **SERVES 4**

COMFORTING CURRIES

Sticky Chicken

This is such a flavourful dish, and my house always smells incredible when it's cooking – it's hard to resist digging in too soon!

Ingredients

- 4 skinless chicken breasts, chopped into chunks
- 120g (4¼oz/scant ½ cup) runny honey
- 120ml (4fl oz/½ cup) dark soy sauce
- 120g (4¼ oz/½ cup) tomato ketchup
- 120ml (4fl oz/½ cup) rice wine vinegar
- 120g (4¼oz/heaped ½ cup) light brown sugar
- 2 garlic cloves, crushed
- 2.5cm (1 inch) piece root ginger, grated
- 2 tbsp cornflour (cornstarch)
- 2 tbsp sesame seeds
- Salt and black pepper
- Rice and stir-fried vegetables, to serve

Method

1. Put all the ingredients except the sesame seeds in a bowl, and season with salt and pepper. Mix well to combine everything, then add to the grab bag.

2. Remove as much air as you can from the bag before sealing. Label the bag with the contents and the date you prepared it. Write on the front that you need to add the sesame seeds at the time of cooking (or a note to refer to this page number). Freeze the bag, making sure it lies as flat as possible.

3. Defrost the bag thoroughly in the fridge for approximately 8–10 hours before cooking.

4. To cook, empty the contents of the bag into your slow cooker. (You can wash the bag and reuse, but don't forget to re-label.) Cook on high for 4 hours or on low for 8 hours.

5. Ten minutes before the end of the cooking time, add the sesame seeds. Stir well and continue to cook for the remaining cooking time.

6. Serve the sticky chicken with rice and stir-fried vegetables.

---

3 MONTHS | **8–10 HOURS** | **LOW 8 hours** | **HIGH 4 hours** | **SERVES 4**

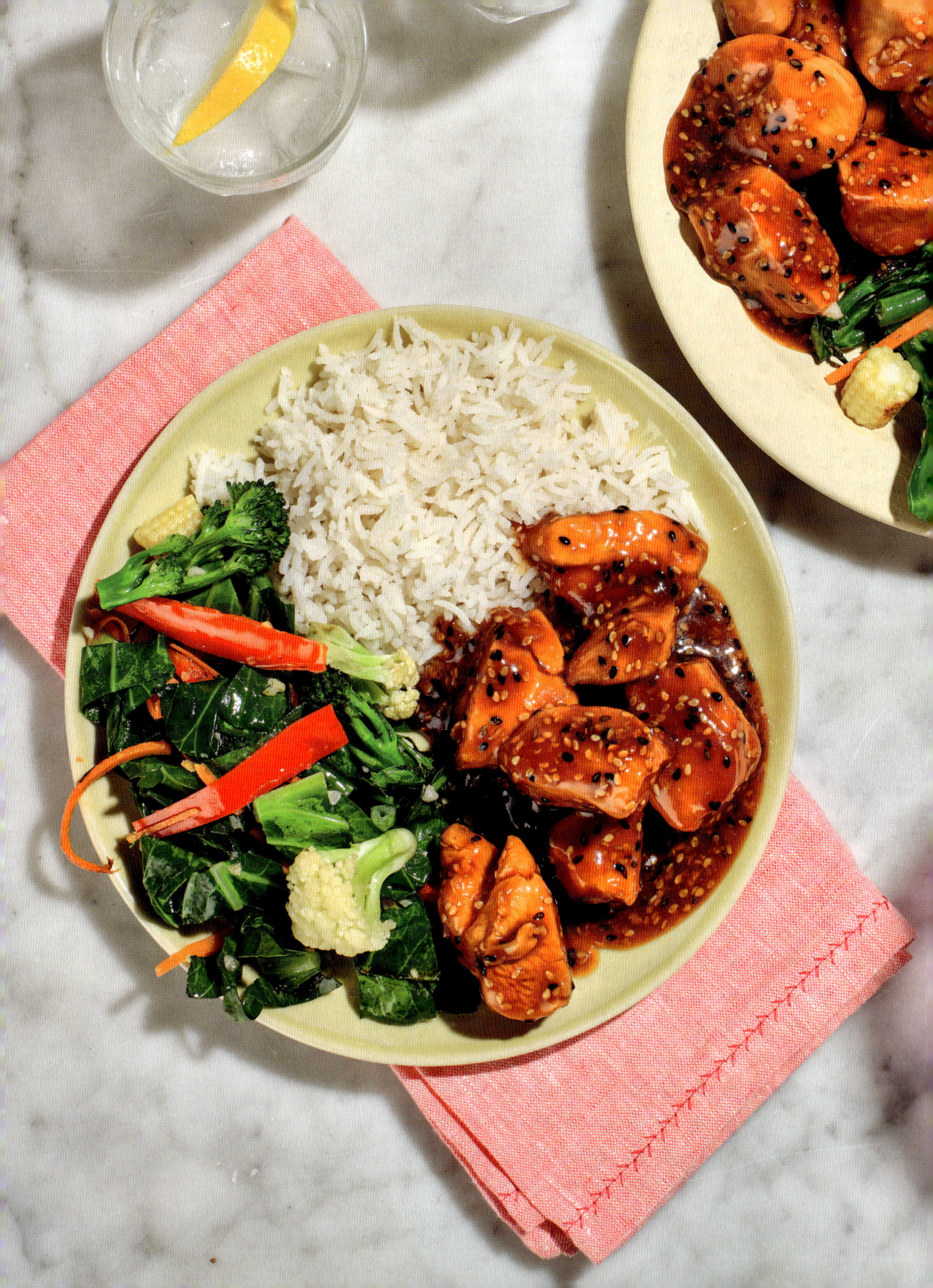

COMFORTING CURRIES

Spicy Honey Chicken

If, like me, you like a really spicy dish, you can add more sriracha to taste. I always make this up then add more when serving, to just my portion. I give it a good stir to combine and then pour over my rice.

- 4 skinless chicken breasts, chopped into chunks
- 120g (4¼oz/scant ½ cup) runny honey
- 120ml (4fl oz/½ cup) sriracha
- 120ml (4fl oz/½ cup) rice wine vinegar
- 120ml (4fl oz/½ cup) light soy sauce
- ½ tsp grated fresh root ginger
- 3 garlic cloves, crushed
- 2 tbsp cornflour (cornstarch)
- 200ml (7fl oz/scant 1 cup) chicken stock
- Rice, to serve

1. Put the chicken in a grab bag. Pour in the honey, sriracha, rice wine vinegar and light soy sauce. Mix together, then add the ginger and garlic.

2. Put the cornflour in a jug and add 2 tablespoons of cold water. Mix well, then pour into the chicken stock. Add this to the bag and mix well.

3. Remove as much air as you can from the bag before sealing. Label the bag with the contents and the date you prepared it, then place it in the freezer, making sure it lies as flat as possible.

4. Defrost the bag thoroughly in the fridge for approximately 8–10 hours before cooking.

5. To cook, empty the contents of the bag into your slow cooker. (You can wash the bag and reuse, but don't forget to re-label.) Cook on high for 4 hours on high or on low for 8 hours.

6. Serve the spicy chicken with rice.

3 MONTHS | **8–10 HOURS** | **LOW 8 hours / HIGH 4 hours** | **SERVES 4**

COMFORTING CURRIES

Chicken & Potato Curry

Chicken thighs are the best part of a chicken. So flavourful, juicy and just downright delicious. They are also cheaper than chicken breast, so even better for making a really decent meal if you're on a budget.

- 1 x 400g (14oz) can chopped tomatoes
- 1 tbsp tomato purée (paste)
- 2 tbsp garam masala
- 2 tsp ground cumin
- 2 tsp ground turmeric
- 1 tsp black pepper
- 1 tsp salt
- ½ tsp chilli powder
- 1kg (2lb 4oz) skinless, boneless chicken thighs
- 500g (1lb 2oz) new potatoes, halved
- 1 onion, finely sliced
- 4 garlic cloves, crushed
- 2.5cm (1 inch) piece root ginger, peeled and grated
- 2 tbsp mango chutney, plus extra to serve
- 1 x 400g (14oz) can coconut milk
- Naan bread and rice, to serve

1. Open the can of tomatoes and add the tomato purée, garam masala, cumin, turmeric, pepper, salt and chilli powder and stir well.

2. Open your grab bag and add the chicken thighs, potatoes, onion, garlic, ginger and mango chutney. Mix it all together, then add the can of tomatoes and mix again. Remove as much air as you can from the bag before sealing. Label the bag with the contents and the date you prepared it. Write on the front that you need to add the coconut milk at the time of cooking (or a note to refer to this page number). Place the bag in the freezer, making sure it lies as flat as possible.

3. Defrost the bag thoroughly in the fridge for approximately 8–10 hours before cooking.

4. To cook, empty the contents of the bag into your slow cooker. (You can wash the bag and reuse, but don't forget to re-label.) Cook on low for 8 hours or on high for 4 hours.

5. Once this cooking time is up, add the coconut milk and stir well. Leave to cook for a further 20 minutes on low.

6. Serve with naan bread, rice and mango chutney.

3 MONTHS | **8–10 HOURS** | **LOW 8 hours** | **HIGH 4 hours** | **SERVES 4**

COMFORTING CURRIES

Thai Red Curry

Thai food is among my favourites. Preparing Thai curries in the slow cooker is a quick and easy way of getting a burst of that flavour without the effort. Will it taste exactly the same as a takeaway? No. But it's my version and it's very close.

1kg (2lb 4oz) boneless, skinless chicken thighs
1 red (bell) pepper, deseeded and thinly sliced
1 onion, thinly sliced
3 garlic cloves, minced
2 tsp grated fresh root ginger
2 tsp fish sauce
1 chicken stock cube
2 tbsp red curry paste
1 tsp salt
½ tsp black pepper
300ml (10½fl oz/1¼ cups) boiling water
1 x 400ml (14oz) can of coconut milk
200g (7oz) green beans, ends removed
A handful of Thai basil leaves, thinly sliced
2 tbsp cornflour (cornstarch)
Jasmine rice, to serve

1. Put the chicken, red pepper, onion, garlic, ginger, fish sauce, stock cube, curry paste, salt and black pepper in a grab bag. Mix the ingredients well.

2. Remove as much air as you can from the bag before sealing. Label the bag with the contents and the date you prepared it. Write on the front that you need to add boiling water and the other ingredients at the time of cooking (or a note to refer to this page number). Place the bag in the freezer, making sure it lies as flat as possible.

3. Defrost the bag thoroughly in the fridge for approximately 8–10 hours before cooking.

4. To cook, empty the contents of the bag into your slow cooker, add the boiling water and stir well. (You can wash the bag and reuse, but don't forget to re-label.) Cook on low for 7 hours or on high for 3½ hours.

5. Once the cooking time is up, add the coconut milk and stir well. Now add the beans and basil leaves. Mix the cornflour with 3 tablespoons of cold water to form a slurry, then stir into the pot. Replace the lid and cook on high for 30 minutes.

6. Serve with jasmine rice.

3 MONTHS | **8–10 HOURS** | **LOW 7 hours** | **HIGH 3½ hours** | **SERVES 4**

COMFORTING CURRIES

Chinese Chicken Curry

My classic chicken curry. The whole family enjoys this recipe, especially as a takeaway alternative on a Friday night.

- 4 large chicken breasts, chopped into chunks
- 3 garlic cloves, minced
- 2 tsp curry powder
- 1 tsp ground turmeric
- 1 tsp Chinese five spice
- 1 tsp grated fresh root ginger
- 1 tsp sugar
- 1 chicken stock cube
- 2 tsp soy sauce
- 400ml (14fl oz/1¾ cups) boiling water
- 175g (6oz/1½ cups) frozen peas
- 3 tbsp cornflour (cornstarch)
- Rice, to serve

1. Put the chicken in a grab bag and add the garlic, curry powder, turmeric, Chinese five spice, ginger, sugar, stock cube and soy sauce. Mix well.

2. Remove as much air as you can from the bag before sealing. Label the bag with the contents and the date you prepared it. Write on the front that you need to add the relevant quantities of boiling water, peas and cornflour at the time of cooking (or a note to refer to this page number). Place the bag in the freezer, making sure it lies as flat as possible.

3. Defrost the bag thoroughly in the fridge for approximately 8–10 hours before cooking.

4. To cook, empty the contents of the bag into your slow cooker and add the boiling water. (You can wash the bag and reuse, but don't forget to re-label.) Mix well until the stock cube is dissolved. Cook on low for 7½ hours or on high for 3½ hours.

5. Once the cooking time is up, add the frozen peas. Mix the cornflour with 6 tablespoons of cold water and stir this in too. Cook for a further 30 minutes.

6. Serve with rice.

3 MONTHS | **8–10 HOURS** | **LOW** 7½ hours | **HIGH** 3½ hours | **SERVES 4**

COMFORTING CURRIES

Thai Yellow Curry

This is my version of a Thai curry. When I was 15, I worked in a Thai restaurant washing the pots. It was the best job I've ever had! They paid me and fed me every night. I don't claim to have taken any skills away from the job, but it did nurture an obsession with Thai food.

8 skinless, boneless chicken thighs, chopped into chunks
4 tbsp Thai yellow curry paste
1 tbsp dark soy sauce
1 tbsp brown sugar
1 tbsp grated root ginger
1 tbsp fish sauce
3 garlic cloves, crushed
1 red (bell) pepper, deseeded and chopped
1 yellow (bell) pepper, deseeded and chopped
½ butternut squash, peeled and chopped
1 chicken jelly stock pot
100ml (3½fl oz/scant ½ cup) boiling water
1 x 400ml (14oz) can of coconut milk

TO SERVE:
Rice
Lime slices or wedges
Basil leaves, to garnish, optional

1. Put all the ingredients except the boiling water and coconut milk in your grab bag. Mix together well.

2. Remove as much air as you can from the bag before sealing. Label the bag with the contents and the date you prepared it. Write on the front that you need to add the boiling water and coconut milk at the time of cooking (or a note to refer to this page number). Place the bag in the freezer, making sure it lies as flat as possible.

3. Defrost the bag thoroughly in the fridge for approximately 8–10 hours before cooking.

4. To cook, empty the contents of the bag into your slow cooker and add the boiling water. (You can wash the bag and reuse, but don't forget to re-label.) Cook for 4 hours on high or 8 hours on low.

5. Thirty minutes before the end of the cooking time, add the coconut milk to the slow cooker and stir well. Continue to cook for the remaining time.

6. Serve the curry with rice and lime, and garnish with basil, if liked.

---

3 MONTHS | **8–10 HOURS** | **LOW** 8 hours | **HIGH** 4 hours | **SERVES 4**

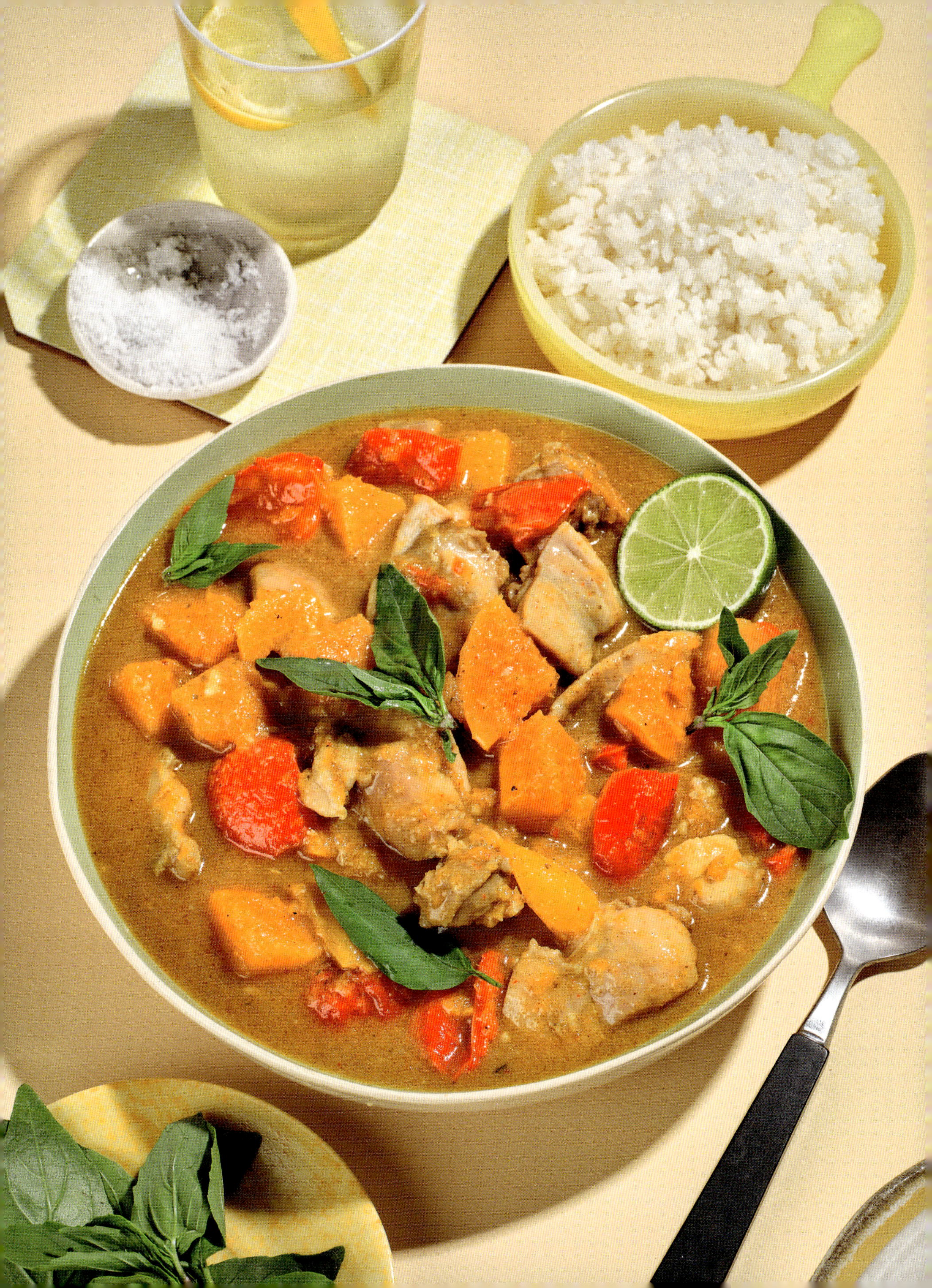

COMFORTING CURRIES

Kung Pao Chicken

Kung Pao chicken is a beautifully sweet and savoury dish. The added cashew nuts give a lovely contrast to the soft chicken, but if you are allergic or don't like them, feel free to omit them.

- 4 skinless chicken breasts, chopped
- 80ml (2½fl oz ⅓ cup) light soy sauce
- 2 tbsp runny honey
- 2 tbsp hoisin sauce
- 2.5cm (1 inch) piece of root ginger, peeled and grated
- 3 garlic cloves, crushed
- 1 tsp chilli powder
- ½ tsp salt
- 1 tsp Szechuan pepper
- 1 red chilli, deseeded and chopped
- 2 red (bell) peppers, deseeded and chopped, (or 1 red and 1 yellow)
- 75g (2½oz) unsalted cashews
- Rice, to serve

1. Put the chicken, soy sauce, honey, hoisin sauce and 50ml (1¾fl oz/3½ tablespoons) water into a grab bag. Mix well.

2. Now add the ginger, garlic, chilli powder, salt and Szechuan pepper. Combine the ingredients well.

3. Remove as much air as you can from the bag before sealing. Label the bag with the contents and the date you prepared it. Write on the front that you need to add the chilli, (bell) peppers and cashews at the time of cooking (or a note to refer to this page number). Place the bag in the freezer, making sure it lies as flat as possible.

4. Defrost the bag thoroughly in the fridge for approximately 8–10 hours before cooking.

5. To cook, empty the contents of the bag into your slow cooker. (You can wash the bag and reuse, but don't forget to re-label.) Cook on high for 4 hours or on low for 8 hours.

6. Thirty minutes before the end of the cooking time, stir in the chilli, peppers and cashew nuts. Continue cooking for the remaining time, then serve with rice.

3 MONTHS | **8–10 HOURS** | **LOW 8 hours | HIGH 4 hours** | **SERVES 4**

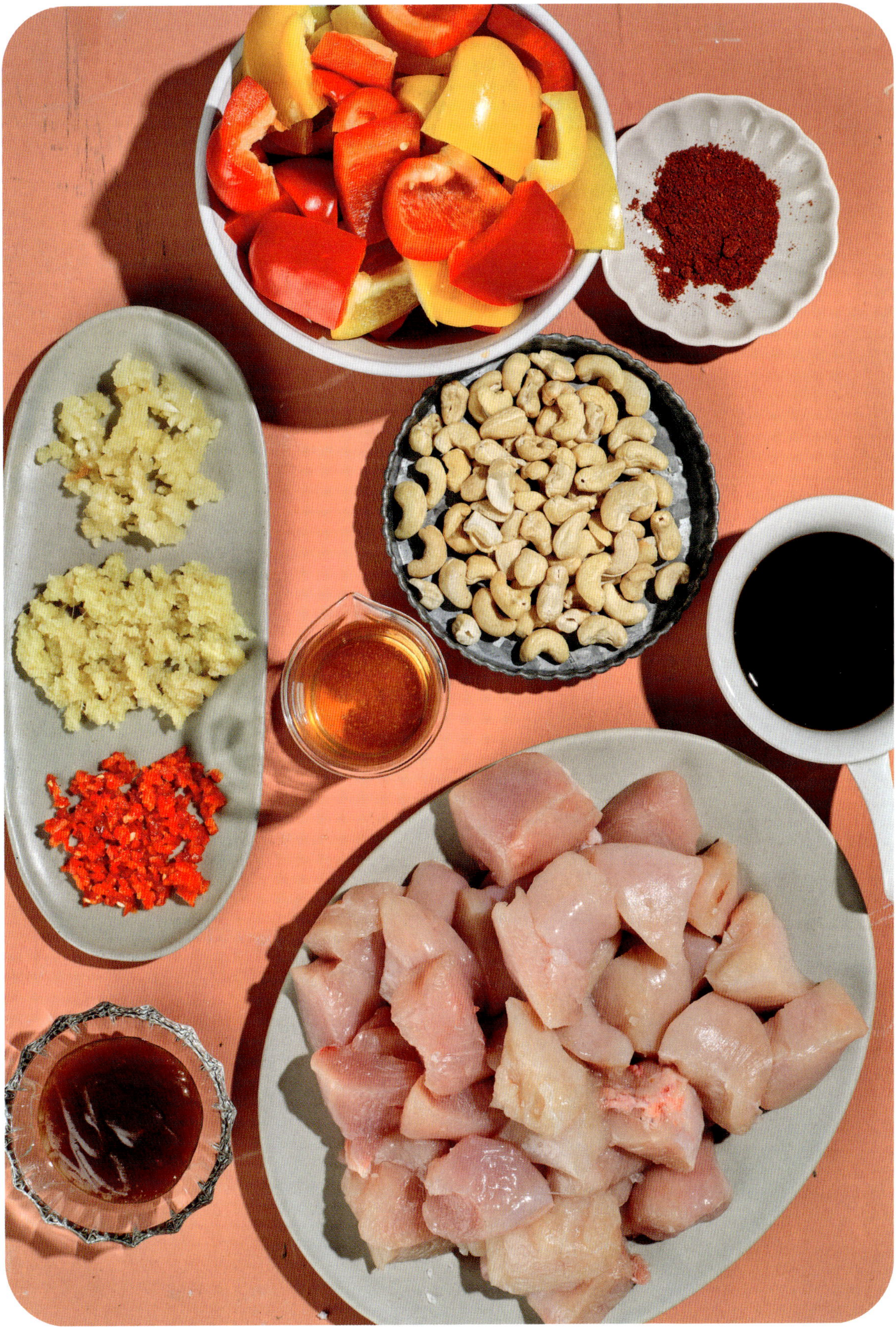

COMFORTING CURRIES

Pork Vindaloo

Don't be scared by the name – my take is not as spicy as you might expect. Although feel free to add more spice if that's your vibe!

- 800g (1lb 12oz) pork shoulder, cut into cubes
- 3 large potatoes, peeled and chopped
- 1 large onion, chopped
- 2 tbsp tomato purée (paste)
- 1 chicken jelly stock pot
- 1 x 400g (14oz) can chopped tomatoes
- 2.5cm (1 inch) piece root ginger, peeled and sliced
- 1 tsp ground cumin
- 1 tsp ground turmeric
- 2 tsp chilli powder
- ½ tsp salt
- ½ tsp pepper
- Rice, to serve

1. Put the pork, potatoes and onion in a grab bag, close the bag and shake to combine.

2. In a jug, combine the tomato purée, chicken stock pot and chopped tomatoes and stir well. Add this mixture to the bag and stir to combine.

3. Now add the ginger, cumin, turmeric, chilli powder, salt and pepper. Stir well.

4. Remove as much air as you can from the bag before sealing. Label the bag with the contents and the date you prepared it, then place it in the freezer, making sure it lies as flat as possible.

5. Defrost the bag thoroughly in the fridge for approximately 8–10 hours before cooking.

6. To cook, empty the contents of the bag into your slow cooker. (You can wash the bag and reuse, but don't forget to re-label.) Cook on high for 4 hours, or on low for 8 hours.

7. Serve the curry with rice.

---

3 MONTHS | **8–10 HOURS** | **LOW 8 hours** | **HIGH 4 hours** | **SERVES 4**

COMFORTING CURRIES

Lamb Vindaloo

I am able to buy my curry pastes from most supermarkets. Go to the biggest one in your area if you can as they have more of a selection for you to rummage through and find some good ones!

1kg (2lb 4oz) lamb shoulder, cut into chunks
4 tbsp vindaloo spice paste
2 garlic cloves, minced
1 onion, chopped finely
2 x 400g (14oz) cans chopped tomatoes
2 tbsp tomato purée (paste)
1 tsp salt
1 tsp sugar
Rice, to serve

1. Put all the ingredients in a grab bag and close the bag. Shake to combine all the ingredients.

2. Remove as much air as you can from the bag before sealing. Label the bag with the contents and the date you prepared it, then place it in the freezer, making sure it lies as flat as possible.

3. Defrost the bag thoroughly in the fridge for approximately 8–10 hours before cooking.

4. To cook, empty the contents of the bag into your slow cooker. (You can wash the bag and reuse, but don't forget to re-label.) Cook on low for 4 hours or on high for 8 hours.

5. Serve with rice.

3 MONTHS | **8–10 HOURS** | **LOW 8 hours | HIGH 4 hours** | **SERVES 4**

COMFORTING CURRIES

Lamb Curry

I've alread said I don't eat lamb but my family loves it. So I'll prepare this for them and when they are having it, find a leftover portion of something else for me.

- 300g (10½oz) natural yoghurt
- 1 tsp ground turmeric
- 1 tsp salt
- 1 garlic clove, chopped
- 1 tsp fresh root ginger, chopped
- 1 tbsp chilli powder
- 1 tsp garam masala
- ½ tsp salt
- 1kg (2lb 4oz) stewing lamb, cut into pieces
- 1 onion, chopped
- 2 green chillies, deseeded and finely chopped
- 1 x 400g (14oz) can chopped tomatoes
- 2 tbsp tomato purée (paste)
- 300ml (10½fl oz/1¼ cups) boiling water

TO SERVE:
Rice
Mango chutney
Poppadums
Chopped coriander (cilantro), to garnish

1. Put the yoghurt in a bowl and add the turmeric, salt, garlic, ginger, chilli powder, garam masala, and salt. Mix together, then add the lamb pieces. Stir to coat the lamb in the yoghurt, then transfer everything to your grab bag.

2. Add all the remaining ingredients except the boiling water. Close the bag and shake to combine the ingredients.

3. Remove as much air as you can from the bag before sealing. Label the bag with the contents and the date you prepared it. Write on the front that you need to add the relevant quantity of boiling water at the time of cooking. Place the bag in the freezer, making sure it lies as flat as possible.

4. Defrost the bag thoroughly in the fridge for approximately 8–10 hours before cooking.

5. To cook, empty the contents of the bag into your slow cooker and add the boiling water. Stir well. Cook on high for 4 hours or on low for 8 hours.

6. Serve with rice, mango chutney, poppadums and garnish with chopped coriander, if liked.

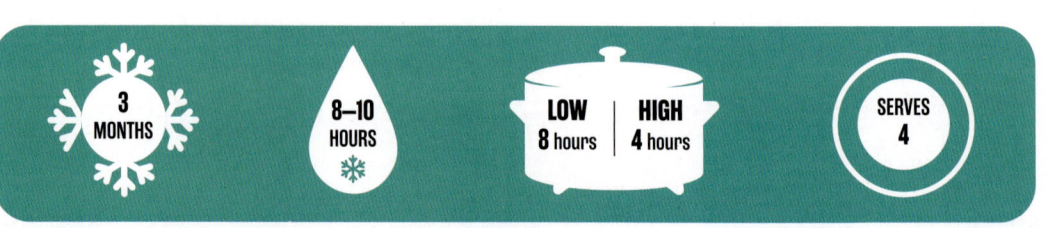

3 MONTHS | 8–10 HOURS | LOW 8 hours | HIGH 4 hours | SERVES 4

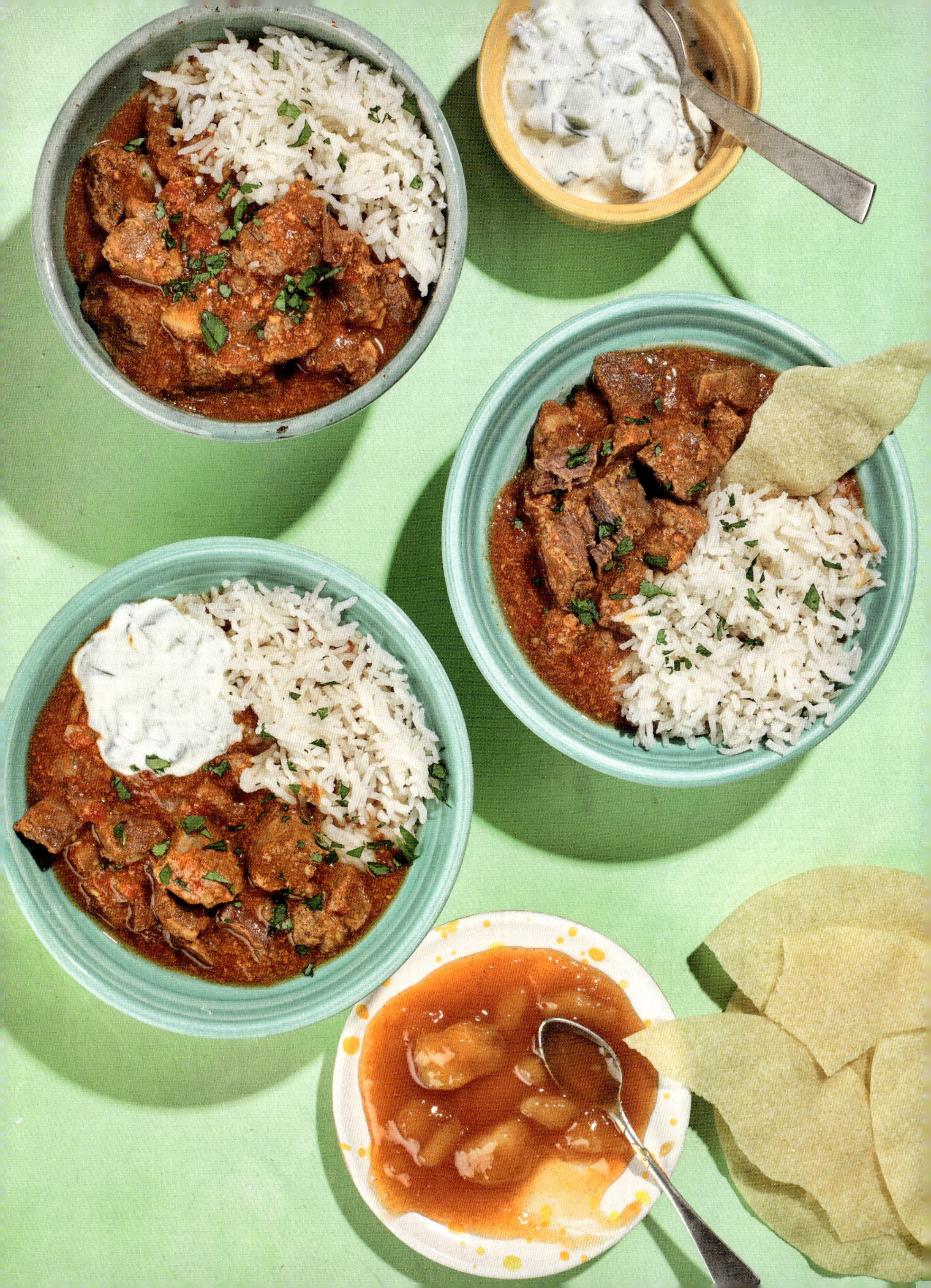

COMFORTING CURRIES

Chicken Tikka Masala

I love preparing curries in the slow cooker. The defrosting process allows for the meat to be marinated in the lovely spices and makes such a difference to the flavour. Chicken tikka is a win for the whole family.

3 tbsp natural yoghurt
1 tbsp chilli powder
½ tsp ground turmeric
1½ tsp garam masala
1 tbsp grated fresh root ginger
1 tbsp garlic, minced
1kg (2lb 4oz) chicken breasts, cut into chunks
2 onions, finely diced
1 x 400g (14oz) can chopped tomatoes
2 tbsp tomato purée (paste)
1 tsp salt
300ml (10½fl oz/1¼ cups) double (heavy) cream
Rice and naan bread, to serve

1. Put the yoghurt in a bowl and add the chilli powder, turmeric, garam masala, ginger and garlic and mix well. Add the chicken breast chunks and stir to coat the chicken in the yoghurt. Put the chicken and yoghurt in a grab bag and add the onions, chopped tomatoes, tomato purée and salt. Mix well.

2. Put the cream into another small freezer bag (or you can use fresh cream and skip this step).

3. Remove as much air as you can from the bags before sealing. Label the bags with the contents and the date you prepared them and clip them together. Place the bags in the freezer, making sure they lie as flat as possible.

4. Defrost the bag thoroughly in the fridge for approximately 8–10 hours before cooking.

5. To cook, empty the contents of the bag into your slow cooker. Cook on low for 8 hours or on high for 4 hours.

6. Once cooking time has finished, add the cream and stir. Leave the lid off and continue cooking for 10–15 minutes until piping hot. Serve with rice.

3 MONTHS | **8–10 HOURS** | **LOW 8 hours / HIGH 4 hours** | **SERVES 4**

· 120 ·

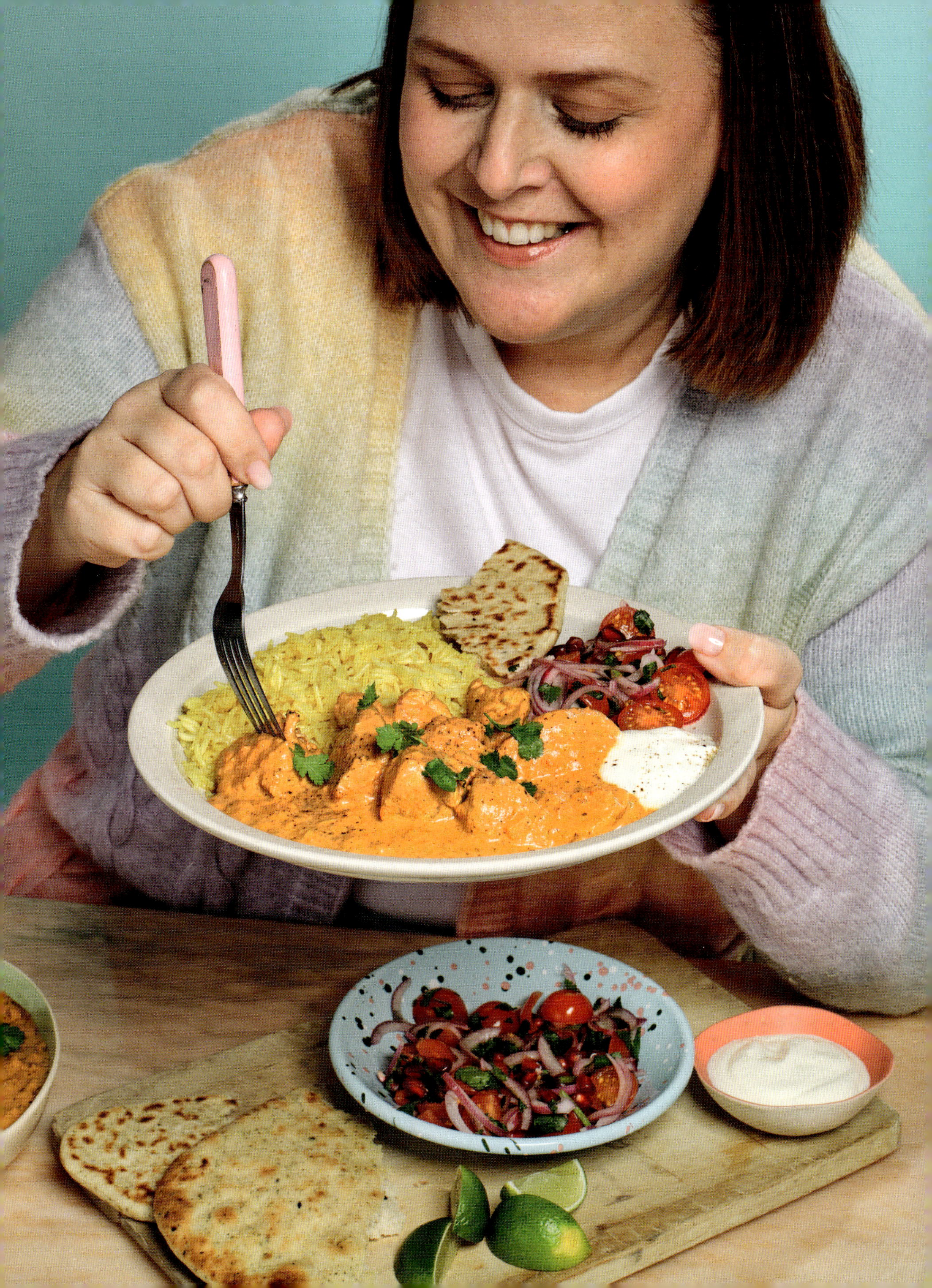

COMFORTING CURRIES

Chicken Balti

Seriously, if you are going to cook this, make sure it's a day where you either have a lot to do or you won't be home, because the smell of this cooking will be very hard to resist!

- 2 x 400g (14oz) cans chopped tomatoes
- 1 tsp paprika
- 1 tsp garam masala
- 2 tsp ground cumin
- 2 tsp ground coriander
- 1 tsp ground turmeric
- 1 tsp salt
- 1 tsp black pepper
- 8 skinless and boneless chicken thighs
- 1 onion, diced
- 1 red (bell) pepper, deseeded and cut into small chunks
- 2 green chillies, deseeded and finely chopped
- 2.5cm (1 inch) piece of root ginger, grated
- 4 garlic cloves, crushed
- Naan bread, to serve
- Coriander (cilantro) leaves and green chillies, to garnish

1. Open one of the cans of tomatoes and add the paprika, garam masala, cumin, coriander, turmeric, salt and pepper. Mix well.

2. Put the chicken in a grab bag and add both cans of tomatoes along with the onion, red pepper, chillies, ginger and garlic. Close the bag and shake to combine all the ingredients.

3. Remove as much air as you can from the bag before sealing. Label the bag with the contents and the date you prepared it, then place it in the freezer, making sure it lies as flat as possible.

4. Defrost the bag thoroughly in the fridge for approximately 8–10 hours before cooking.

5. To cook, empty the contents of the bag into your slow cooker. (You can wash the bag and reuse, but don't forget to re-label.) Cook on low for 8 hours or on low for 4 hours.

6. Serve the curry with naan bread.

---

3 MONTHS | **8–10 HOURS** | **LOW 8 hours** | **HIGH 4 hours** | **SERVES 4**

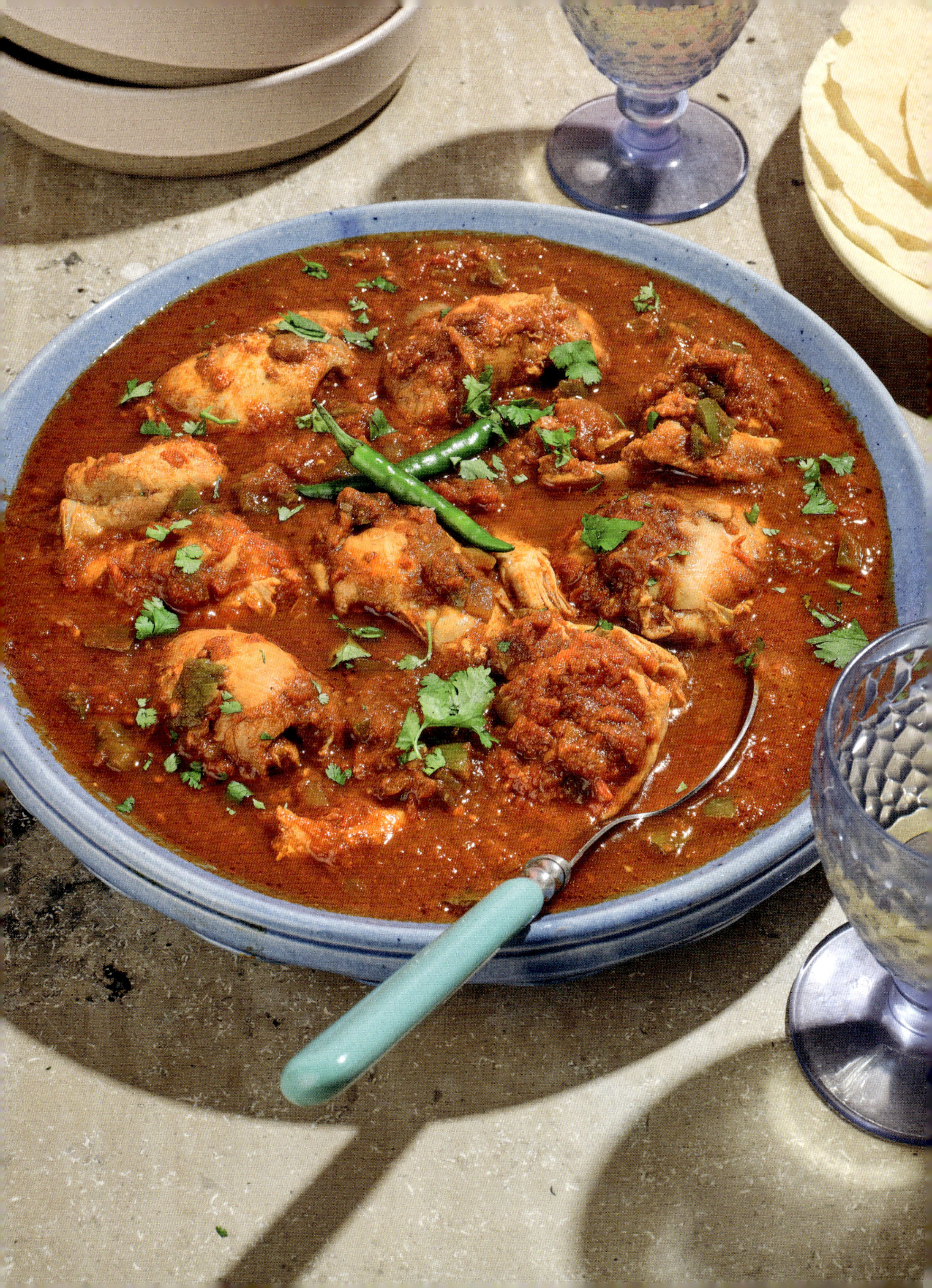

COMFORTING CURRIES

Turkey Curry

If you've got 10 minutes on Christmas Day, get this prepped for Boxing Day to use up your leftover turkey. Instead of freezing, just pop the bag in the fridge overnight and set off in the morning. Of course if you want to store this for longer, then it will need to be frozen.

2 x 400g (14oz) cans chopped tomatoes
1 tsp garam masala
1 tsp ground turmeric
1 tsp ground cumin
½ tsp paprika
½ tsp chilli powder
¼ tsp salt
2 tbsp tomato purée (paste)
500g (1lb 2oz) skinless turkey breast, diced into chunks
1 red (bell) pepper, deseeded and chopped into chunks
1 courgette (zucchini), thickly sliced
2 handfuls of fresh spinach
1 onion, peeled and diced
3 garlic cloves, minced
5cm (2 inch) piece fresh root ginger, grated
Rice, to serve

1. Open one can of tomatoes, add all the spices and salt and mix well. Add the tomato purée to the second can and mix well.

2. Open the grab bag and add the turkey and all the vegetables along with the garlic and ginger. Add both cans of tomatoes, close the bag and shake to coat the meat and vegetables in the spices.

3. Remove as much air as you can from the bag before sealing. Label the bag with the contents and the date you prepared it, then place it in the freezer, making sure it lies as flat as possible.

4. Defrost the bag thoroughly in the fridge for approximately 8–10 hours before cooking.

5. To cook, empty the contents of the bag into your slow cooker. (You can wash the bag and reuse, but don't forget to re-label.) Cook on low for 8 hours or on high for 4 hours.

6. Serve the curry with rice.

3 MONTHS | **8–10 HOURS** | **LOW** 8 hours / **HIGH** 4 hours | **SERVES 4**

COMFORTING CURRIES

Spicy Chicken Curry

I like to shred up the chicken and serve this piled into a jacket potato – it's such a good combination. You can always add extra spice if this isn't hot enough for you!

400g (14oz/1¾ cups) natural yoghurt
1 tbsp garam masala
1 tsp hot chilli powder
1 tsp ground turmeric
2 tsp ground cumin
2 tsp chilli flakes
2 onions, finely sliced
2.5cm (1 inch) piece root ginger, peeled and grated
4 garlic cloves, minced
4 chicken breasts (about 600g/1lb 5oz)
Salt
Rice, couscous or jacket potatoes, to serve

1. Put the yoghurt in a bowl and add all the spices, onion, ginger and garlic, and season with salt. Mix well, then add the chicken breasts. Ensure the chicken is coated in the marinade, then transfer to a grab bag.

2. Remove as much air as you can from the bag before sealing. Label the bag with the contents and the date you prepared it, then place it in the freezer, making sure it lies as flat as possible.

3. Defrost the bag thoroughly in the fridge for approximately 8–10 hours before cooking.

4. To cook, empty the contents of the bag into your slow cooker. (You can wash the bag and reuse, but don't forget to re-label.) Cook on low for 6 hours or on high for 3 hours. Halfway through cooking, baste the chicken with the juices in the slow cooker, then continue cooking.

5. You can serve the chicken breasts whole and spoon the sauce over, or shred them in the pot and mix in with all the juices. Serve the curry with rice or couscous, or in a jacket potato.

3 MONTHS | 8–10 HOURS | LOW 6 hours | HIGH 3 hours | SERVES 4

COMFORTING CURRIES

Beef & Coconut Curry

I always recommend searing your beef off for this curry as it helps the meat hold together in lovely big chunks and also adds lots of nice caramelized flavours.

- 1 tbsp olive oil
- 1.5kg (3¼lb) braising beef, chopped into chunks
- 1 onion, peeled and chopped
- 2 red (bell) peppers, deseeded and chopped
- 3 garlic cloves, minced
- 2 tsp finely grated root ginger
- 2 tbsp curry paste
- 1 beef stock cube
- 1 x 400g (14oz) can chopped tomatoes
- 2 tbsp tomato purée (paste)
- 2 tsp sugar
- ½ tsp salt
- ½ tsp black pepper
- 1 x 400ml (14oz) can coconut milk
- 2 tbsp cornflour (cornstarch)
- Rice, to serve

1. Heat the olive oil in a frying pan and sear the beef (in batches if necessary) for around 2 minutes until browned. Cover a plate with a piece of kitchen roll and transfer the beef to the plate to drain. Allow to cool completely.

2. Put the beef in a grab bag and add all the remaining ingredients except the coconut milk and cornflour. Close the bag and shake well to combine.

3. Remove as much air as you can from the bag before sealing. Label the bag with the contents and the date you prepared it. Write on the front that you need to add the coconut milk and cornflour at the time of cooking. Place the bag in the freezer, making sure it lies as flat as possible.

4. Defrost the bag thoroughly in the fridge for approximately 8-10 hours before cooking.

5. To cook, empty the contents of the bag into your slow cooker. Cook on low for 6 hours or on high for 3 hours.

6. Once the cooking time is up, add the coconut milk and stir well. Mix the cornflour with 6 tablespoons of cold water and stir this in too. Replace the lid and cook for a further 20-30 minutes. Serve the curry with rice.

3 MONTHS | **8–10 HOURS** | **LOW 6 hours** | **HIGH 3 hours** | **SERVES 4**

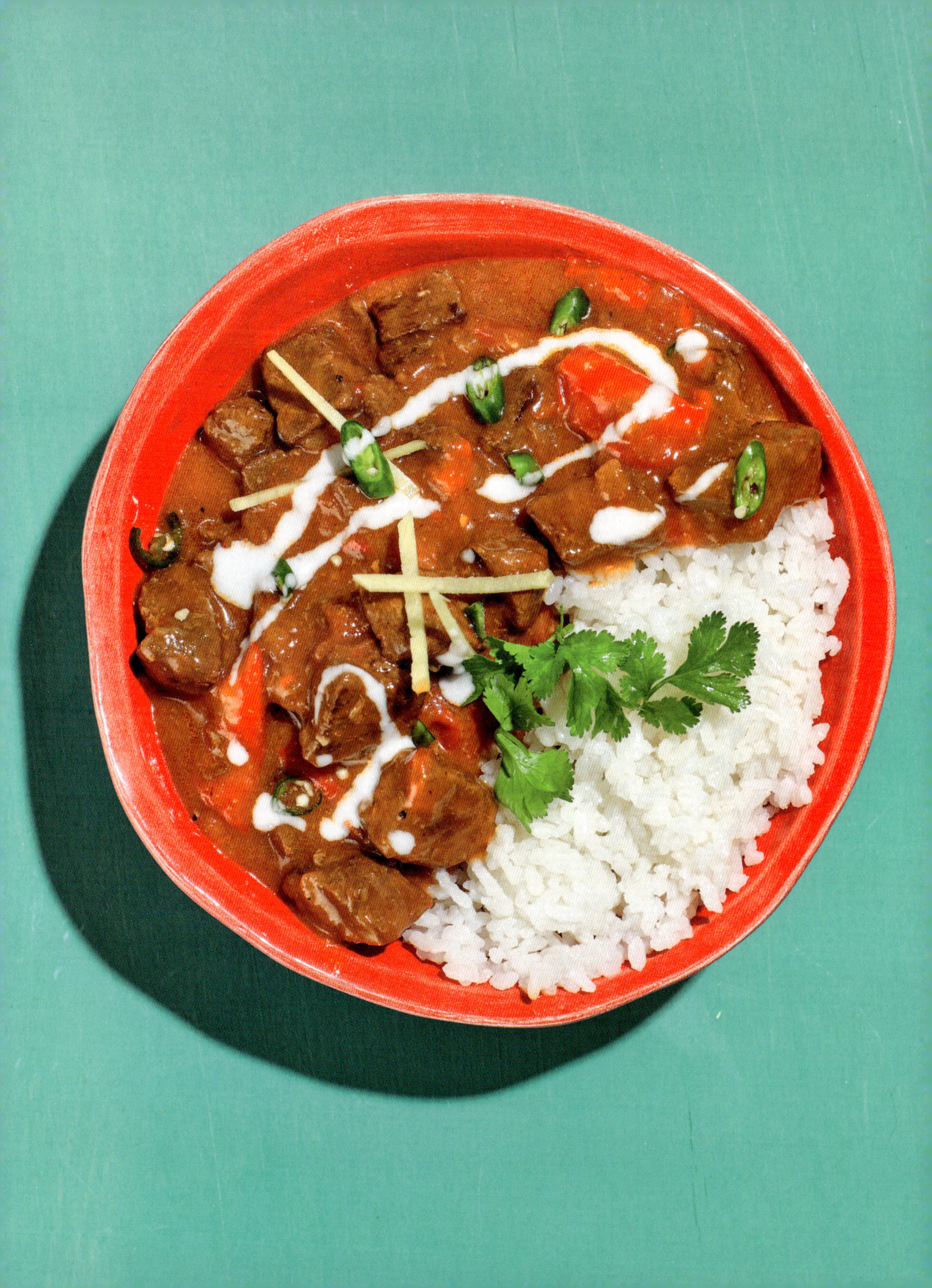

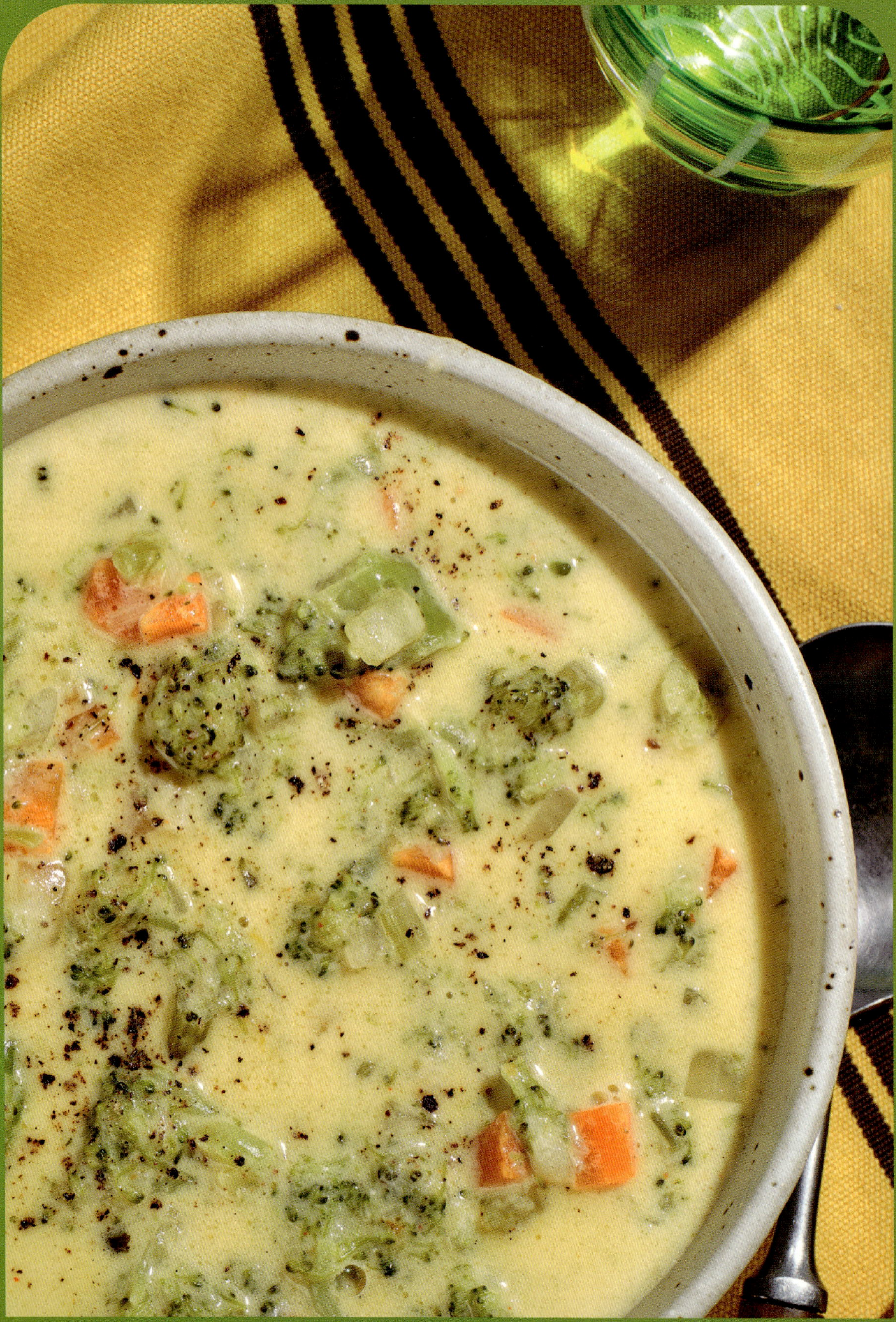

HEARTY
4
SOUPS

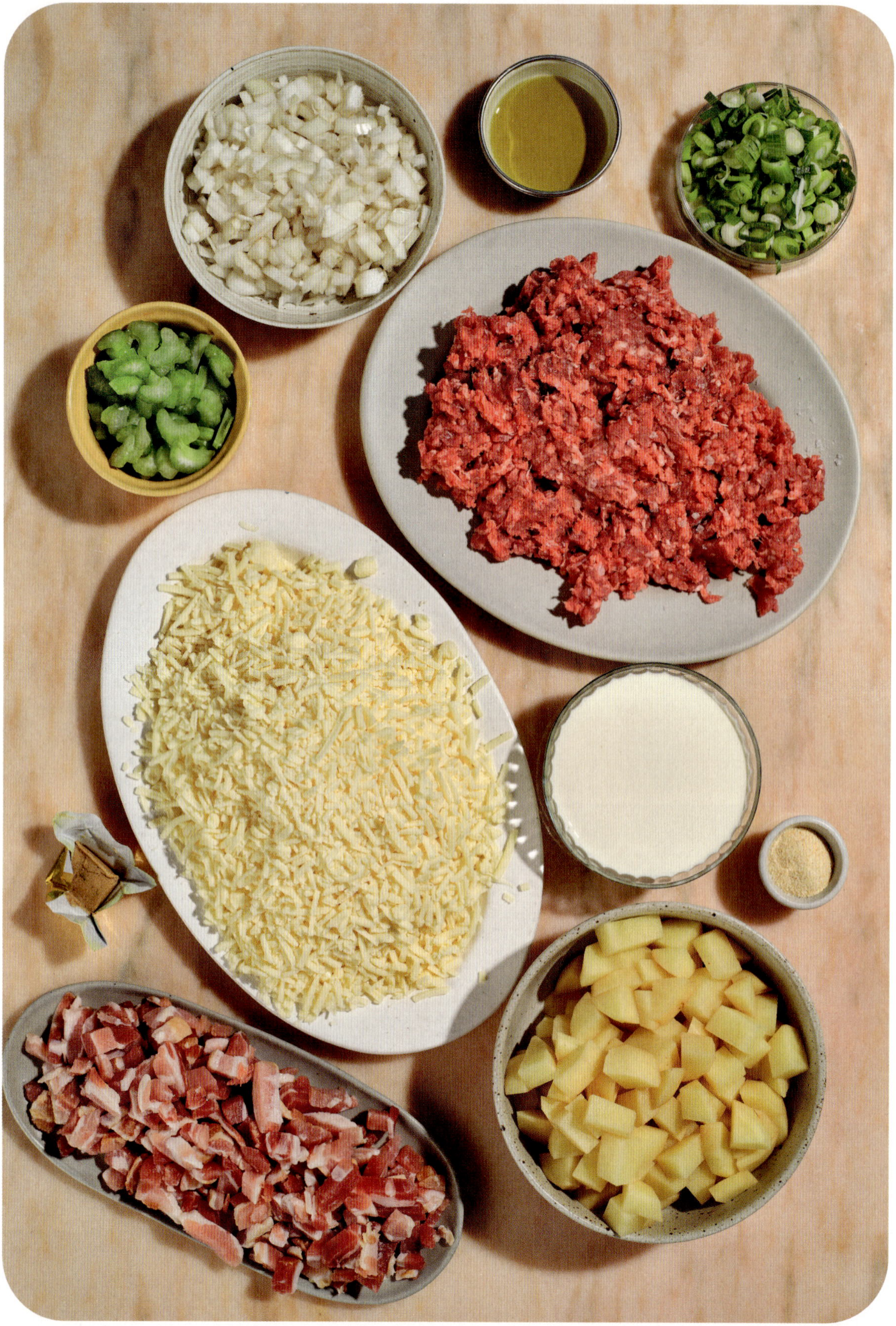

HEARTY SOUPS

Cheeseburger Soup

This is such a flavourful soup that can be eaten on its own or with a nice crusty roll that will really heighten the cheeseburger feel. Scrumptious!

1 tbsp olive oil
500g (1lb 2oz) minced beef (5% fat)
200g (7oz) bacon lardons
500g (1lb 2oz) potatoes, peeled and diced
1 onion, diced
1 celery stalk, chopped
2 tsp garlic powder
1 chicken stock cube
500ml (17fl oz/2 cups) boiling water
200ml (7oz/scant 1 cup) double (heavy) cream
450g (1lb) Cheddar cheese, grated
3 spring onions (scallions), chopped
Salt and black pepper
Crusty rolls, to serve

1. Heat the olive oil in a frying pan and fry the minced beef until just browned. Once cooked, remove from the pan. Now cook the bacon lardons until golden. Allow everything to cool.

2. Put the potatoes, onion, celery, garlic powder, chicken stock cube and cooked beef and lardons in your grab bag. Mix well. Remove as much air as you can from the bag before sealing. Label the bag with the contents and the date you prepared it. Write on the front that you need to add the relevant quantities of boiling water, cream, cheese and spring onions at the time of cooking (or a note to refer to this page number). Place the bag in the freezer, making sure it lies as flat as possible.

3. Defrost the bag thoroughly in the fridge for approximately 8–10 hours before cooking.

4. To cook, empty the contents of the bag into your slow cooker, add the boiling water and stir well. (You can wash the bag and reuse, but don't forget to re-label.) Cook on high for 3½ hours or on low for 7½ hours.

5. Add the cream, cheese and spring onions and season with salt and pepper. Stir well and continue cooking for a further 30 minutes.

6. Serve the soup with crusty rolls.

| 3 MONTHS | 8–10 HOURS | LOW 7½ hours | HIGH 3½ hours | SERVES 6 |

HEARTY SOUPS

Red Pepper & Sweet Potato Soup

Having a family that thinks they don't like sweet potato can sometimes be a challenge, but little do they know that they eat it a lot! I just cut the chunks a little smaller and they don't even question it. Aren't kids funny?

6 red (bell) peppers, halved and deseeded

Olive oil, for drizzling

3 garlic cloves, crushed

2 onions, chopped into chunks

1 tsp chilli flakes

3 sweet potatoes (about 380g/13½oz), peeled and chopped into cubes

1 chicken stock cube

1 tsp black pepper

350ml (12fl oz/1½ cups) boiling water

1 x 400ml (14oz) can coconut milk

French bread and butter, to serve

Coriander (cilantro) sprigs, to garnish

1. Preheat the oven to 200ºC (400ºF) fan/Gas 6. Lay the red peppers on a roasting tray and drizzle with olive oil. Roast for 30–35 minutes, until softened and browning. Allow to cool completely.

2. Once cooled, chop the peppers and put them in a grab bag along with all the remaining ingredients except the boiling water and coconut milk. Remove as much air as you can from the bag before sealing. Label the bag with the contents and the date you prepared it. Write on the front that you need to add the relevant quantity of boiling water and the coconut milk at the time of cooking. Place the bag in the freezer, making sure it lies as flat as possible.

3. Defrost the bag thoroughly in the fridge for approximately 8–10 hours before cooking.

4. To cook, empty the contents of the bag into your slow cooker. Add the boiling water and stir until the stock cube is completely dissolved. Cook on low for 6 hours or on high for 3 hours

5. Add the coconut milk, stir well and continue cooking on low for an additional 30 minutes.

6. Serve with French bread and butter, and garnish with coriander sprigs.

3 MONTHS | **8–10 HOURS** | **LOW 6 hours** | **HIGH 3 hours** | **SERVES 4**

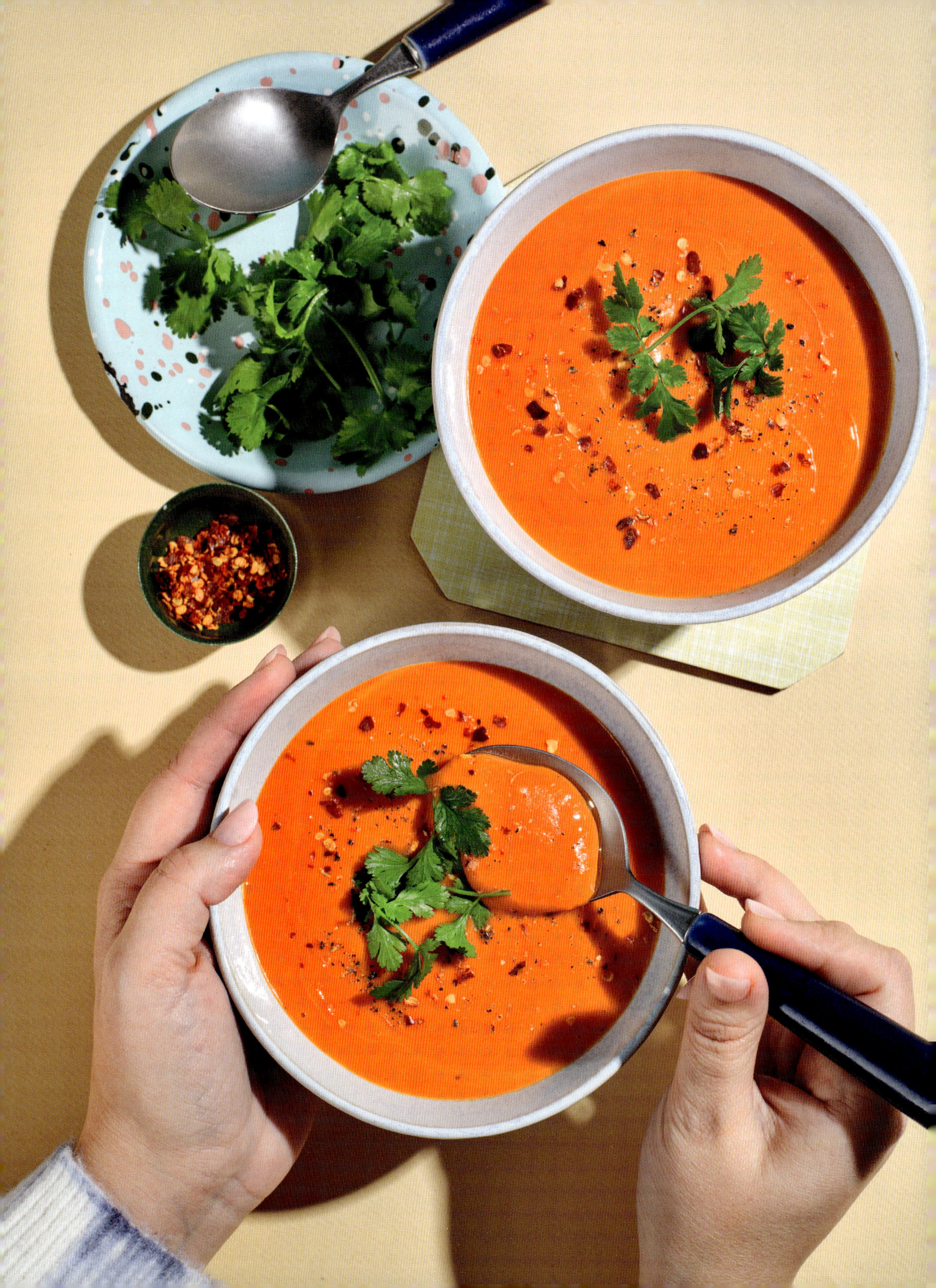

HEARTY SOUPS

Taco Soup

My family are suckers for anything Mexican inspired and I can guarantee empty bowls. This soup works wonders on cold days, filling up their tummies.

- 1 tbsp olive oil
- 350g (12oz) minced beef (5% fat)
- 1 beef stock cube
- 2 x 400g (14oz) cans chopped tomatoes
- 1 x 400g (14oz) can kidney beans, drained and rinsed
- 1 x 400g (14oz) can black beans, drained and rinsed
- 300g (10½oz) frozen sweetcorn
- 1½ tsp onion powder
- 1 tsp garlic powder
- 2 green chillies, deseeded and finely chopped
- ½ tsp salt
- 1 x 25g (1oz) packet of taco seasoning
- 300ml (10½fl oz/1¼ cups) boiling water

TO SERVE:
Sour cream
Tortilla chips
Grated Cheddar cheese

1. Heat the olive oil in a frying pan and fry the minced beef until just browned. Once cooked, remove from the pan and allow to cool.

2. Put all the ingredients, including the cooked mince, but not the boiling water, in a grab bag and mix thoroughly. Remove as much air as you can from the bag before sealing. Label the bag with the contents and the date you prepared it. Write on the front that you need to add the relevant quantity of boiling water at the time of cooking (or a note to refer to this page number). Place the bag in the freezer, making sure it lies as flat as possible.

3. Defrost the bag thoroughly in the fridge for approximately 8–10 hours before cooking.

4. You can wash the bag and reuse, don't forget to relabel.

5. To cook, empty the contents of the bag into the slow cooker. and add the boiling water (You can wash the bag and reuse, but don't forget to re-label.) Cook on low for 8 hours or on high for 4 hours.

6. Serve the soup topped with a blob of sour cream, some tortilla chips and a sprinkling of grated cheese on top.

3 MONTHS | **8–10 HOURS** | **LOW** 8 hours | **HIGH** 4 hours | **SERVES 4**

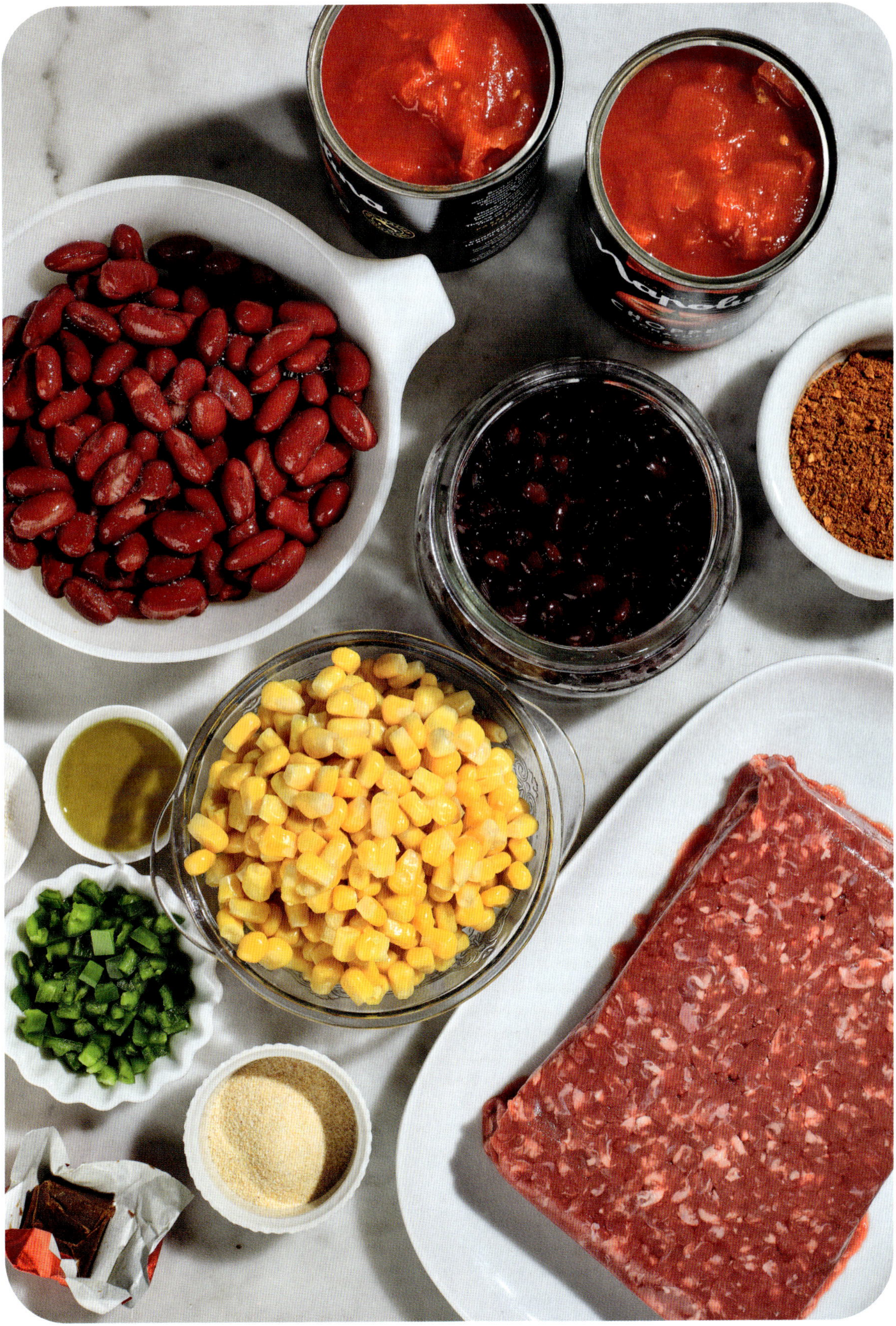

HEARTY SOUPS

Rich Tomato Soup

Picture the scene: it's a cold autumn day, you've been out for a long walk and you come home to this cooking in the slow cooker. Wonderful – warming and delicious, this will be a hit with everyone. You can also freeze any soup you don't eat for another day. I love to serve this with slices of cheese on toast for dunking.

- 18 salad tomatoes (about 1kg/2lb 4oz), blanched, peeled and chopped
- ½ tsp dried oregano
- 1 tsp salt
- ½ tsp pepper
- 1 tsp onion powder
- 1 tsp garlic powder
- 2 basil leaves
- 1 vegetable stock cube
- 250ml (9fl oz/1 cup) boiling water
- Single (light) cream, to drizzle

1. Add all the ingredients except the boiling water to a grab bag and mix well.

2. Remove as much air as you can from the bag before sealing. Label the bag with the contents and the date you prepared it. Write on the front that you need to add the relevant quantity of boiling water at the time of cooking (or a note to refer to this page number). Place the bag in the freezer, making sure it lies as flat as possible.

3. Defrost the bag thoroughly in the fridge for approximately 8–10 hours before cooking.

4. To cook, empty the contents of the bag into your slow cooker and add the boiling water. (You can wash the bag and reuse, but don't forget to re-label.) Cook on low for 8 hours or on high for 4 hours.

5. Spoon into bowls and finish with a drizzle of cream to serve.

3 MONTHS | **8–10 HOURS** | **LOW** 8 hours | **HIGH** 4 hours | **SERVES 4**

HEARTY SOUPS

Sausage & Pepper Soup

One of my favourites. You can omit frying the sausage but I find the meat breaks down a little too much if you don't and I enjoy the bite of chunky fried pieces which also preserves the flavour of the sausage. Yum.

1 tbsp olive oil
12 pork sausages, skins removed and cut into 2.5cm (1 inch) pieces
1 green (bell) pepper, deseeded and sliced
1 red (bell) pepper, deseeded and sliced
1 onion, sliced
5 potatoes, peeled and cut in chunks
3 tomatoes, chopped
1 tsp garlic powder
1 vegetable jelly stock pot
300ml (10½fl oz/1¼ cups) boiling water
Salt and black pepper
Crusty bread, to serve

1. Heat the olive oil in a frying pan and fry the sausage pieces until browned. Once cooked, allow to cool completely.

2. Put the cooled sausage in a grab bag and add the rest of the ingredients except the boiling water.

3. Remove as much air as you can from the bag before sealing. Label the bag with the contents and the date you prepared it. Write on the front that you need to add the relevant quantity of boiling water at the time of cooking (or a note to refer to this page number). Place the bag in the freezer, making sure it lies as flat as possible.

4. Defrost the bag thoroughly in the fridge for approximately 8–10 hours before cooking.

5. To cook, empty the contents of the bag into the slow cooker and add the boiling water. (You can wash the bag and reuse, but don't forget to re-label.) Cook on low for 6 hours or on high for 3 hours.

6. Season the soup to taste and serve with crusty bread.

3 MONTHS | **8–10 HOURS** | **LOW 6 hours | HIGH 3 hours** | **SERVES 4**

HEARTY SOUPS

Cheese & Broccoli Soup

There's a reason cheese and broccoli are a classic combination – it just works! I love how broccoli absorbs all the flavours of what it's been cooking in and then when you bite into it it's a taste sensation!

500g (1lb 2oz) frozen broccoli florets
1 onion, diced
2 carrots, peeled and diced
2 celery stalks, chopped
2 chicken stock cubes
¼ tsp salt
½ tsp pepper
1/8 tsp cayenne pepper
500g (1lb 2oz) mature Cheddar cheese
200ml (7fl oz/scant 1 cup) double (heavy) cream
800ml (28fl oz/3½ cups) boiling water

1. To your first large freezer bag, add the frozen broccoli, and the onion, carrots, celery, chicken stock cubes, salt, pepper, cayenne pepper and cheese. Shake to combine the ingredients.

2. Put the cream in a second smaller bag. If you know you'll have fresh cream in the fridge when you'd like to cook this meal, then just skip this step, but it's so handy to have some cream in the freezer for soups. Remove as much air as you can from the bags before sealing. Label the bags with the contents and the date you prepared it, then clip them together. Write on the front that you need to add the relevant quantity of boiling water and the cream at the time of cooking (or a note to refer to this page number). Place the bags in the freezer, making sure they lie as flat as possible.

3. Defrost the bags thoroughly in the fridge for approximately 8–10 hours before cooking.

4. To cook, empty the contents of the large bag into the slow cooker and add the boiling water. (You can wash the bag and reuse, but don't forget to re-label.) Stir until the chicken stock cubes have dissolved. Cook on low for 6 hours or on high for 3 hours.

5. Once the cooking time is up, add the cream, stir well and cook for 30 minutes on low, then serve.

3 MONTHS | 8–10 HOURS | LOW 6 hours | HIGH 3 hours | SERVES 4

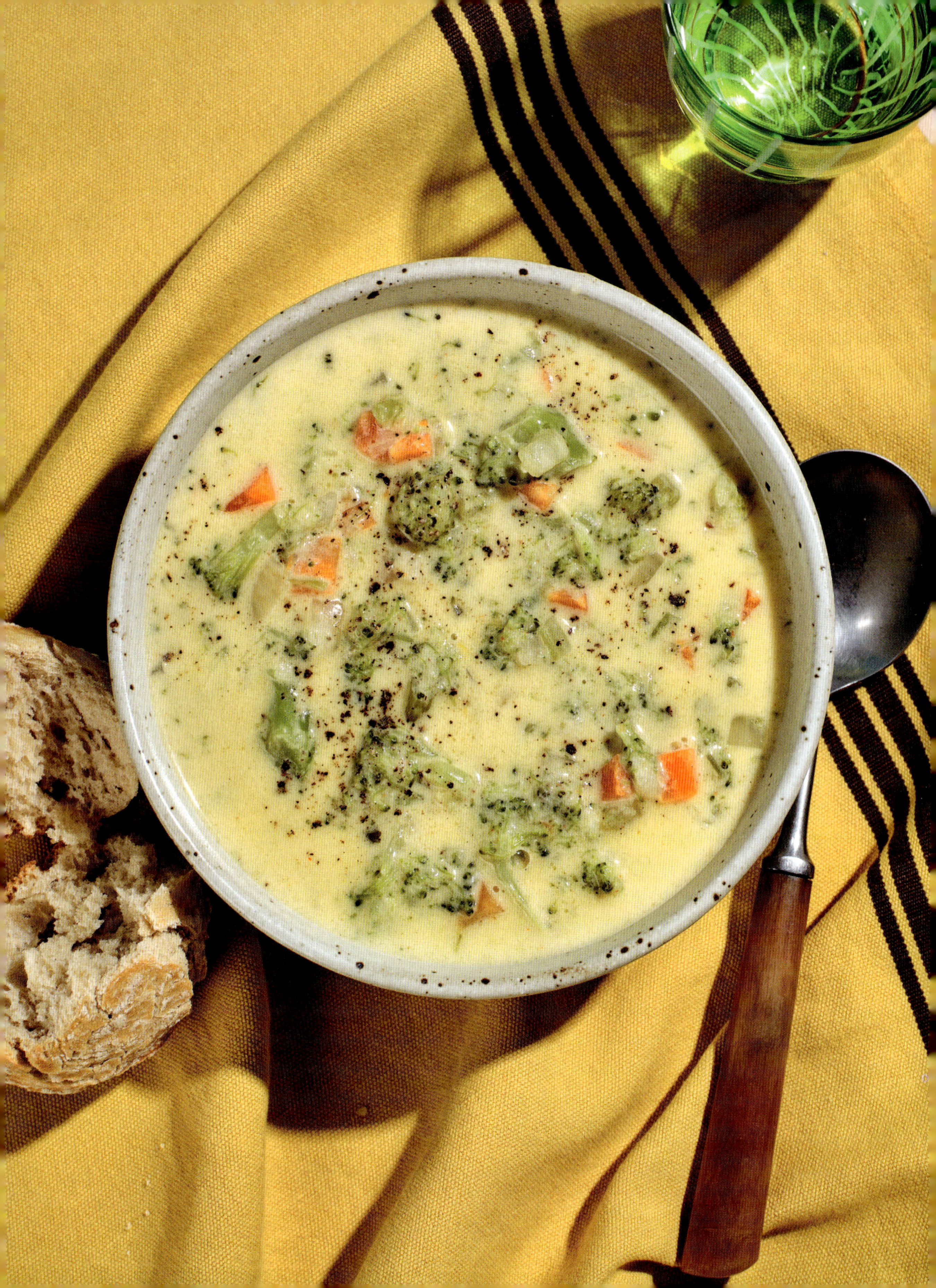

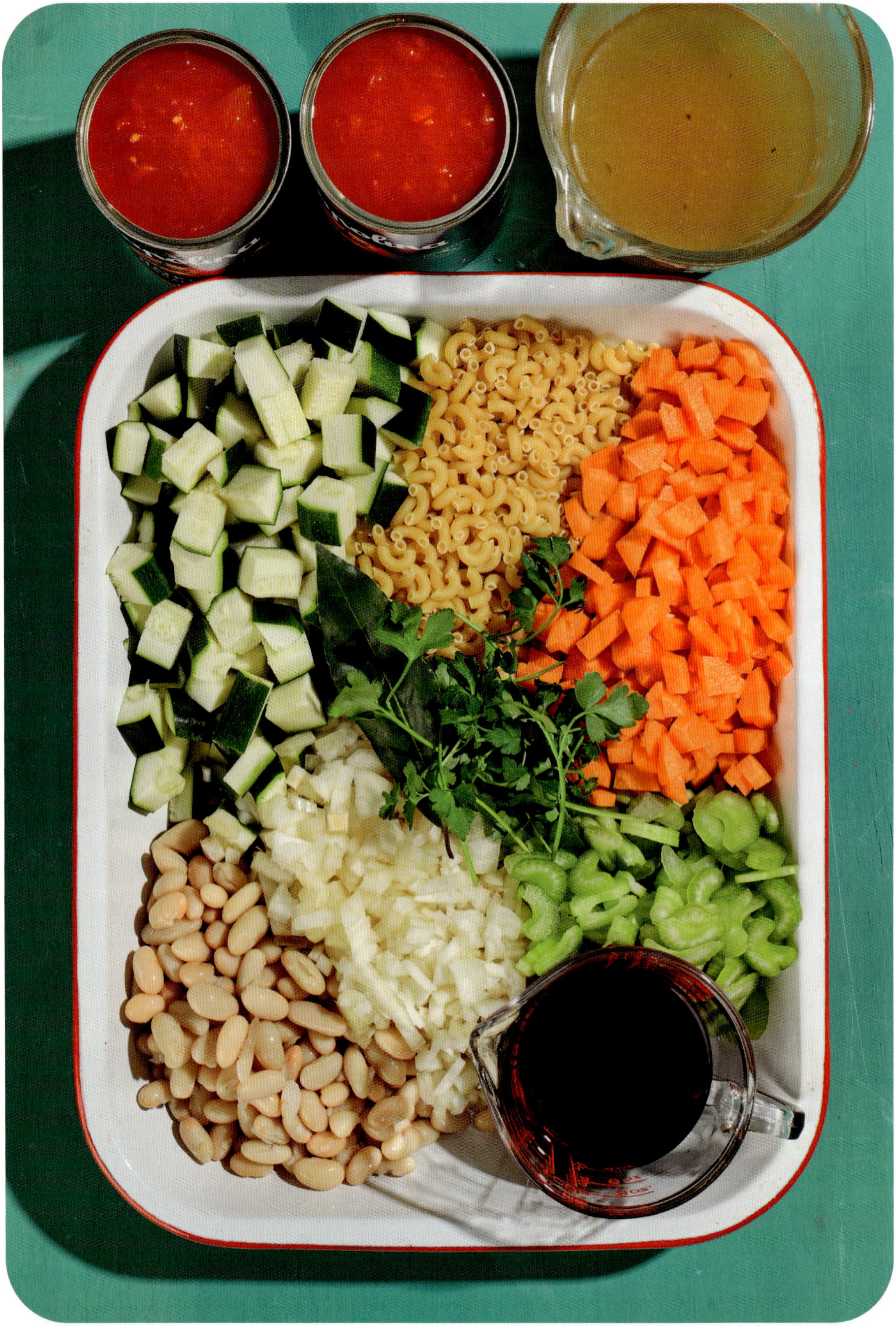

HEARTY SOUPS

Italian Vegetable Soup

This is a great soup if you're looking to get a good portion of vegetables into your system – think of all those vitamins! And adding the macaroni means this is also very filling.

- 1 large onion, chopped
- 2 carrots, peeled and diced
- 2 celery stalks, chopped
- 2 courgettes (zucchini), cubed
- 1 x 400g (14oz) can cannellini beans, rinsed and drained
- 10g fresh parsley leaves, chopped
- 2 x 400g (14oz) cans chopped tomatoes
- 120ml (4fl oz/½ cup) red wine
- 1 chicken jelly stock pot
- 1 tsp salt
- 1 bay leaf
- 300ml (10½fl oz/1¼ cups) boiling water
- 40g (1½oz) dried macaroni
- Black pepper
- Grated Parmesan cheese, to serve

1. Put all the ingredients except the boiling water and macaroni into a grab bag and season with pepper. Mix together well.

2. Remove as much air as you can from the bag before sealing. Label the bag with the contents and the date you prepared it. Write on the front that you need to add the relevant quantities of boiling water and macaroni at the time of cooking (or a note to refer to this page number). Place the bag in the freezer, making sure it lies as flat as possible.

3. Defrost the bag thoroughly in the fridge for approximately 8–10 hours before cooking.

4. To cook, empty the contents of the bag into your slow cooker. (You can wash the bag and reuse, but don't forget to re-label.) Cook on low for 6 hours or on high for 3 hours.

5. Once the cooking time is up, add the macaroni and stir. Leave to cook on high for 30 minutes further, or until the macaroni is cooked through.

6. Serve the soup in bowls with a good sprinkle of Parmesan cheese.

3 MONTHS | **8–10 HOURS** | **LOW** 6 hours | **HIGH** 3 hours | **SERVES 4**

HEARTY SOUPS

Split Pea & Ham Soup

Give me gammon in any form and I'm sold, so a big bowl of this hits the spot nicely. I tend to make a large batch of this, then split it evenly between single-serving-sized freezer bags so that I can have this for lunch when I'm working. When I've sent my kids off with packed lunches it always feels like a I'm having a bit of a cheeky treat as it's so good!

450g (1lb) split peas

350g (12oz) gammon, chopped into small chunks

1 large onion, chopped

1 celery stalk, chopped

1 carrot, peeled and chopped

1 red (bell) pepper, deseeded and chopped into small chunks

3 garlic cloves, crushed

1 tsp Italian seasoning

2 bay leaves

1 chicken stock cube

300ml (10½fl oz/1¼ cups) boiling water

1. Put all the ingredients except the boiling water into a grab bag and mix well.

2. Remove as much air as you can from the bag before sealing. Label the bag with the contents and the date you prepared it. Write on the front that you need to add the relevant quantity of boiling water at the time of cooking (or a note to refer to this page number). Place the bag in the freezer, making sure it lies as flat as possible.

3. Defrost the bag thoroughly in the fridge for approximately 8–10 hours before cooking.

4. To cook, empty the contents of the bag into your slow cooker and add the boiling water. (You can wash the bag and reuse, but don't forget to re-label.) Stir until the stock cube is completely dissolved. Cook on low for 8 hours or on high for 4 hours, and serve.

3 MONTHS | **8–10 HOURS** | **LOW** 8 hours | **HIGH** 4 hours | **SERVES 4**

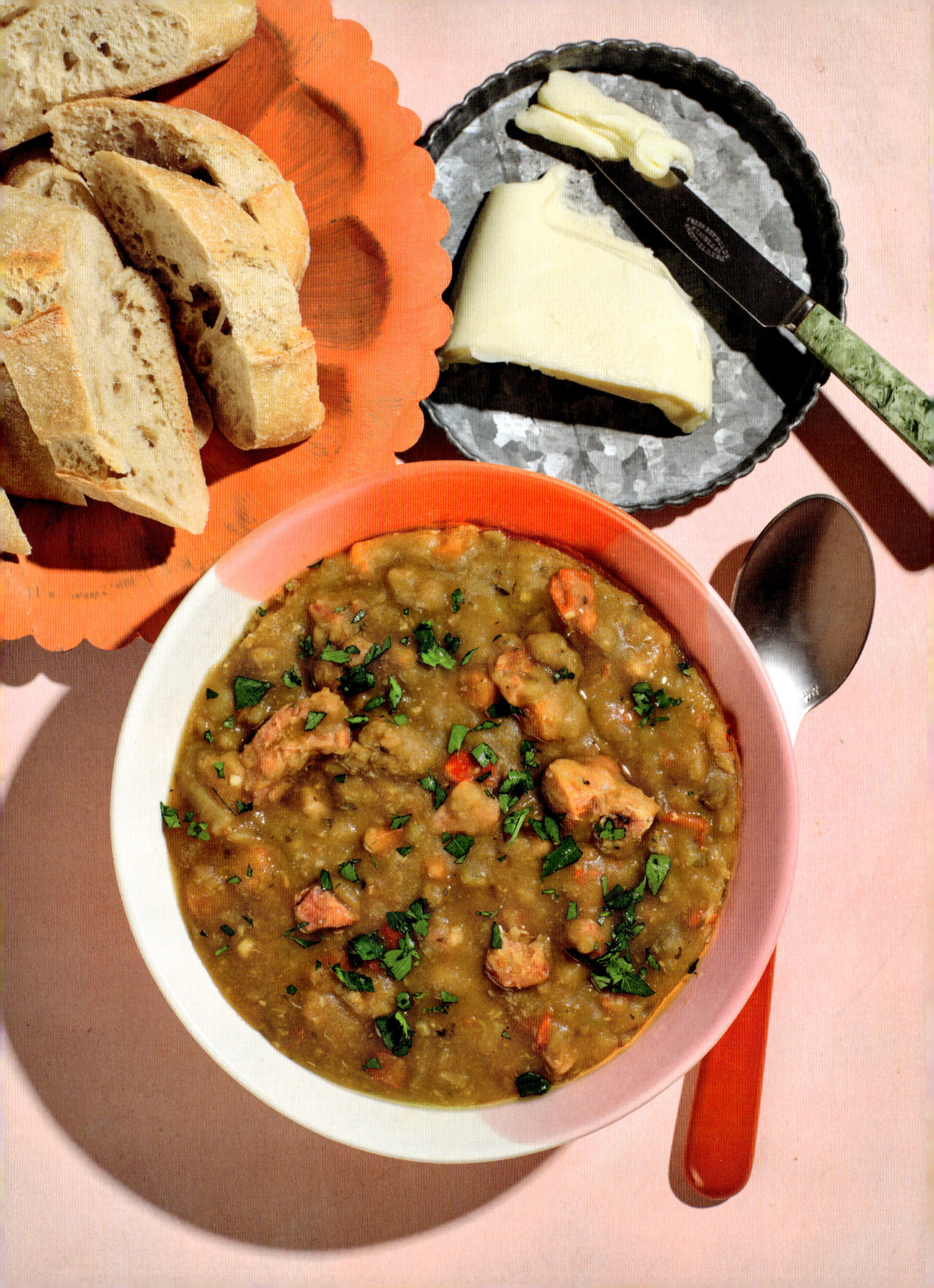

HEARTY SOUPS

Mulligatawny Soup

This soup definitely has a grown-up flavour thanks to the swede and carrot combination. It always reminds me of the mash my mum served us as kids that I used to hate and now really love.

- 1 carrot, peeled and chopped into small chunks
- 1 onion, chopped into small chunks
- ½ turnip, peeled and chopped into small chunks
- ½ swede, peeled and chopped into small chunks
- 1 tbsp curry powder
- 2 chicken stock cubes
- 1 tbsp finely chopped fresh coriander (cilantro)
- 500ml (17fl oz/2 cups) boiling water
- 1 x 250g (9oz) pouch microwave rice
- Salt and black pepper
- Crusty bread, to serve

1. Put all the ingredients except the rice and boiling water in a grab bag and season with salt and pepper. Mix well.

2. Remove as much air as you can from the bag before sealing. Label the bag with the contents and the date you prepared it. Write on the front that you need to add the relevant quantity of boiling water and pouch of rice at the time of cooking (or a note to refer to this page number). Place the bag in the freezer, making sure it lies as flat as possible.

3. Defrost the bag thoroughly in the fridge for approximately 8–10 hours before cooking.

4. To cook, empty the contents of the bag into your slow cooker and add the boiling water. (You can wash the bag and reuse, but don't forget to re-label.) Cook on low for 6 hours or high for 3 hours.

5. Thirty minutes before the end of the cooking time, add the packet of rice to the soup and stir well. Cook for the remaining time.

6. Serve the soup in bowls with nice crusty bread. Stir through chopped coriander to garnish.

3 MONTHS | **8–10 HOURS** | **LOW 6 hours** | **HIGH 3 hours** | **SERVES 4**

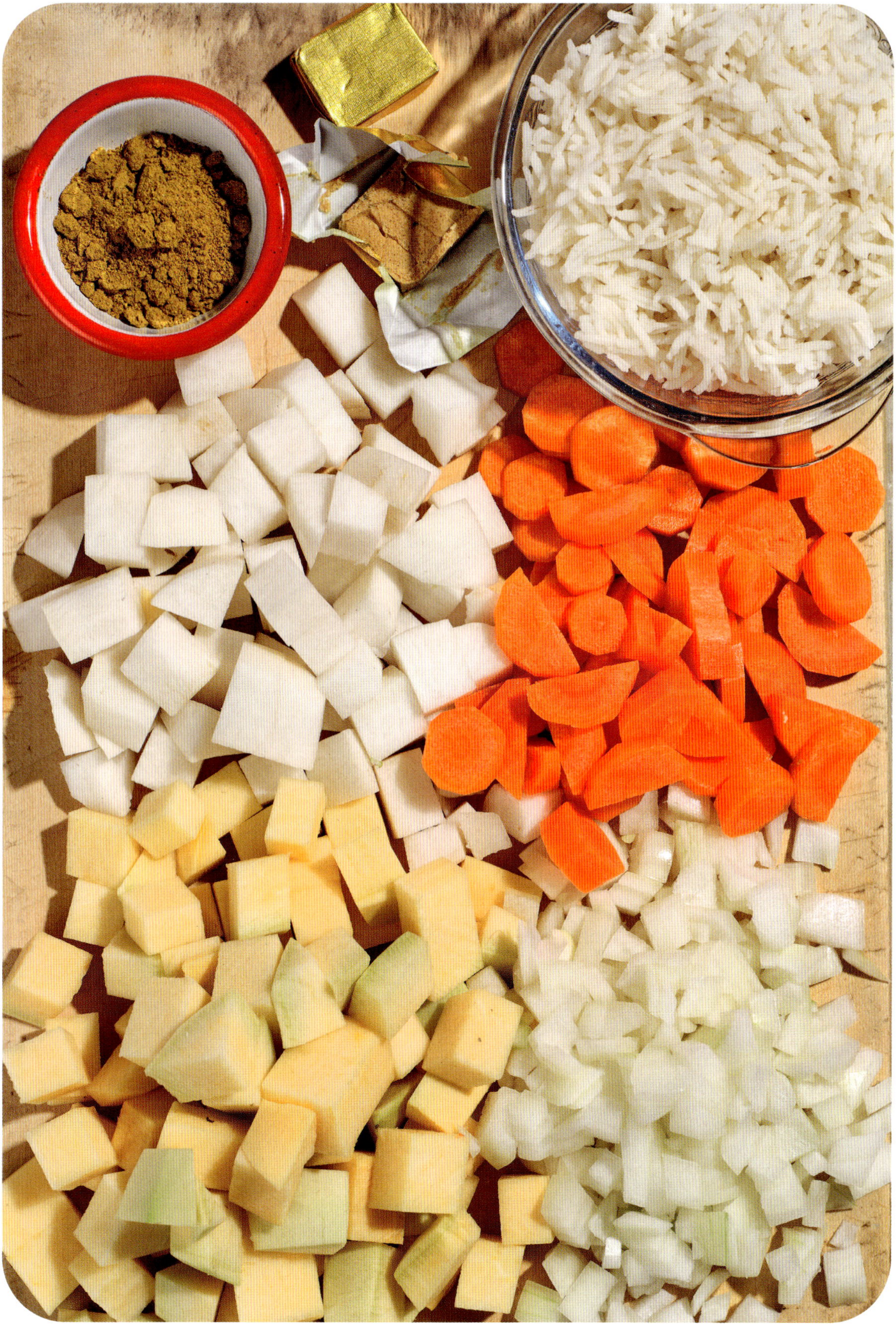

HEARTY SOUPS

Chicken Noodle Soup

A sick day classic: filling, full of nutrients and warming. Keep a stash of this in your freezer and the moment you start feeling under the weather, get it cooking! You could also freeze it in smaller portions and take a portion round to a loved one when they are ill – they are sure to feel better immediately!

- 2 carrots, peeled and chopped
- 2 celery stalks, chopped
- 1 onion, chopped
- 2 garlic cloves, finely chopped
- 1kg (2lb 4oz) bone-in, skinless chicken thighs
- 2 chicken stock cubes
- 800ml (28fl oz/3½ cups) boiling water
- 200ml (7fl oz/scant 1 cup) dry white wine
- 300g (10½oz) fresh egg noodles (from the chilled aisle)
- 2 tbsp chopped fresh flat-leaf parsley
- 2 tbsp chopped fresh dill
- 2 tbsp fresh lemon juice
- Salt and black pepper

1. Put the carrots, celery, onion, garlic, chicken thighs and stock cubes in a grab bag, season with salt and pepper and mix well. Remove as much air as you can from the bag before sealing. Label the bag with the contents and the date you prepared it. Write on the front that you need to add the other ingredients and boiling water at the time of cooking (or a note to refer to this page number). Place the bag in the freezer, making sure it lies as flat as possible.

2. Defrost the bag thoroughly in the fridge for approximately 8–10 hours before cooking.

3. To cook, empty the contents of the bag into your slow cooker, add the boiling water and dry white wine and stir everything together well. (You can wash the bag and reuse, but don't forget to re-label.) Cook on high for 3½ hours or on low for 6½ hours.

4. Once the cooking time is up, remove the chicken from the slow cooker, debone it and shred the meat. Return the meat to the slow cooker and add the noodles. Cook for a further 20 minutes on low or until the noodles are cooked through.

5. Stir in the parsley, dill and lemon juice and serve.

3 MONTHS | 8–10 HOURS | LOW 6½ hours | HIGH 3½ hours | SERVES 4

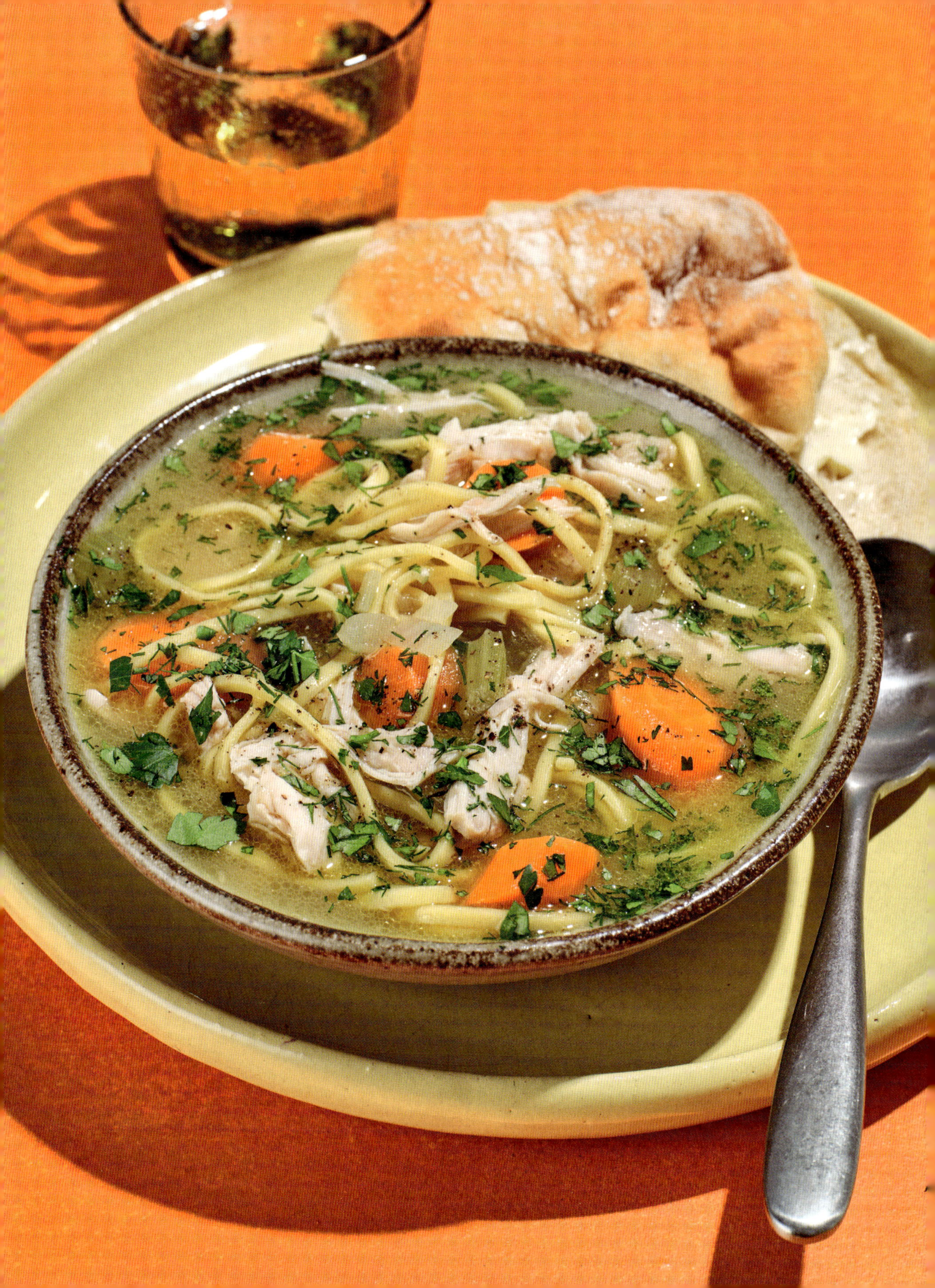

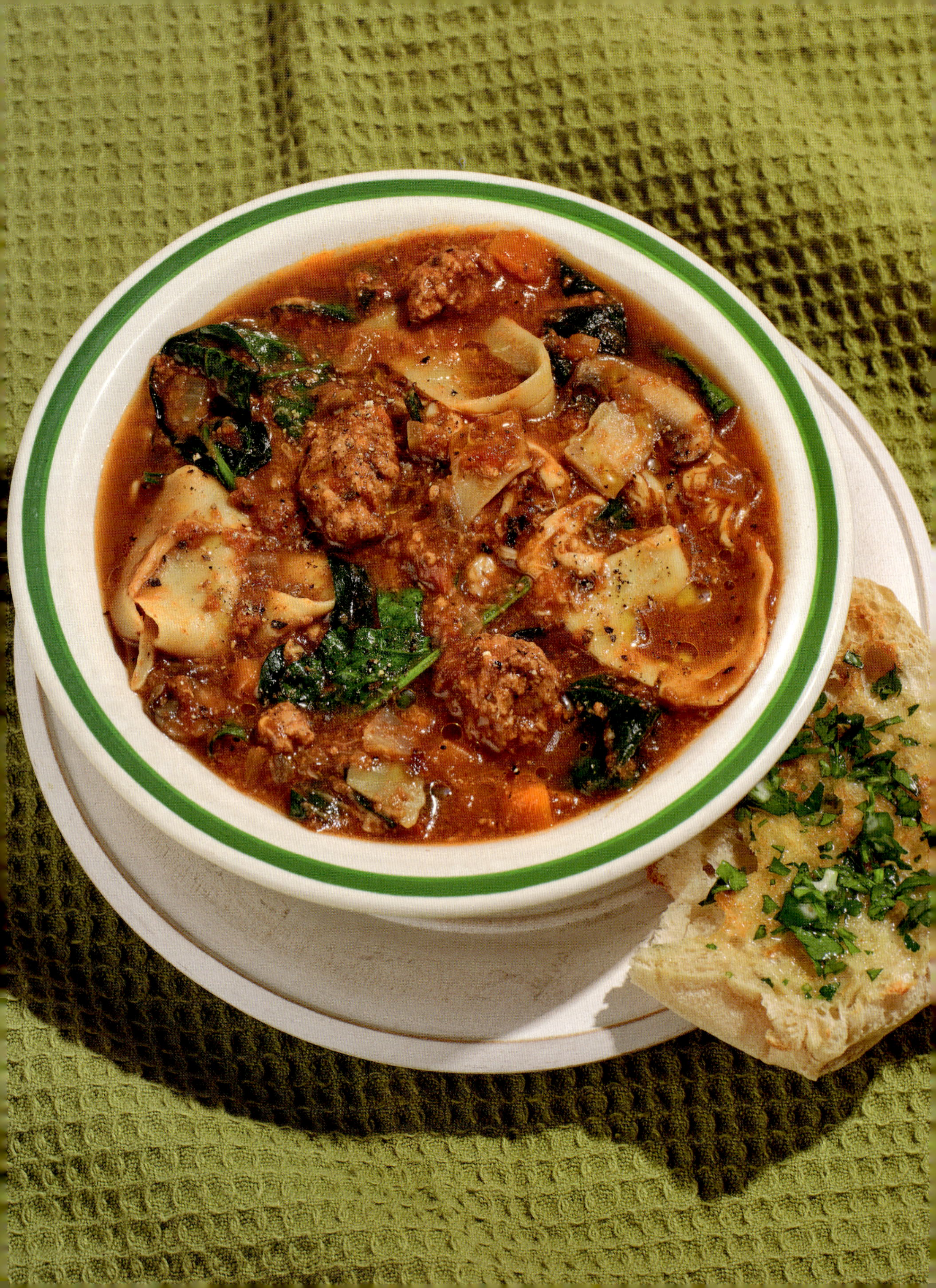

HEARTY SOUPS

Lasagna Soup

This dish was all over TikTok in October 2024; it. I'm not one to jump on viral trends or replicate recipes, but this just looked so good. My version includes some carrots for texture and a nice amount of mozzarella to finish. Scrummy!

- 500g (1lb 2oz) lean minced beef
- 1 large onion, chopped
- 2 carrots, peeled and chopped
- 3 garlic cloves, minced
- 1 beef stock cube
- 2 x 400g (14oz) cans chopped tomatoes
- 2 tbsp tomato purée (paste)
- 2 tsp Italian seasoning
- 400ml (14fl oz/1¾ cups) boiling water
- 200g (7oz) mushrooms, sliced
- Handful of fresh spinach, coarsely chopped
- 6 dried lasagna sheets, broken into pieces
- 250g (9oz) shredded mozzarella cheese
- Salt and black pepper
- Crusty bread, to serve

1. Add the beef, onion, carrots, garlic, stock cube, chopped tomatoes, tomato purée and seasoning into the grab bag and mix well. Remove as much air as you can from the bag before sealing. Label the bag with the contents and the date you prepared it. Write on the front that you need to add the relevant quantities of boiling water and other ingredients at the time of cooking (or a note to refer to this page number). Place the bag in the freezer, making sure it lies as flat as possible.

2. Defrost the bag thoroughly in the fridge for approximately 8–10 hours before cooking.

3. To cook, empty the contents of the bag into your slow cooker and add the boiling water. (You can wash the bag and reuse, but don't forget to re-label.) Cook on high for 3½ hours or on low for 7½ hours.

4. Once the cooking time is up, add the mushrooms, spinach and lasagna sheet pieces. Continue cooking on high for a further 30 minutes, or until the lasagna sheets are cooked through.

5. Just before serving, season to taste with salt and pepper, add the mozzarella and stir in. Serve in bowls with crusty bread.

3 MONTHS | **8–10 HOURS** | **LOW 7½ hours** / **HIGH 3½ hours** | **SERVES 4**

HEARTY SOUPS

Beef & Vegetable Soup

I used to babysit a young Polish boy and his mum would drop him off with a Tupperware box filled with soup. It always looked and smelt so good I had to recreate it. My version always reminds me of him and the way we couldn't understand each other at all, but we liked each other immensely.

- 500g (1lb 2oz) lean minced beef (5% fat)
- 1 tsp salt
- ½ tsp pepper
- 2 onions, chopped
- 1 white cabbage, chopped
- 400g (14oz) frozen mixed vegetables
- 1 beef stock cube
- 1 x 400g (14oz) can chopped tomatoes
- 1 bay leaf
- 2 tsp Italian seasoning
- 400ml (14fl oz/1¾ cups) boiling water

1. Put all the ingredients except the boiling water in a grab bag and mix well.

2. Remove as much air as you can from the bag before sealing. Label the bag with the contents and the date you prepared it. Write on the front that you need to add the relevant quantity of boiling water at the time of cooking (or a note to refer to this page number). Place the bag in the freezer, making sure it lies as flat as possible.

3. Defrost the bag thoroughly in the fridge for approximately 8–10 hours before cooking.

4. To cook, empty the contents of the bag into your slow cooker and add the boiling water. (You can wash the bag and reuse, but don't forget to re-label.) Stir well until the stock cube has dissolved. Cook on low for 8 hours or on high for 4 hours.

3 MONTHS | **8–10 HOURS** | **LOW 8 hours** | **HIGH 4 hours** | **SERVES 6–8**

HEARTY SOUPS

Cauliflower Soup

Cauliflower is packed full of vitamins and is so good for you. This is a really tasty way of having a meat-free meal. You can also freeze any leftovers to have another day.

1 whole cauliflower, chopped into florets
2 leeks, washed and sliced
2 celery stalks, diced
3 garlic cloves, minced
1 chicken stock cube
½ tsp salt
½ teaspoon black pepper
200g (7oz) Cheddar cheese, grated, plus extra to serve
150g double (heavy) cream
800ml (28fl oz/3½ cups) boiling water
Sour cream , to serve

1. Put the cauliflower, leeks, celery, garlic, stock cube and salt and pepper into a grab bag.

2. Put the cheese in a second smaller bag, and the cream in another small bag. (You can use fresh cheese and cream if you'd prefer and skip this step).

3. Remove as much air as you can from the bags before sealing. Label the bags with the contents and the date you prepared them and clip them all together. Write on the front that you need to add the relevant quantity of boiling water at the time of cooking (or a note to refer to this page number). Place the bags in the freezer, making sure they lie as flat as possible.

4. Defrost the bags thoroughly in the fridge for approximately 8–10 hours before cooking.

5. To cook, empty the contents of the large bag into the slow cooker and add the boiling water. (You can wash the bag and reuse, but don't forget to re-label.) Cook on low for 6 hours or on high for 3 hours.

6. Once this cooking time is up, add the cheese and cream. Mix well and cook for a further 30 minutes.

7. Serve in bowls with a dollop of sour cream and a sprinkle of cheese.

3 MONTHS | **8–10 HOURS** | **LOW 6 hours / HIGH 3 hours** | **SERVES 4**

HEARTY SOUPS

Butternut Squash Soup

Butternut squash is so delicious, especially after roasting (see my tip). It's sweet with a hint of nutty flavour that goes perfectly in soup.

- 1 onion, diced
- 3 garlic cloves, crushed
- 1 large butternut squash, peeled and cut into chunks
- 1 carrot, peeled and chopped
- 1 vegetable stock cube
- ½ tsp cayenne pepper, plus extra to garnish
- ½ tsp salt
- ½ tsp black pepper
- 300ml (10½fl oz/1¼ cups) double (heavy) cream
- 800ml (28fl oz/3½ cups) boiling water

1. Put all the ingredients except the cream and boiling water into a grab bag. Mix the ingredients together

2. Put the cream into another small freezer bag (or you can use fresh cream if you'd prefer and skip this step). Remove as much air as you can from the bags before sealing. Label the bags with the contents and the date you prepared them and clip them together. Write on the front that you need to add the relevant quantity of boiling water at the time of cooking (or a note to refer to this page number). Place the bags in the freezer, making sure they lie as flat as possible.

3. Defrost the bags thoroughly in the fridge for approximately 8–10 hours before cooking.

4. To cook, empty the contents of the large bag into your slow cooker and add the boiling water. (You can wash the bag and reuse, but don't forget to re-label.) Mix well until the stock cube has dissolved. Cook on low for 8 hours or on high for 4 hours.

5. Once the cooking time is up, add the cream and stir in. Leave to cook for a further 10 minutes until piping hot.

6. Serve the soup in bowls with a sprinkle of cayenne pepper on top.

3 MONTHS | **8–10 HOURS** | **LOW 8 hours | HIGH 4 hours** | **SERVES 4**

TIP:
To add additional flavour, (if you have time!) you could drizzle the butternut squash with oil and roast it in the oven for 30 minutes. Let cool completely, then follow the instructions above.

HEARTY SOUPS

Pork Shoulder Soup

Pork can go tough when it's overcooked, but cooking this in the slow cooker will give you a lovely soft meat and a yummy broth to enjoy on a chilly day.

- 500g (1lb 2oz) pork shoulder, chopped into chunks
- 500g (1lb 2oz) potatoes, peeled and chopped into chunks
- 4 carrots, peeled and sliced thickly
- 1 leek, finely sliced
- 1 onion, diced
- 1 beef stock cube
- 4 garlic cloves, crushed
- 1 tbsp tomato puree (paste)
- ½ tsp salt
- ½ tsp pepper
- 1 tsp Italian seasoning
- 600ml (21fl oz/2½ cups) boiling water
- 250ml (9fl oz/1 cup) red wine
- 2 tbsp cornflour (cornstarch)
- Crusty bread, to serve

1. Put all the ingredients, except the wine, boiling water and cornflour, into a grab bag. Mix the ingredients well. Remove as much air as you can from the bag before sealing. Label the bag with the contents and the date you prepared it. Write on the front that you need to add the relevant quantities of boiling water, wine and cornflour at the time of cooking (or a note to refer to this page number). Place the bag in the freezer, making sure it lies as flat as possible.

2. Defrost the bag thoroughly in the fridge for approximately 8–10 hours before cooking.

3. To cook, empty the contents of the bag into your slow cooker and add the boiling water and red wine. (You can wash the bag and reuse, but don't forget to re-label.) Mix thoroughly so that the stock cube completely dissolves. Cook on low for 7 hours or on high for 4 hours.

4. Once the cooking time is up, mix the cornflour with 5 tablespoons of water. Add to the stew, stir and leave to cook for a further 30 minutes so that the stew is nice and thick.

5. Serve with crusty bread.

3 MONTHS | **8–10 HOURS** | **LOW 7 hours | HIGH 4 hours** | **SERVES 4**

HEARTY SOUPS

Leek & Potato Soup

Words cannot express how much I love leek and potato soup. I had never had it before my mother-in-law once bought me a fancy carton, but since then I've been somewhat of a fan. She sadly passed during the creation of this cookbook and so I dedicate this recipe to her, Natasha Burne.

- 30g (1oz/2 tbsp) butter
- 2 onions, chopped
- 4 leeks, trimmed and sliced
- 3 large potatoes, peeled and cut into chunks
- 1 tsp dried mixed herbs
- 1 vegetable or chicken stock cube
- 800ml (28fl oz/3½ cups) boiling water
- 100ml (3½fl oz/scant ½ cup) double (heavy) cream
- Salt and black pepper
- Bread and butter, to serve

1. Add the butter, onions, leeks and potatoes to the bag and mix well. Add the herbs and stock cube. Season with salt and pepper and mix well.

2. Remove as much air as you can from the bag before sealing. Label the bag with the contents and the date you prepared it. Write on the front that you need to add the relevant quantities of boiling water and cream at the time of cooking (or a note to refer to this page number). Place the bag in the freezer, making sure it lies as flat as possible.

3. Defrost the bag thoroughly in the fridge for approximately 8–10 hours before cooking.

4. To cook, empty the contents of the bag into your slow cooker and add the boiling water. (You can wash the bag and reuse, but don't forget to re-label.) Stir until the stock cube has completely dissolved. Cook on low for 6 hours or on high for 3 hours.

5. Once the cooking time is up, add the cream and cook on low for a further 20 minutes.

6. Serve with fresh bread and butter.

3 MONTHS | **8–10 HOURS** | **LOW 6 hours** | **HIGH 3 hours** | **SERVES 4**

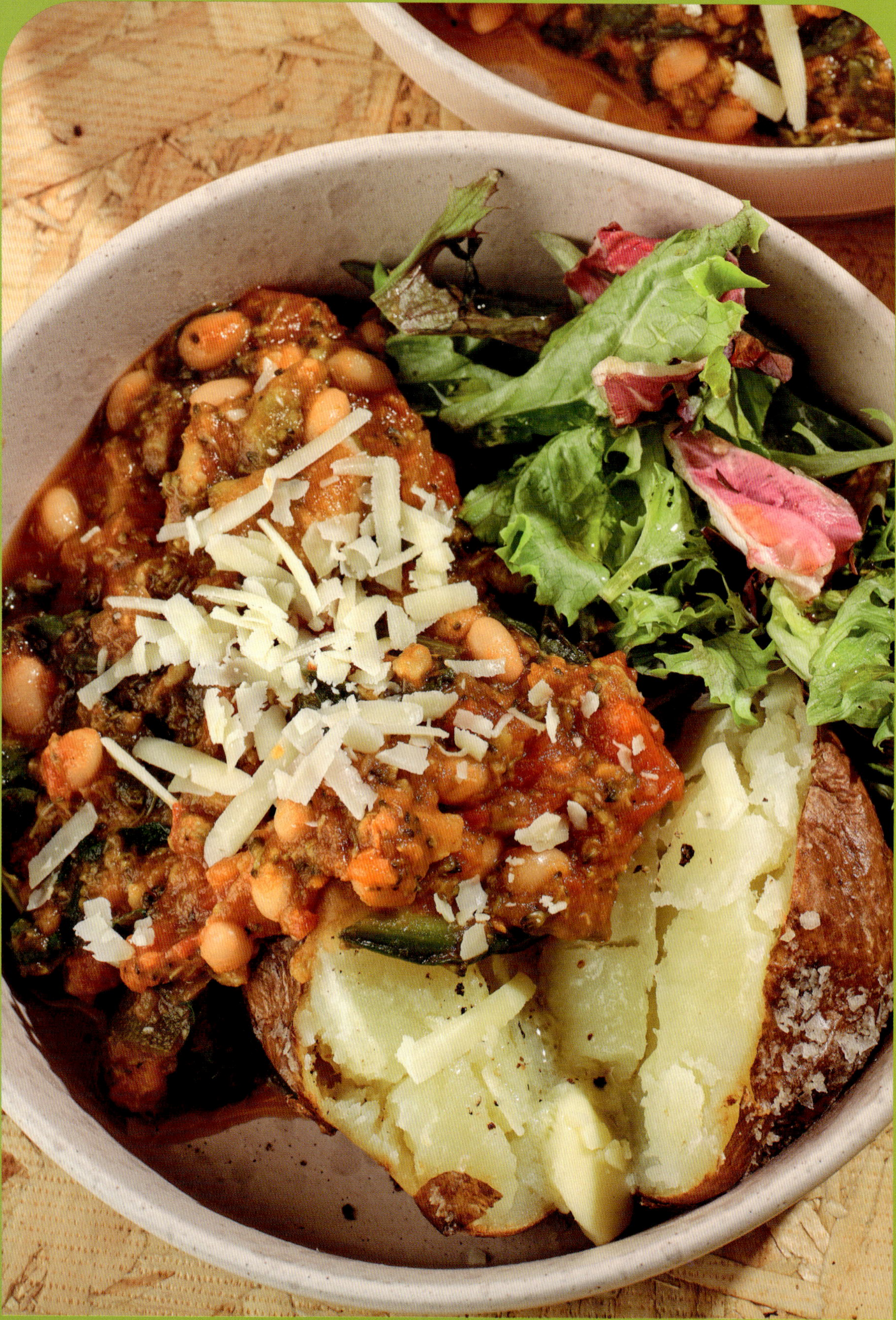

VEGETARIAN

5

VEGAN

VEGETARIAN VEGAN

Sweet Potato Curry

This is a lovely vegan curry, and one which is so filling. You could roast the butternut squash before adding (once completely cooled) to the grab bag, if you'd like to add some additional flavour.

400g (14oz) sweet potatoes, peeled and chopped
½ butternut squash, peeled and chopped
1 onion, chopped
2 garlic cloves, crushed
200g (7oz) drained canned chickpeas, rinsed
1 x 400g (14oz) can chopped tomatoes
½ tsp ground cumin
1 tsp paprika
1 tsp mild curry powder
2 tsp garam masala
1 x 400ml (14oz) can coconut milk
Roti and mango chutney, to serve

1. Put the sweet potatoes, butternut squash, onion, garlic and chickpeas in a grab bag.

2. In a jug or bowl, combine the chopped tomatoes, cumin, paprika, curry powder and garam masala. Mix well, then pour into the bag.

3. Remove as much air as you can from the bag before sealing. Label the bag with the contents and the date you prepared it. Write on the front that you need to add the coconut milk at the time of cooking (or a note to refer to this page number). Place the bag in the freezer, making sure it lies as flat as possible.

4. Defrost the bag thoroughly in the fridge for approximately 8–10 hours before cooking.

5. To cook, empty the contents of the bag into your slow cooker. (You can wash the bag and reuse, but don't forget to re-label.) Cook on high for 4 hours or on low for 8 hours.

6. Thirty minutes before the end of the cooking time, add the coconut milk to the slow cooker, stir well and continue cooking for the remaining time.

7. Serve the curry with roti and mango chutney.

3 MONTHS | **8–10 HOURS** | **LOW 8 hours | HIGH 4 hours** | **SERVES 4**

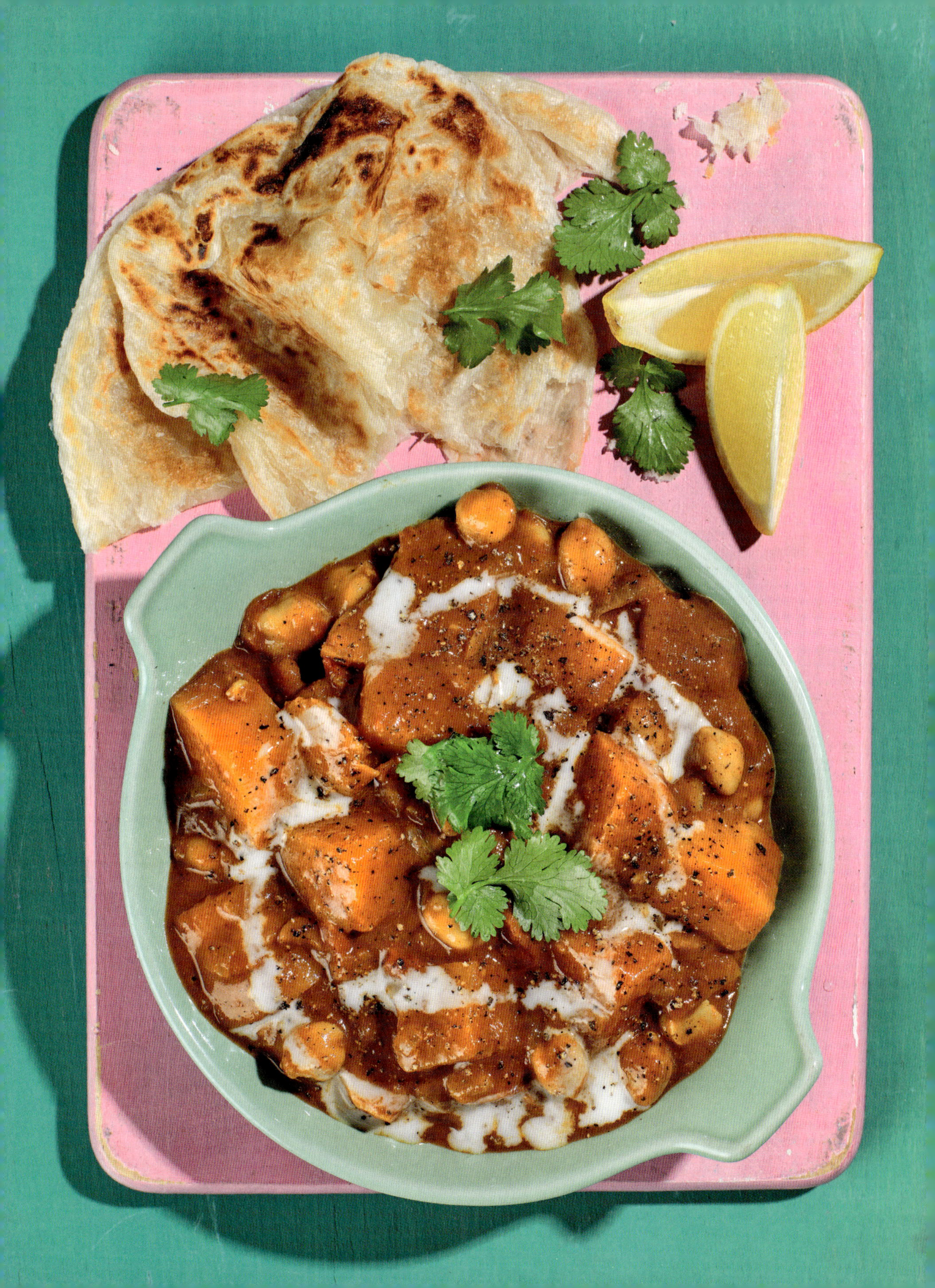

VEGETARIAN VEGAN

Vegetable Curry

Even if you eat meat, why not try a meat free day? Once you try this curry (which is actually vegan) and see how inexpensive it works out to be, I can almost guarantee you'll be making a few of these grab bags to keep in stock!

- 1 courgette (zucchini), chopped
- 3 potatoes, peeled and chopped peeled
- ½ aubergine (eggplant), chopped
- ½ cauliflower, chopped into small florets
- 1 yellow (bell) pepper, deseeded and chopped
- 1 green (bell) pepper, deseeded and chopped
- 3 tbsp mild curry paste
- 2 tbsp mango chutney
- 1 vegetable jelly stock pot
- 1 x 400g (14oz) can chopped tomatoes
- 200ml (7fl oz/scant 1 cup) coconut milk
- Rice, to serve

1. Put all the vegetables in a grab bag, close the bag and shake to combine.

2. In a jug, combine the curry paste, mango chutney, vegetable stock pot and chopped tomatoes. Whisk to combine, then add to the grab bag.

3. Remove as much air as you can from the bag before sealing. Label the bag with the contents and the date you prepared it. Write on the front that you need to add the coconut milk at the time of cooking (or a note to refer to this page number). Place the bag in the freezer, making sure it lies as flat as possible.

4. Defrost the bag thoroughly in the fridge for approximately 8–10 hours before cooking.

5. To cook, empty the contents of the bag into your slow cooker. (You can wash the bag and reuse, but don't forget to re-label.) Cook on high for 4 hours, or on low for 8 hours.

6. Thirty minutes before the end of the cooking time, add the coconut milk, stir well, and cook for the remaining time.

7. Serve the curry with rice.

3 MONTHS | **8–10 HOURS** | **LOW 8 hours / HIGH 4 hours** | **SERVES 4**

VEGETARIAN VEGAN

Tofu Tikka Masala

You can make this up in a batch, cook and then freeze what you don't eat to have another day. Defrost, then take it in some Tupperware to work and just reheat in the microwave. Lovely!

- 1 x 400g (14oz) can of chopped tomatoes
- 1 tbsp garam masala
- 1 ½ tsp ground cumin
- ½ tsp ground turmeric
- ¼ tsp paprika
- ½ tsp salt
- ½ tsp black pepper
- 280g (10oz) extra firm tofu, drained and cut into chunks
- 2 garlic cloves, crushed
- 2.5cm (1 inch) piece fresh root ginger, grated
- 1 red (bell) pepper, deseeded and cut into chunks
- 1 onion, diced
- 2 carrots, peeled and sliced
- 3 medium-sized potatoes, peeled and chopped into small chunks
- 200g (7oz) frozen cauliflower florets
- 1 x 400g (14oz) can coconut milk
- Rice, to serve

1. Open the can of tomatoes, add all the spices and salt and pepper and stir to combine.

2. Put the tofu in a grab bag and pour in the canned tomatoes. Close the bag and shake well to coat the tofu. Reopen the bag and add all the remaining ingredients except the coconut milk. Shake well.

3. Remove as much air as you can from the bag before sealing. Label the bag with the contents and the date you prepared it. Write on the front that you need to add the coconut milk at the time of cooking (or a note to refer to this page number). Place the bag in the freezer, making sure it lies as flat as possible.

4. Defrost the bag thoroughly in the fridge for approximately 8–10 hours before cooking.

5. To cook, empty the contents of the bag into your slow cooker. Cook on low for 8 hours or on high for 4 hours.

6. Once the cooking time is up, add the coconut milk, stir and leave to cook for a further 20 minutes on low. Serve the curry with rice.

3 MONTHS | **8–10 HOURS** | **LOW 8 hours | HIGH 4 hours** | **SERVES 4**

VEGETARIAN VEGAN

Vegan Chickpea Curry

Do I like chickpeas? No. Do I like this curry? Yes. It's a weird one! I think it must be because the sauce is so delicious and it blends so well with the chickpeas. Whatever it is, it makes for a yummy curry.

- 1 x 400g (14oz) can chickpeas, drained and rinsed
- 2 tsp mild curry powder
- 2.5cm (1 inch) piece root ginger, grated
- 3 garlic cloves, crushed
- 1 tsp salt
- ½ tsp black pepper
- 1 x 400g (14oz) can chopped tomatoes
- 2 yellow (bell) peppers, deseeded and chopped
- 1 large onion, sliced
- 1 x 400ml (14oz) can coconut milk

1. Put the chickpeas in a bowl and add the curry powder, ginger, garlic, salt and pepper. Mix well and pour into the grab bag.

2. Add the chopped tomatoes, yellow peppers and onion to the bag and shake to combine.

3. Remove as much air as you can from the bag before sealing. Label the bag with the contents and the date you prepared it. Write on the front that you need to add the coconut milk at the time of cooking (or a note to refer to this page number). Place the bag in the freezer, making sure it lies as flat as possible.

4. Defrost the bag thoroughly in the fridge for approximately 8–10 hours before cooking.

5. To cook, empty the contents of the bag into your slow cooker. (You can wash the bag and reuse, but don't forget to re-label.) Cook on high for 4 hours or on low for 8 hours.

6. Thirty minutes before the end of the cooking time, add the coconut milk, stir well, and cook for the remaining time.

7. Serve the curry with rice.

3 MONTHS | **8–10 HOURS** | **LOW 8 hours** | **HIGH 4 hours** | **SERVES 4**

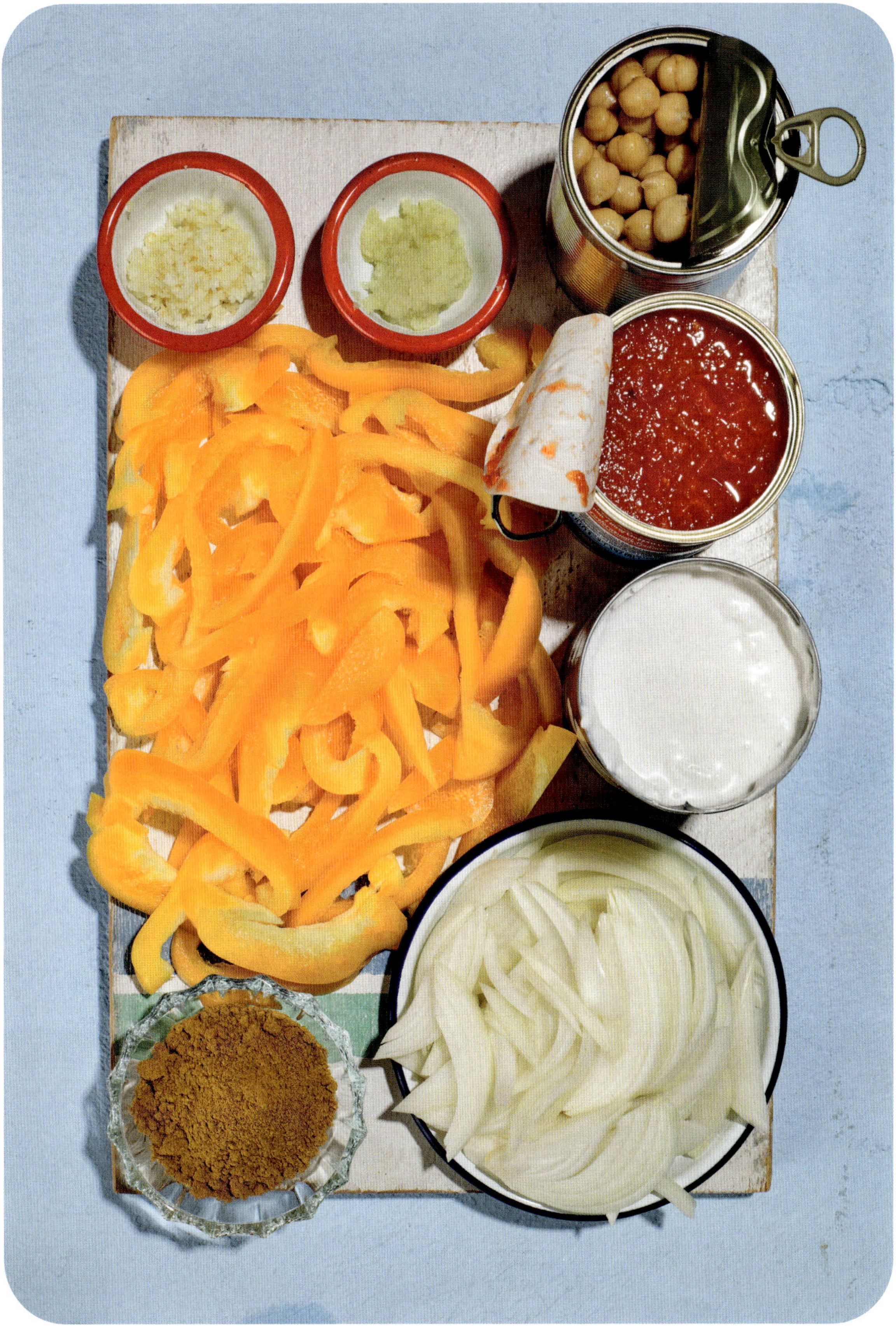

VEGETARIAN VEGAN

Vegetable Tagine

I absolutely love couscous, and I always have a supply for meals like this. Delicious fresh vegetables served over couscous is my idea of heaven, but this tagine is also great in a jacket potato.

- 4 carrots, peeled and cut into chunks
- 4 small parsnips (or 3 large), cut into chunks
- 3 red onions, cut into wedges
- 2 red (bell) peppers, deseeded and cut into chunks
- 2 tbsp olive oil
- 2 tbsp runny honey
- 1 x 400g (14oz) can chopped tomatoes
- 1 tsp ground cumin
- 1 tsp paprika
- 1 tsp chilli powder
- Salt and black pepper
- Couscous, jacket potatoes or crusty bread, to serve
- Flaked almonds and herbs, to garnish

1. Preheat the oven to 180°C/160°C fan/350°F/Gas 4. Spread the vegetables over a baking tray and drizzle with the olive oil and honey. Bake for 35-40 minutes, until softened and golden, then allow to cool completely.

2. Open the canned tomatoes and add the cumin, paprika and chilli powder. Mix well.

3. Add the cooled vegetables to your freezer bag, then add the canned tomatoes and mix well.

4. Remove as much air as you can from the bag before sealing. Label the bag with the contents and the date you prepared it, then place it in the freezer, making sure it lies as flat as possible.

5. Defrost the bag thoroughly in the fridge for approximately 8-10 hours before cooking.

6. To cook, empty the contents of the bag into your slow cooker. (You can wash the bag and reuse, but don't forget to re-label.) Cook on high for 3 hours, or on low for 6 hours.

7. Season to taste with salt and pepper and serve with couscous, jacket potatoes or custy bread.

3 MONTHS | 8–10 HOURS | LOW 6 hours | HIGH 3 hours | SERVES 4

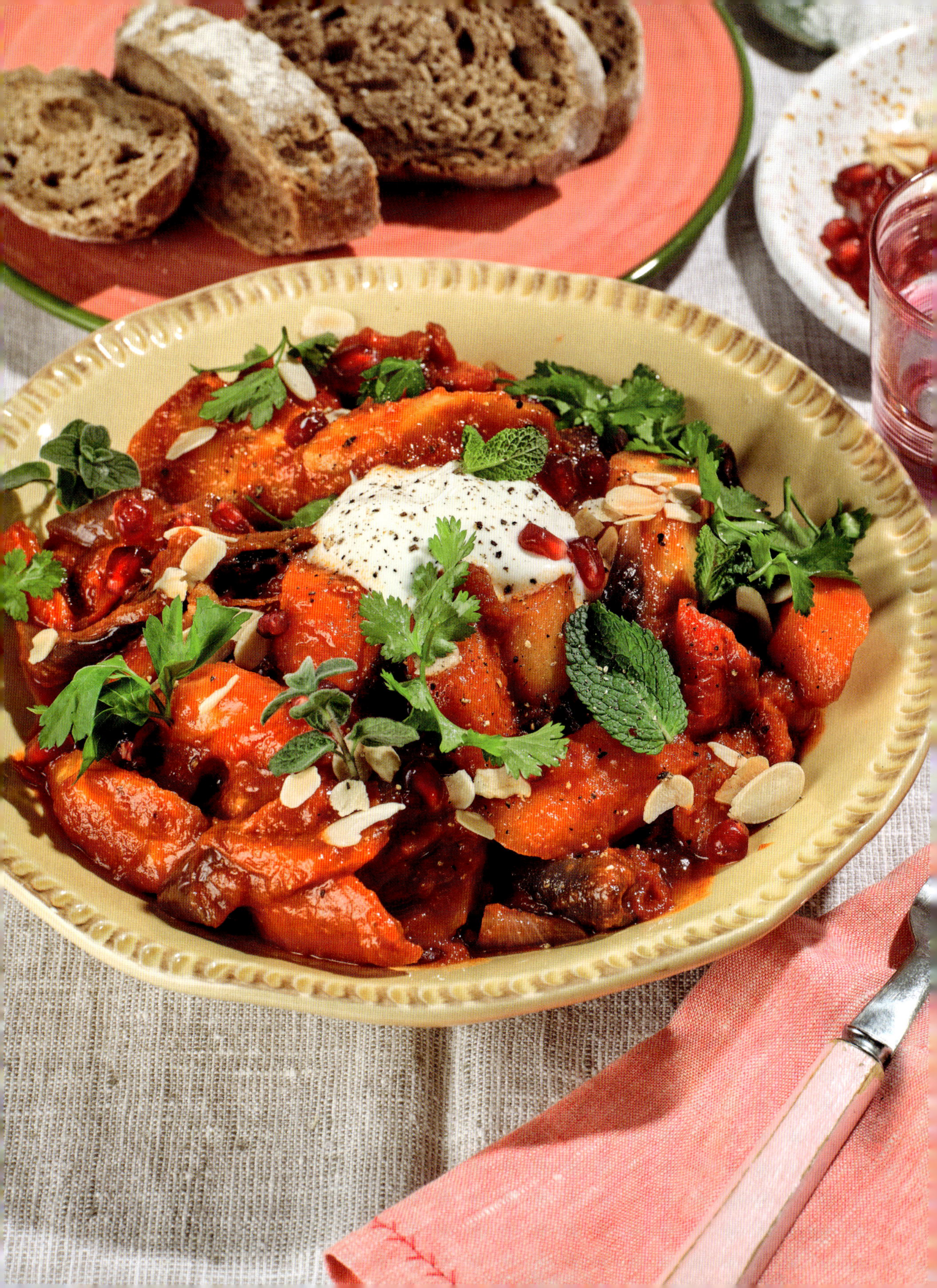

VEGETARIAN VEGAN

Vegetarian Chilli

Trust me, you don't miss the meat in this delicious meal. The beans are such good source of protein and will fill up even the hungriest of tummies.

- 2 x 400g (14oz) cans chopped tomatoes
- 2 tsp ground cumin
- 2 tsp paprika
- 1 tsp ground coriander
- ¼ tsp sea salt
- ¼ tsp black pepper
- 2 celery stalks, chopped
- 2 garlic cloves, finely chopped
- 2 red onions, diced
- 4 carrots, peeled and diced
- 1 x 400g (14oz) can cannellini beans, drained and rinsed
- 2 green (bell) peppers, deseeded and chopped into chunks
- 1 red (bell) pepper, deseeded and chopped into chunks
- Bread, to serve

1. Open the cans of chopped tomatoes and into one of them add the cumin, paprika, coriander, salt and pepper. Stir well.

2. Add all the remaining ingredients to your grab bag along with both cans of tomatoes and mix well.

3. Remove as much air as you can from the bag before sealing. Label the bag with the contents and the date you prepared it, then place it in the freezer, making sure it lies as flat as possible.

4. Defrost the bag thoroughly in the fridge for approximately 8–10 hours before cooking.

5. To cook, empty the contents of the bag into your slow cooker. (You can wash the bag and reuse, but don't forget to re-label.) Cook on low for 6 hours or on high for 3 hours.

6. Serve the chilli in bowls with chunks of fresh bread for dunking.

3 MONTHS | **8–10 HOURS** | **LOW 6 hours** | **HIGH 3 hours** | **SERVES 4**

VEGETARIAN VEGAN

Vegetable Korma

This is my version of a vegetarian korma. The spices give it an authentic flavour, while the cauliflower and butternut squash provide the bite you'd normally get from the chicken. If you are cooking for vegetarians, then you can serve with naan bread, but be aware that most naan breads aren't vegan.

- A splash of vegetable oil
- 1 onion, peeled and finely chopped
- 2 red chillies, deseeded and finely sliced
- 2 garlic cloves, minced
- 1 tbsp freshly grated ginger
- 1 tsp ground turmeric
- 1 tsp garam masala
- 2 tbsp tomato purée (paste)
- 1 carrot, peeled and chopped
- 1 red (bell) pepper, deseeded and diced
- 300g (10½oz) cauliflower, chopped into small pieces
- 300g (10½oz) butternut squash, peeled, deseeded and diced
- 1 meat-free chicken-flavour stock cube
- 2 heaped tbsp ground almonds
- 200ml (7fl oz/scant 1 cup) boiling water
- Salt and black pepper
- White rice and/or naan bread, to serve

1. Heat the vegetable oil in a pan and fry the onion on a medium heat for around 8 minutes until softened. Add the chillies, garlic, ginger, turmeric, garam masala and tomato purée and continue to cook for another 2 minutes. Remove from the heat and allow to cool completely.

2. Add the cooled mixture to your grab bag, then add the carrot, red pepper, cauliflower, butternut squash and the stock cube. Close the bag and shake to combine all the ingredients. Remove as much air as you can from the bag before sealing. Label the bag with the contents and the date you prepared it. Write on the front that you need to add the relevant quantities of ground almonds and boiling water at the time of cooking. Place the bag in the freezer, making sure it lies as flat as possible.

3. Defrost the bag thoroughly in the fridge for approximately 8–10 hours before cooking.

4. To cook, empty the contents of the bag into your slow cooker, add the ground almonds and boiling water and stir well. Cook on low for 8 hours or on high for 4 hours.

5. Serve the korma with white rice and/or naan bread.

3 MONTHS | **8–10 HOURS** | **LOW 8 hours / HIGH 4 hours** | **SERVES 4**

VEGETARIAN VEGAN

Red Tofu & Green Bean Curry

There's so much going on here that if you aren't a fan of the flavour of tofu but want or need the protein it provides then this is the recipe for you.

- 560g (1lb 4oz) firm tofu, drained and cut into 2.5cm (1 inch) pieces
- 250g (9oz) green beans, trimmed
- 1 vegetable stock cube
- 1 red onion, finely sliced
- 2 plum tomatoes, diced
- 2.5cm (1 inch) piece of root ginger, peeled and finely chopped
- 2 garlic cloves, crushed
- 2 tbsp vegan red curry paste
- 400ml (14fl oz/1¾ cups) boiling water
- 1 x 400g (14oz) can coconut milk
- Salt and black pepper
- Rice, to serve
- Coriander (cilantro), to garnish

1. Put all the ingredients except the boiling water and coconut milk into a grab bag, season with salt and pepper and mix well.

2. Remove as much air as you can from the bag before sealing. Label the bag with the contents and the date you prepared it. Write on the front that you need to add the boiling water and coconut milk at the time of cooking (or a note to refer to this page number). Place the bag in the freezer, making sure it lies as flat as possible.

3. Defrost the bag thoroughly in the fridge for approximately 8–10 hours before cooking.

4. To cook, empty the contents of the bag into your slow cooker, add the boiling water and mix everything well. (You can wash the bag and reuse, but don't forget to re-label.) Cook on low for 6 hours or on high for 3 hours.

5. Thirty minutes before the end of the cooking time, add the coconut milk and continue cooking for the remaining time.

6. Serve with rice, and garnish with coriander sprigs.

---

3 MONTHS | **8–10 HOURS** | **LOW** 6 hours | **HIGH** 3 hours | **SERVES 4**

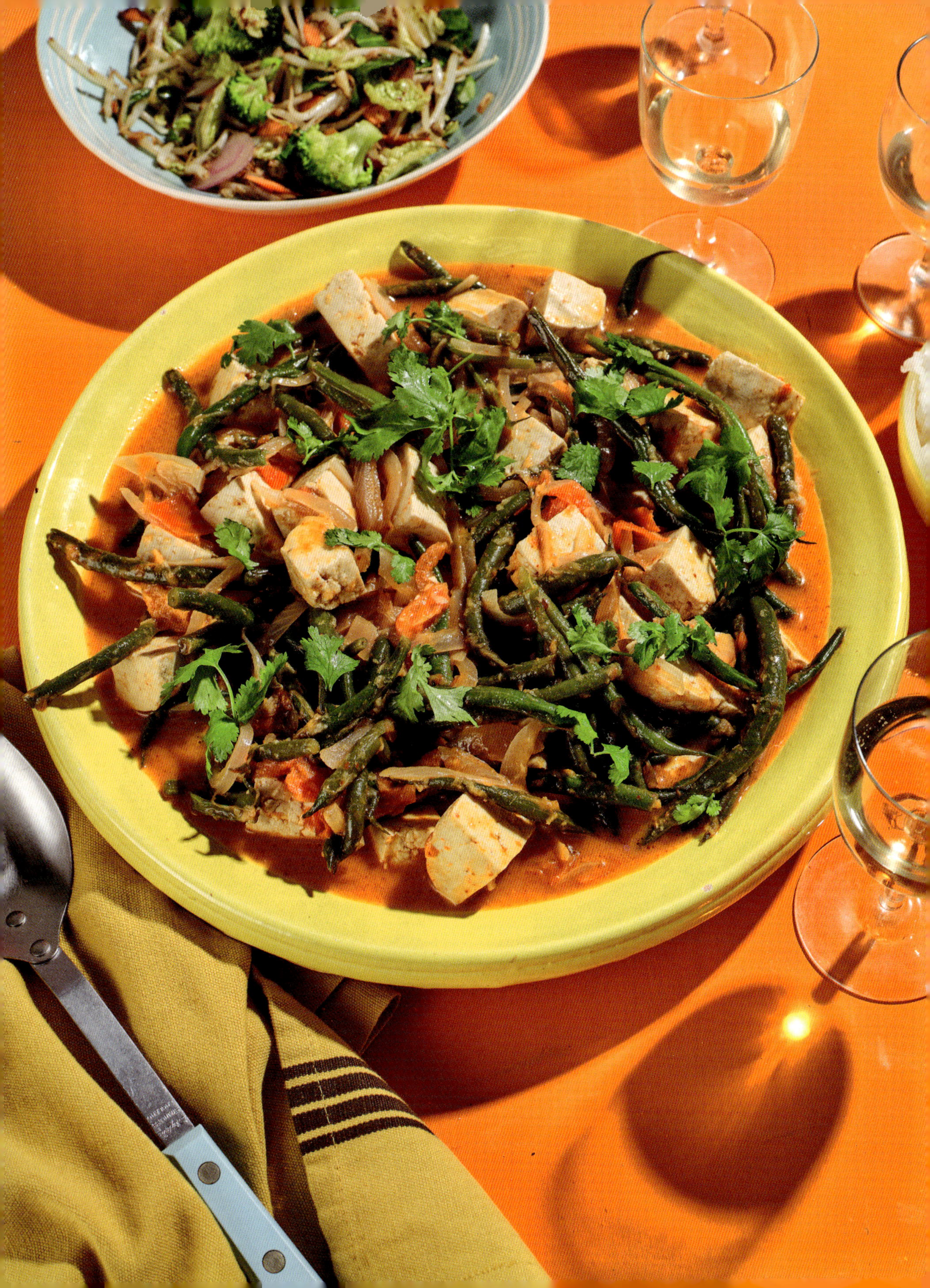

VEGETARIAN VEGAN

Veggie Lasagna

You won't miss the meat in this lasagna, I promise! I like to serve this with a crisp cold salad and will get empty plates every time.

250g (9oz) baby spinach, roughly chopped

2 courgettes (zucchini), chopped into chunks

400g (14oz) closed cup mushrooms, chopped into chunks

3 carrots, peeled and chopped into small dice

1 red (bell) pepper, deseeded and chopped into small pieces

250g (9oz) ricotta cheese

1 large egg

2 x 400g (14oz) cans chopped tomatoes

2 garlic cloves, finely chopped

8 dried whole-wheat lasagna sheets

100g (3½oz) mozzarella cheese, torn into pieces

Salt and black pepper

Side salad of lettuce, cucumber and tomatoes, to serve

1. Put the spinach, courgettes, mushrooms, carrots, red (bell) pepper, ricotta and egg in a bowl. Season and mix well, then tip into a grab bag.

2. In a second grab bag, combine both cans of tomatoes and the garlic. Remove as much air as you can from the bags before sealing. Label the bags with the contents and the date you prepared it, then clip them together. Write on the front that you need to add the lasagne sheets and relevant quantity of mozzarella at the time of cooking (or a note to refer to this page number). Place in the freezer, making sure they lie as flat as possible.

3. Defrost the bags thoroughly in the fridge for approximately 6–8 hours before cooking.

4. To cook, tip half of the first bag (with the spinach and courgettes) into the bottom of the slow cooker and spread out evenly. Lay four lasagna sheets over the top to cover, then top with half of the contents of the second bag (containing the tomato mixture). Repeat to use up all the ingredients. Cook on low for 4 hours or on high for 2 hours.

5. Once the cooking time is up, sprinkle the mozzarella over the top and leave to cook, uncovered, for a further 20 minutes. Serve the lasagna with a side salad.

---

3 MONTHS | **6–8 HOURS** | **LOW 4 hours / HIGH 2 hours** | **SERVES 4**

VEGETARIAN VEGAN

Potato & Cauliflower Hash

This is so filling that we normally have leftovers, which I'll freeze for my lunch one day or send into work with my eldest for him to have warm on a cold day.

- 1 large cauliflower, roughly chopped
- 6 medium potatoes, peeled and chopped
- 1 tsp chilli powder
- 200ml (7fl oz/scant 1 cup) whole (full-fat) milk
- 100ml (3½fl oz/scant ½ cup) boiling water
- 90g (3¼oz) mature Cheddar cheese, grated
- Crusty bread, green beans and sweetcorn, to serve

1. Put the cauliflower, potatoes and chilli powder in the grab bag. Closer the bag and shake well to combine the ingredients. Open the bag and pour in the milk.

2. Remove as much air as you can from the bag before sealing. Label the bag with the contents and the date you prepared it. Write on the front that you need to add the relevant quantities of boiling water and Cheddar cheese at the time of cooking (or a note to refer to this page number). Place the bag in the freezer, making sure it lies as flat as possible.

3. Defrost the bag thoroughly in the fridge for approximately 8–10 hours before cooking.

4. To cook, empty the contents of the bag into your slow cooker, add the boiling water and stir. (You can wash the bag and reuse, but don't forget to re-label.) Top with the grated cheese. Cook on low for 4 hours or on high for 2 hours.

5. Serve the hash with crusty bread, green beans and sweetcorn.

3 MONTHS | **8–10 HOURS** | **LOW 4 hours | HIGH 2 hours** | **SERVES 4**

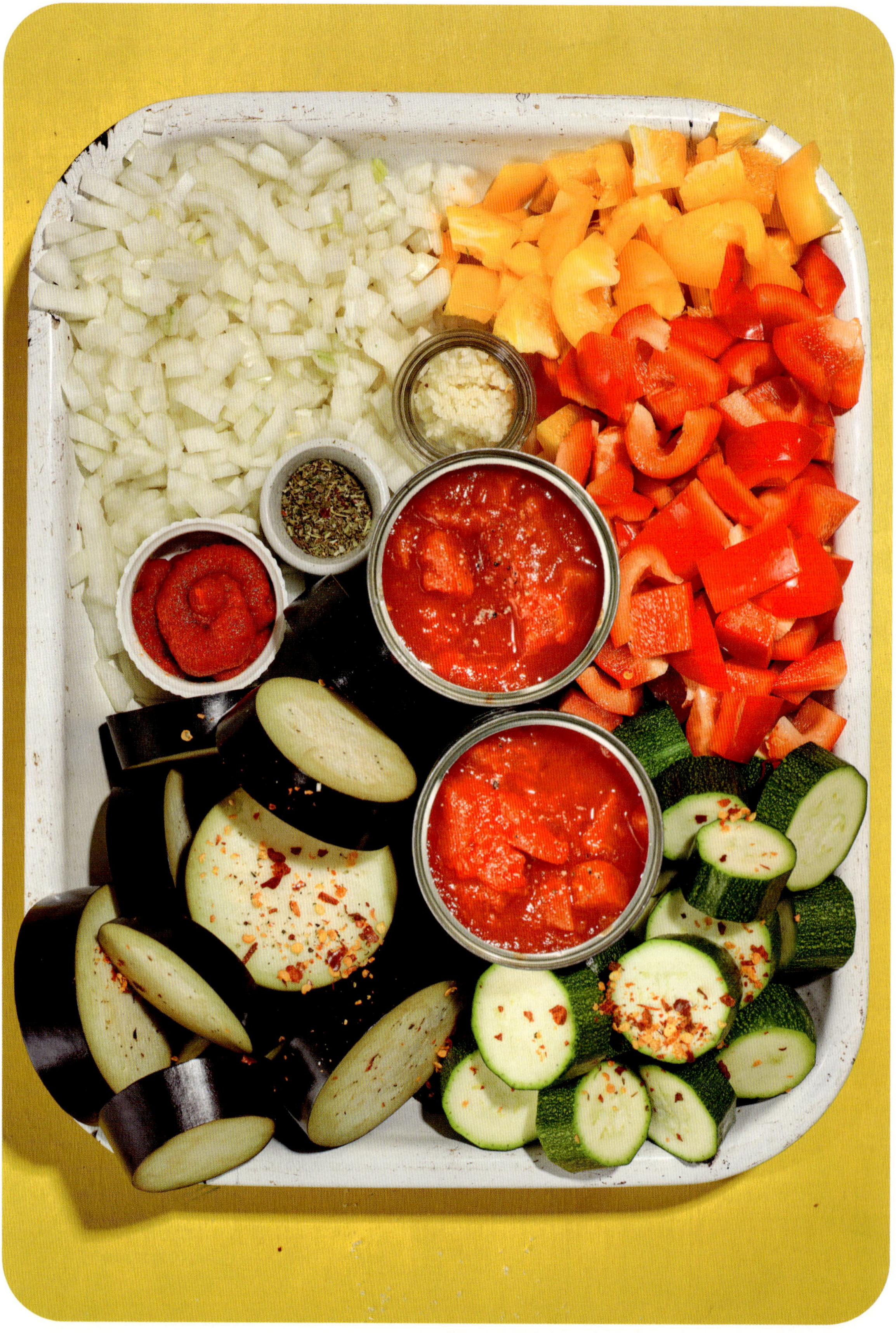

VEGETARIAN VEGAN

Deliciously Vegan Ratatouille

Unfortunately, this recipe doesn't come with a rat under your hat to prepare it for you! There's a bit of chopping but it's worth it in the end as this is jam packed with vitamins and flavour.

- 2 x 400g (14oz) cans chopped tomatoes
- 1 tsp Italian seasoning
- 1 tbsp tomato purée (paste)
- ¼ tsp chilli flakes
- 1½ tsp salt
- ¼ tsp pepper
- 2 courgettes (zucchini), cut into thick slices
- 2 red (bell) peppers, deseeded chopped into chunks
- 1 yellow (bell) pepper, deseeded and chopped into chunks
- 1 aubergine (eggplant), chopped into thick slices
- 1 onion, diced
- 2 garlic cloves, crushed
- Crusty bread, to serve

1. Open one of the cans of tomatoes and add the Italian seasoning, tomato purée, chilli flakes, salt and pepper and stir well.

2. Put the remaining ingredients in a grab bag, then pour in both cans of tomatoes. Close the bag and shake to combine.

3. Remove as much air as you can from the bag before sealing. Label the bag with the contents and the date you prepared it, then place it in the freezer, making sure it lies as flat as possible.

4. Defrost the bag thoroughly in the fridge for approximately 8–10 hours before cooking.

5. To cook, empty the contents of the bag into your slow cooker. (You can wash the bag and reuse, but don't forget to re-label.) Cook on low for 6 hours or on high for 3 hours.

6. Serve in bowls with crusty bread.

3 MONTHS | **8–10 HOURS** | **LOW 6 hours | HIGH 3 hours** | **SERVES 4**

VEGETARIAN VEGAN

Vegan Bolognese

This recipe is easy to make and has the goodness of lots of vegetables, meaning it's packed full of vitamins! Serve with spaghetti and some vegan cheese on top – delicious!

- ½ cauliflower, chopped into small chunks
- ½ aubergine (eggplant), diced
- 4 carrots, peeled and diced
- 8 mushrooms, diced
- 3 garlic cloves, minced
- 2 x 400g (14oz) cans chopped tomatoes
- 1 tbsp balsamic vinegar
- 1 tbsp dried oregano
- Salt and black pepper
- Spaghetti and grated vegan cheese, to serve

1. Put all the ingredients into a grab bag. Close the bag and shake well to combine.

2. Remove as much air as you can from the bag before sealing. Label the bag with the contents and the date you prepared it, then place it in the freezer, making sure it lies as flat as possible.

3. Defrost the bag thoroughly in the fridge for approximately 8–10 hours before cooking.

4. To cook, empty the contents of the bag into your slow cooker. (You can wash the bag and reuse, but don't forget to re-label.) Cook on low for 8 hours or on high for 4 hours.

5. Taste and season the bolognese, then serve with spaghetti and a sprinkle of grated cheese.

3 MONTHS | **8–10 HOURS** | **LOW** 8 hours / **HIGH** 4 hours | **SERVES 4**

VEGETARIAN VEGAN

Broccoli Casserole

I've said it before and I'll say it again, broccoli is the most underrated vegetable! It's not only good for you, it's also so tasty.

- 750g (1lb 10oz) broccoli, chopped into chunks
- 1 onion, peeled and chopped into chunks
- 3 carrots, peeled and chopped
- 2 leeks, diced
- 1 vegetable jelly stock pot
- 2 bay leaves
- 250ml (9fl oz/1 cup) boiling water
- 100g (3½oz/scant ½ cup) oat-based crème fraîche
- Salt and black pepper
- Crusty bread and vegan butter, to serve

1. Put all the vegetables in the grab bag, then add the stock pot and bay leaves and season with salt and pepper. Close the bag and shake well to combine all the ingredients.

2. Remove as much air as you can from the bag before sealing. Label the bag with the contents and the date you prepared it. Write a note on the front to add the relevant quantities of boiling water and crème fraîche at the time of cooking (or a note to refer to this page number). Place the bag in the freezer, making sure it lies as flat as possible.

3. Defrost the bag thoroughly in the fridge for approximately 8–10 hours before cooking.

4. To cook, empty the contents of the bag into your slow cooker, add the boiling water and stir. (You can wash the bag and reuse, but don't forget to re-label.) Cook on low for 8 hours or on high for 4 hours.

5. When the cooking is completed, add the crème fraîche and stir well. Serve with crusty bread and vegan butter.

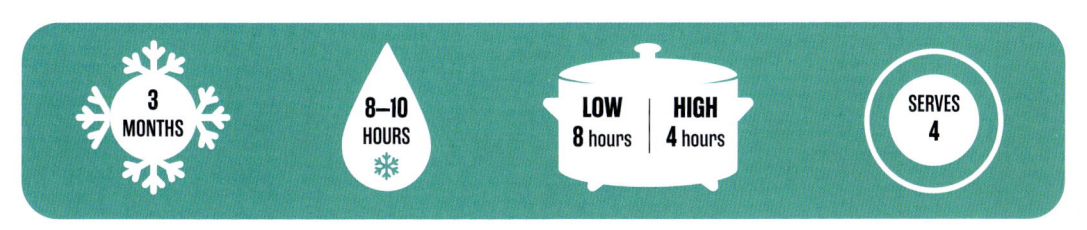

---

3 MONTHS | 8–10 HOURS | LOW 8 hours | HIGH 4 hours | SERVES 4

VEGETARIAN VEGAN

Spinach & Pumpkin Chilli

Chilli is just one of the most comforting foods. I'll cook this when everyone is on different schedules and they can just help themselves when they get home. It's great with a salad and jacket potatoes or chunks of bread to dunk.

- 2 x 400g (14oz) cans chopped tomatoes
- ½ tsp chilli powder
- ½ tsp salt
- 375g (13oz) broccoli, chopped
- 1 courgette (zucchini), diced
- 1 small onion, peeled and diced
- 200g (7oz) canned pumpkin purée
- 1 vegetable jelly stock pot
- 300ml (10½fl oz/1¼ cups) boiling water
- 1 x 400g (14oz) can haricot beans, drained and rinsed
- 220g (7¾oz) baby spinach, washed
- Jacket potatoes or crusty bread and salad, to serve

1. Open one can of tomatoes, add the chilli powder and salt and stir to combine. Add the broccoli, courgette and onion to the grab bag, then pour in the two cans of tomatoes. Add the pumpkin purée and stock pot.

2. Remove as much air as you can from the bag before sealing. Label the bag with the contents and the date you prepared it. Write on the front that you need to add the relevant quantities of boiling water, haricot beans and spinach at the time of cooking. Place the bag in the freezer, making sure it lies as flat as possible.

3. Defrost the bag thoroughly in the fridge for approximately 8–10 hours before cooking.

4. To cook, empty the contents of the bag into your slow cooker, add the boiling water and stir well. Cook on low for 7½ hours or on high for 3½ hours.

5. Thirty minutes before the cooking time is up, add the haricot beans and baby spinach. Stir well and continue cooking for the remaining 30 minutes.

6. Serve with jacket potatoes or bread and salad.

3 MONTHS | **8–10 HOURS** | **LOW** 7½ hours | **HIGH** 3½ hours | **SERVES 4**

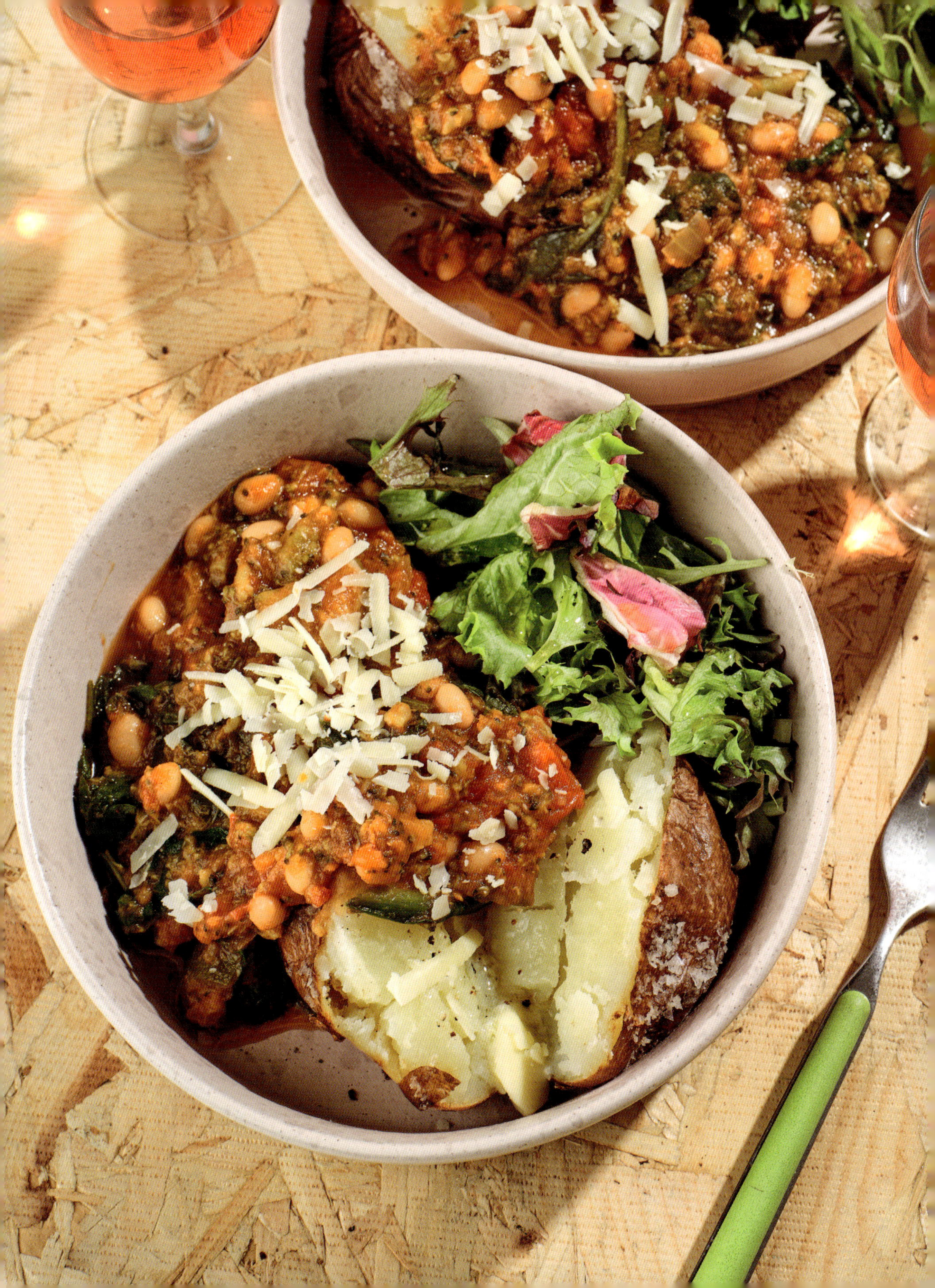

VEGETARIAN VEGAN

Vegetable Fajitas

The mushrooms here act as a great meat alternative as they have quite a meaty taste, especially if you leave the stalks on. I serve fajitas with tortilla wraps, salsa, guacamole and sour cream. You can omit the sour cream if you're vegan.

- 2 red (bell) peppers, deseeded and cut into strips
- 1 yellow (bell) pepper, deseeded cut into strips
- 1 onion, peeled and sliced
- 480g (1lb 1oz) chestnut (cremini) mushrooms, stalks on, sliced
- 300g (10½oz) cherry tomatoes, halved
- 1 tsp paprika
- 1 x 30g (1oz) packet fajita spice mix

TO SERVE:
Tortilla wraps
Guacamole
Salsa
Sour cream (optional)

1. Add all the ingredients to the grab bag, close the bag and shake well to combine.

2. Remove as much air as you can from the bag before sealing. Label the bag with the contents and the date you prepared it, then place it in the freezer, making sure it lies as flat as possible.

3. Defrost the bag thoroughly in the fridge for approximately 8–10 hours before cooking.

4. To cook, empty the contents of the bag into your slow cooker. (You can wash the bag and reuse, but don't forget to re-label.) Cook on high for 3 hours or low for 6 hours.

5. Serve the fajitas with tortilla wraps, guacamole and salsa, and sour cream if wished.

3 MONTHS | **8–10 HOURS** | **LOW 6 hours / HIGH 3 hours** | **SERVES 4**

VEGETARIAN VEGAN

Vegetarian Meatballs

If you're looking for the occasional meat-free day but don't want to lose the sensation of eating meat, then vegetarian 'meatballs' are a great alternative. They still look like meat, and when cooked in the sauce they will take on a lot of that flavour that you're used to. Scrummy!

2 x 400g (14oz) cans chopped tomatoes
2 garlic cloves, crushed
2 tsp dried mixed herbs
2 tbsp tomato purée (paste)
1 celery stalk, diced
1 medium carrot, peeled and diced
1 onion, diced
300g (10½oz) vegetarian Swedish-style meatballs
Salt and black pepper
Spaghetti, to serve

1. Open the cans of tomatoes and into one of them, add the garlic, mixed herbs and tomato purée and season with salt and pepper. Stir well to combine. Add the celery, carrot and onion to the grab bag. Pour in both cans of tomatoes and mix to combine.

2. The meatballs come already frozen and will be cooked from frozen, so they can be left in the packaging in the freezer.

3. Remove as much air as you can from the bag before sealing. Label the bag with the contents and the date you prepared it. Write on the front that you need to add the frozen meatballs at the time of cooking (or a note to refer to this page number). Place the bag in the freezer, making sure it lies as flat as possible.

4. Defrost the bag thoroughly in the fridge for approximately 8–10 hours before cooking.

5. To cook, empty the contents of the bag into your slow cooker and add the frozen meatballs. Stir well. (You can wash the bag and reuse, but don't forget to re-label.) Cook on low for 8 hours or on high for 4 hours.

6. Serve the meatballs and sauce with spaghetti.

| 3 MONTHS | 8–10 HOURS | LOW 8 hours / HIGH 4 hours | SERVES 4 |

VEGETARIAN VEGAN

Butternut Squash & Courgette Casserole

I love butternut squash, it's so hearty and sweet. You could roast it before adding to the casserole for an extra pop of flavour.

- 400g (14oz) butternut squash, peeled and chopped into chunks
- 4 courgettes (zucchini), sliced
- 1 tsp garlic powder
- 1 tsp dried mixed herbs
- 1 vegetable jelly stock pot
- ½ tsp sea salt
- ¼ tsp pepper
- 100ml (3½fl oz/ scant ½ cup) boiling water
- 2 tbsp cornflour (cornstarch)
- 25g (1oz) butter
- 150g (5½oz) vegan Parmesan cheese
- Crusty bread and/or mashed potatoes, to serve

1. Add the butternut squash and courgettes to the grab bag and mix. Next add the garlic powder, mixed herbs, stock pot, salt and pepper. Remove as much air as you can from the bag before sealing. Label the bag with the contents and the date you prepared it. Write on the front that you need to add the relevant quantities of boiling water, cornflour, butter and cheese at time of cooking (or a note to refer to this page number). Place the bag in the freezer, making sure it lies as flat as possible.

2. Defrost the bag thoroughly in the fridge for approximately 8–10 hours before cooking.

3. To cook, empty the contents of the bag into your slow cooker, add the boiling water and stir. (You can wash the bag and reuse, but don't forget to re-label.) Cook on low for 6 hours or high for 3 hours.

4. Once the cooking time has finished, mix the cornflour with 4 tablespoons of cold water in a jug. Add to the casserole and stir. Add the butter to the top of the pot and sprinkle with the cheese. Leave to cook for a final 30 minutes on high.

5. Serve with crusty bread and/or mashed potatoes.

3 MONTHS | **8–10 HOURS** | **LOW 6 hours | HIGH 3 hours** | **SERVES 4**

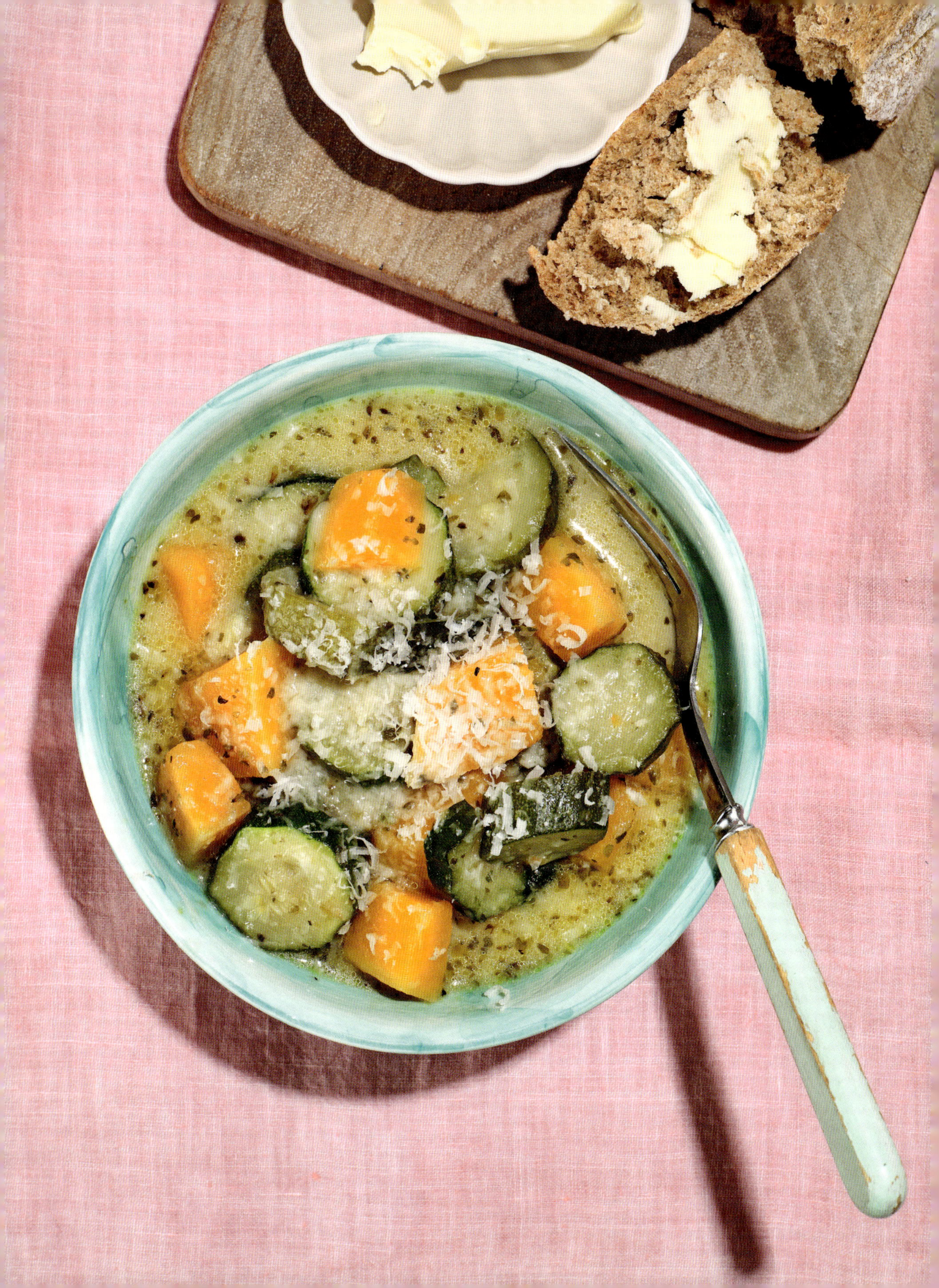

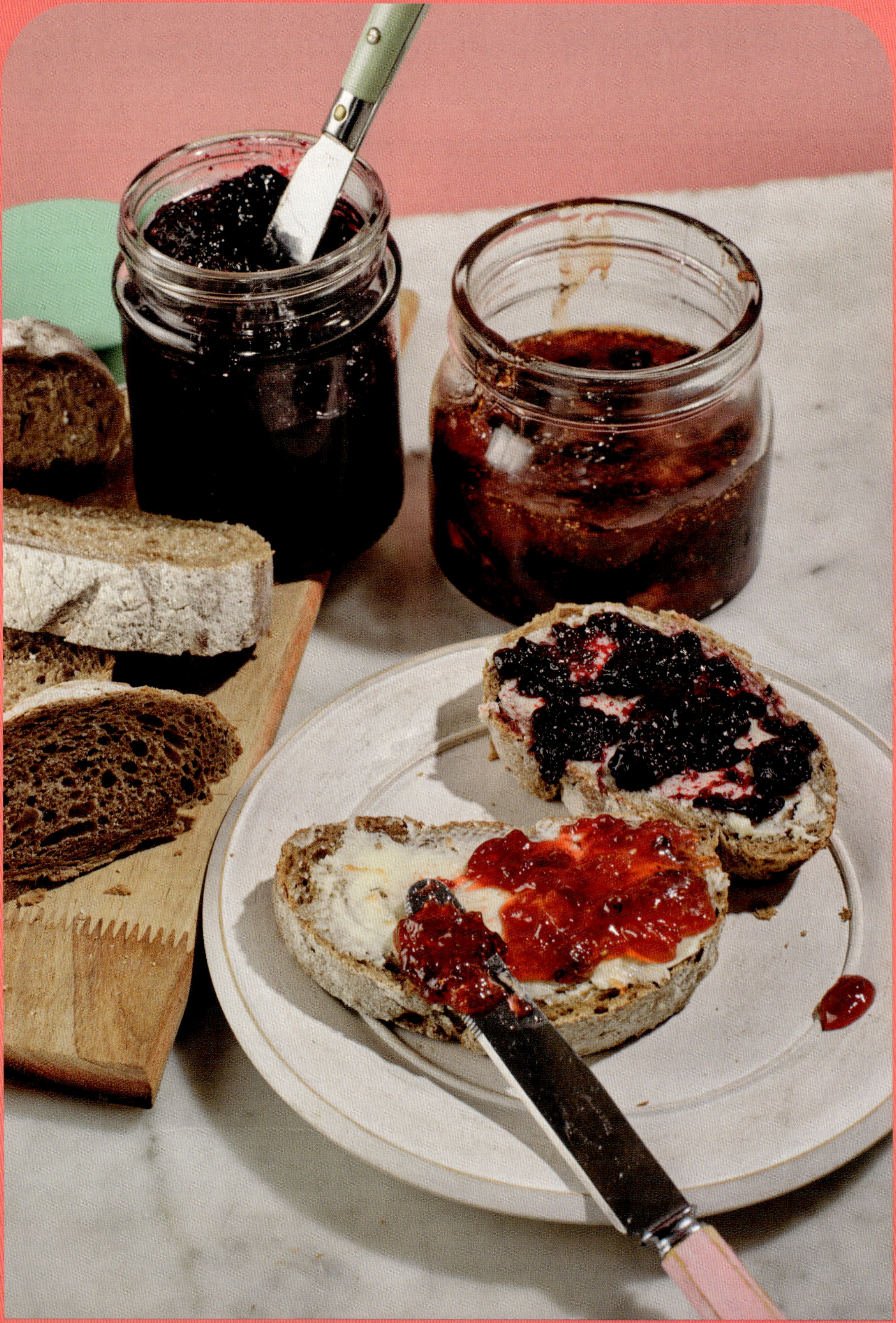

SOMETHING

6

SWEET

SOMETHING SWEET

Blueberry Jam

My youngest is a blueberry menace; he loves them so much. But sometimes I end up buying more than even he can manage to eat, so when that happens they get frozen to use for jam, muffins and smoothies.

500g (1lb 2oz) blueberries
Juice of 1 lemon
125g caster (granulated) sugar
A pinch of salt

1. Put the blueberries in a grab bag and pour in the lemon juice. Mix well, then add the sugar and salt. Seal the bag and shake to coat the blueberries in the sugar and salt.

2. Remove as much air as you can from the bag before sealing. Label the bag with the contents and the date you prepared it, then place it in the freezer, making sure it lies as flat as possible.

3. Defrost the bag thoroughly in the fridge for approximately 8–10 hours before cooking.

4. To cook, empty the contents of the bag into your slow cooker. (You can wash the bag and reuse, but don't forget to re-label.) Cook on low for 4 hours, making sure to stir every hour.

5. To thicken your jam, remove the lid after the above cooking time and leave to cook on low for another 1–2 hours. If you like the fruit in big pieces, then simply jar up once it's cooled a little. If you prefer a smoother consistency, use a hand blender to blitz it until smooth.

6. Transfer to a sterilized jar and seal, then store in a cool place for up to 12 months.

3 MONTHS | **8–10 HOURS** | **LOW 4 + 1–2 hours** | **MAKES 1 x 450ML JAR**

SOMETHING SWEET

Strawberry Jam

After cooking, this can be stored for up to a year in the cupboard, so a jar of it would make an ideal homemade gift at Christmas or for a birthday. Freeze your strawberries when they are on offer in the supermarket, then cook when you've got some spare time.

- 300g (10½oz) strawberries, chopped
- 250g (9oz/1¼ cups) jam sugar
- Grated zest of ½ lemon
- 30g (2oz/heaped ¼ cup) raisins
- 100ml (3½fl oz/scant ½ cup) boiling water

1. Put all the ingredients except the boiling water into the grab bag. Close the bag and shake to cover the strawberries with the sugar.

2. Remove as much air as you can from the bag before sealing. Label the bag with the contents and the date you prepared it. Write on the front that you need to add the relevant quantity of boiling water at the time of cooking (or a note to refer to this page number). Place the bag in the freezer, making sure it lies as flat as possible.

3. This can be cooked from frozen, so just open the bag and empty the contents into the slow cooker, then add the boiling water and stir. Cook on high for 30 minutes, then stir well. Leave to cook on high for a further 3½ hours.

4. Divide the jam among two small sterilized jars and seal. Store in a cool place for up to a year.

6 MONTHS | **0 HOURS** | **HIGH ½ hour + LOW 3½ hours** | **MAKES 2 x 100ML JARS**

SOMETHING SWEET

Walnut Apples

This can be cooked within two hours from frozen, so if you find yourself short on time but want a delicious treat, this is the one for you!

200g (7oz) Granny Smith apples, cored and thicky sliced
2 tsp vanilla extract
1 tbsp sugar
1 tsp ground nutmeg
1 tsp ground cinnamon
125ml (4fl oz/½ cup) double (heavy) cream
80g (2¾oz) walnuts, chopped
Ice cream, to serve

1. Put the apples in a grab bag and add the vanilla.

2. In a small bowl, combine the sugar, nutmeg and cinnamon. Stir together, then add to the grab bag. Close the bag and shake to cover the apples in the spices.

3. Remove as much air as you can from the bag before sealing. Label the bag with the contents and the date you prepared it. Write on the front that you need to add the relevant quantities of cream and walnuts at time of cooking (or a note to refer to this page number). Place the bag in the freezer, making sure it lies as flat as possible.

4. This can be cooked from frozen. Empty the contents of the bag into your slow cooker. (You can wash the bag and reuse, but don't forget to re-label.) Cook for 1 hour on high, then add the cream and stir. Continue cooking for a further 1 hour.

5. Sprinkle over the chopped walnuts and serve with ice cream.

6 MONTHS | **0 HOURS** | **HIGH 1 + 1 hour** | **SERVES 4**

SOMETHING SWEET

Apple Crumble

Freezing fruit is such a great way of preserving it. When you either have too many apples or they are about to go bad, use them up in this delicious crumble.

700g (1lb 9oz) Bramley apples, peeled and chopped into chunks
Juice of 1 lemon
3 tbsp golden caster (granulated) sugar
2 tsp ground cinnamon
1 recipe quantity of crumble topping (see page 188)
Custard, to serve

1. Put the apples in a grab bag and pour in the lemon juice. Shake the bag so that the lemon juice coats the apple pieces. This will not only give the crumble a delicious kick in flavour but also helps prevent the apples turning brown when freezing. Next add the sugar and cinnamon to your bag. Seal and shake well to combine and coat the apples.

2. Remove as much air as you can from the bag before sealing. Label the bag with the contents and the date you prepared it. Write the crumble ingredients on the front (or a note to refer to the crumble recipe), so that you know you need to prepare this to serve with the apples. Place the bag in the freezer, making sure it lies as flat as possible.

3. Defrost the bag thoroughly in the fridge for approximately 8–10 hours before cooking.

4. To cook, empty the contents of the bag into your slow cooker. (You can wash the bag and reuse, but don't forget to re-label.) Cook on low for 5 hours or on high for 3 hours.

5. Towards the end of the cooking time, make the crumble following steps 4 and 5 on page 188.

6. Once the apples are cooked, sprinkle the crumble and serve with hot custard over.

| 6 MONTHS | 8–10 HOURS | LOW 5 hours / HIGH 3 hours | SERVES 4 |

SOMETHING SWEET

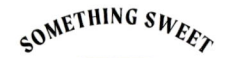

Maple Pear Crumble

Pears have such a subtle taste, but when teamed with maple syrup and spices they really soak up those flavours and come into their own.

4 pears, cut in half and cored
100ml (3½fl oz/scant ½ cup) maple syrup
1 tsp vanilla extract
1 tsp ground cinnamon
½ tsp ground ginger
¼ tsp ground nutmeg
200ml (7fl oz/scant 1 cup) boiling water
Custard, to serve (optional)

FOR THE CRUMBLE:
1 tsp ground cinnamon
50g (1¾oz/3½ tbsp) unsalted butter
100g (3½oz/¾ cup) plain (all-purpose) flour
50g (1¾oz/¼ cup) demerara sugar

1. Place the pears into the grab bag. Add the maple syrup, vanilla extract, cinnamon, ginger and nutmeg to a bowl. Mix until combined, then pour into the bag. Close the bag and rub the maple syrup mixture all over the pears. Remove as much air as you can before sealing. Label the bag with the contents and the date you prepared it. Write the crumble ingredients on the front so that you know you need to prepare this to serve with the pears. Place the bag in the freezer, making sure it lies as flat as possible.

2. Defrost the bag thoroughly in the fridge for approximately 8–10 hours before cooking.

3. To cook, empty the contents of the bag into your slow cooker and add the boiling water to the base of pot. Cook on low for 6 hours or high for 3.

4. Towards the end of the cooking time, make the crumble. Preheat the oven to 180°C/160°C fan/350°F/Gas 4.

5. Rub the cold butter into the flour and cinnamon to create a chunky breadcrumb consistency, then add the sugar and rub in. Spread over a baking tray and bake for about 20 minutes, or until light golden. To serve, place two pear halves into each bowl, spoon over some of the liquid from the slow cooker, then top with crumble. Add custard too if you like!

6 MONTHS | 8–10 HOURS | LOW 6 hours | HIGH 3 hours | SERVES 4

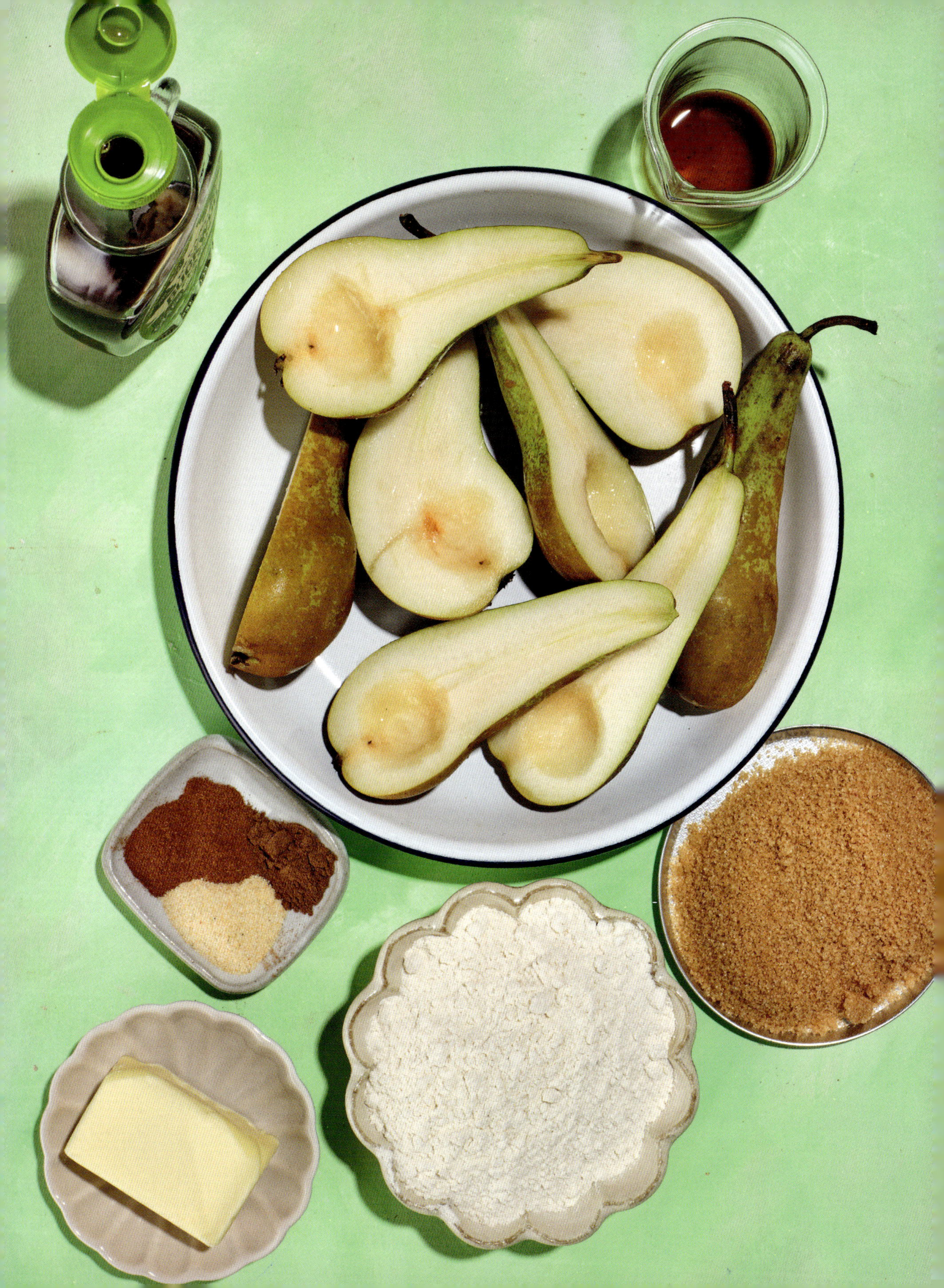

SOMETHING SWEET

Caramel Apple Crispy

This one can be cooked from frozen, so if you need to get something made for pudding on the same day, this is the one for you!

- 8 Granny Smith apples, peeled, cored and thickly sliced
- ½ tsp ground cinnamon
- 1 tbsp cornflour (cornstarch)
- 120g (4¼oz/1 cup less 1½ tbsp) plain (all-purpose) flour
- 50g (1¾oz/½ cup) porridge oats
- 60g (2oz/¼ cup) unsalted butter, chilled
- A pinch of salt
- 150g (5½oz) caramel (I use a shop-bought jar)
- Custard or ice cream, to serve

1. Put the apples in a grab bag, then add the cinnamon and cornflour. Close the bag and shake to coat the apples.

2. Put the flour, oats, butter and salt in a bowl and rub together until the mixture comes together in small clumps. Transfer this mixture to a second grab bag.

3. Remove as much air as you can from the bags before sealing. Label the bags with the contents and the date you prepared them. Write on the front of the apple bag that you need to add the relevant quantity of caramel at the time of cooking (or a note to refer to this page number). Clip the two bags together. Place the bags in the freezer, making sure they lie as flat as possible – this is particularly necessary for the crumble mix.

4. This can be cooked from frozen, so when you're ready to cook, empty the apples into the slow cooker and pour over the caramel sauce, then sprinkle over the topping mix. You may have to break this apart if it's frozen in large pieces. (You can wash the bags and reuse, but don't forget to re-label.) Cook on high for 3 hours or on low for 6 hours. If after cooking the crumble is still soft from excess steam, remove the lid and cook for a further 30 minutes.

5. Serve with custard or ice cream.

---

6 MONTHS | **0 HOUR** | **LOW** 6 hours | **HIGH** 3 hours | **SERVES 4**

SOMETHING SWEET

Cinnamon Baked Apples

At the first sign of autumn, get these made. Buy in some ice cream, or some custard, and you have yourself the ultimate cosy treat.

- 50g (1¾oz/ ¼ cup) dark brown sugar
- 1 tsp lemon juice
- 2 tbsp sultanas (golden raisins)
- 4 medium Golden Delicious or Granny Smith apples, washed and cored
- 20g (¾oz/1½ tbsp) unsalted butter
- 1 tsp ground cinnamon
- 300ml (10½fl oz/1¼ cups) apple juice
- Ice cream or custard, to serve

1. In a bowl, mix together the sugar, lemon juice and sultanas. Stuff the mixture into the centre of the cored apples until they are packed full, then put them in the grab bag. Remove as much air as you can from the bag before sealing. Label the bag with the contents and the date you prepared it. Write on the front that you need to add the relevant quantities of butter, cinnamon and apple juice at the time of cooking. Place the bag in the freezer, making sure it lies as flat as possible.

2. Defrost the bag thoroughly in the fridge for approximately 8–10 hours before cooking.

3. To cook, place the apples into the slow cooker, with the bottom of the apples on the bottom of the dish.

4. Melt the butter in the microwave and add the cinnamon. Mix well, then pour over the apples. Pour the apple juice into the dish. Cook on high for 2 hours or on low for 4 hours until the apples are soft and just starting to collapse. Dish up one apple per person into a bowl and pour over the liquid from the bottom of the slow cooker. Serve along with ice cream or custard.

6 MONTHS | **8–10 HOURS** | **LOW 4 hours / HIGH 2 hours** | **SERVES 4**

SOMETHING SWEET

Mixed Berry Cobbler

I love berries and so does my youngest, Seb, so this is one we are always tempted to serve before its finished cooking because we can't wait!

250g (9oz) raspberries, washed and patted dry
250g (9oz) blueberries, washed and patted dry
2 tbsp granulated sugar
½ tsp ground cinnamon
Non-stick cooking spray
Custard, to serve

FOR THE BATTER:
160g (5¾oz/1¼ cups) plain (all-purpose) flour
1 tsp baking powder
200g (7oz/1 cup) sugar
¼ tsp salt
1 egg, lightly beaten
2 tbsp vegetable oil
60ml (2fl oz/¼ cup) full-fat milk

1. Add the berries to the grab bag and sprinkle over the sugar and cinnamon. Close the bag and shake well to coat the fruit with the sugar. Remove as much air as you can before sealing. Label with the contents and the date you prepared it. Write on the front that you need to add the batter ingredients at the time of cooking. Place the bag in the freezer, making sure it lies as flat as possible.

2. Defrost the bag thoroughly in the fridge for approximately 3–4 hours before cooking.

3. When you are ready to cook, put the flour, baking powder, sugar and salt in a bowl and mix to combine. In a separate bowl, whisk together the egg, oil and milk.

4. Now add the wet ingredients to the dry and stir until you get a nice smooth batter.

5. Add 1 tablespoon of flour mixture to the defrosted fruit in the bag and stir. Now add the fruit to the batter in the bowl and stir to incorporate the fruit.

6. Spray the slow cooker bowl with a non-stick cooking spray. Pour in the batter and spread it evenly across the base. Cook on low for 3 hours, or until a knife inserted into the cobbler comes out clean. Serve with custard.

6 MONTHS | **3–4 HOURS** | **LOW 3 hours** | **SERVES 4**

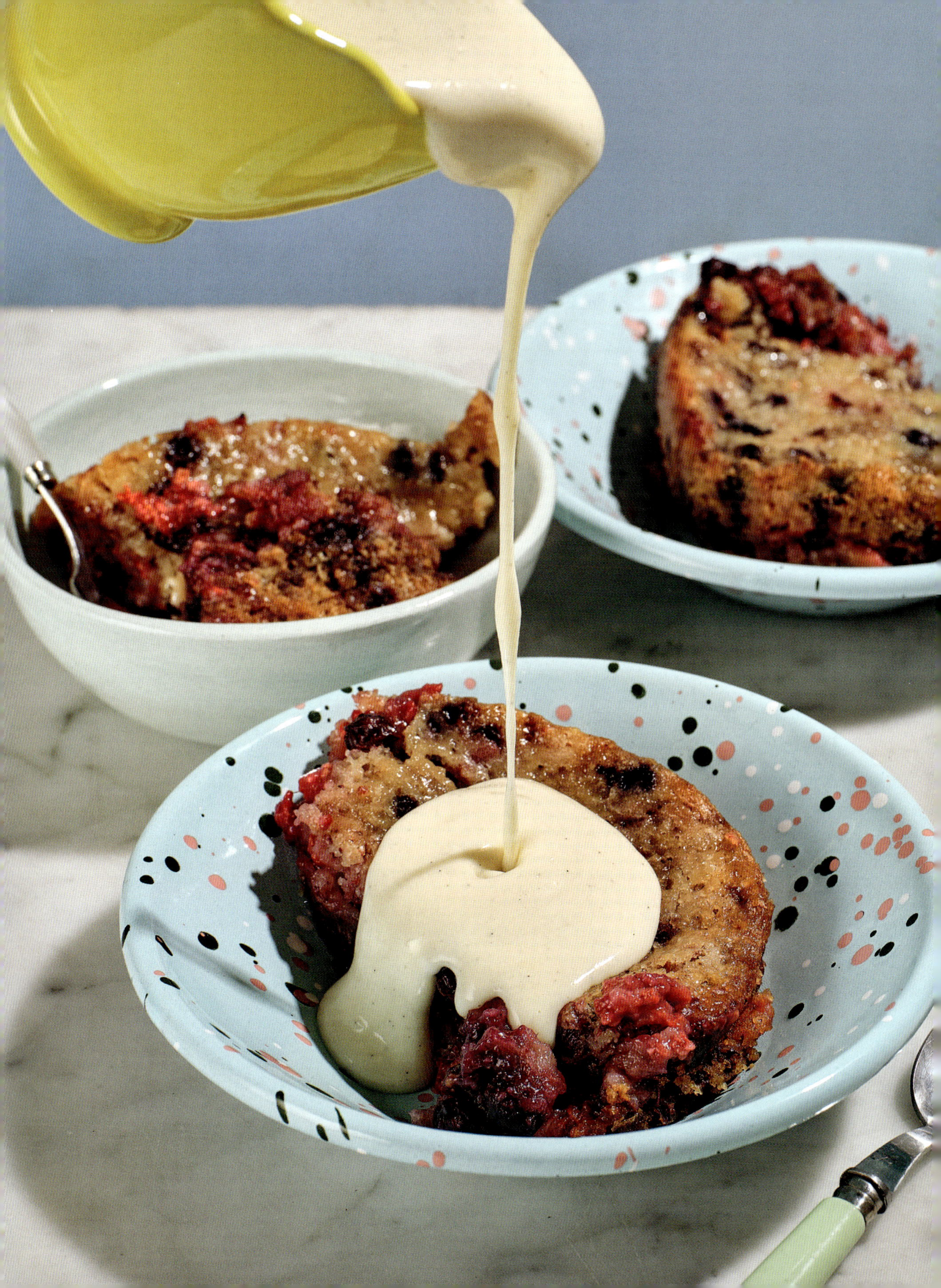

SOMETHING SWEET

Bread & Butter Pudding

A delicious treat to have after dinner, the cinnamon and nutmeg will fill your house with the most incredible smell. Try making this around Christmas time, head out for a nice garden centre trip and then come home to the smell of Christmas from your kitchen!

- 10 slices brioche loaf (about 400g/14oz), cut into 2.5cm (1 inch) square pieces
- 200g (7oz/1 cup) granulated sugar
- 250g (9oz/1 heaped cup) unsalted butter, cut into small cubes, plus optional extra for greasing
- 2 tsp ground cinnamon
- 1 tsp vanilla extract
- 100g (3½oz/¾ cup) raisins
- ½ tsp ground nutmeg
- A pinch of salt
- Non-stick cooking spray, for greasing (optional)
- 4 eggs
- 500ml (17fl oz/2 cups) whole milk
- Custard, cream or fresh fruit, to serve

1. Put the brioche, sugar, butter, cinnamon, vanilla, raisins, nutmeg and salt into a grab bag. Mix together well.

2. Remove as much air as you can from the bag before sealing. Label the bag with the contents and the date you prepared it. Write on the front that you need to add the relevant quantities of eggs and milk at the time of cooking (or a note to refer to this page number). Place the bag in the freezer, making sure it lies as flat as possible.

3. Defrost the bag thoroughly in the fridge for approximately 8–10 hours before cooking.

4. To cook, spray the bottom of the slow cooker bowl with the non-stick cooking spray, or grease with a thin coating of butter. Empty the contents of the bag into your slow cooker. (You can wash the bag and reuse, but don't forget to re-label.)

5. In a bowl beat the eggs with the milk, then add to the slow cooker. Stir everything together well. Set the temperature to low and cook for 3 hours, giving it a stir after the first 30 minutes.

6. Serve the pudding with custard, cream or fresh fruit.

3 MONTHS | **8–10 HOURS** | **LOW 3 hours** | **SERVES 6**

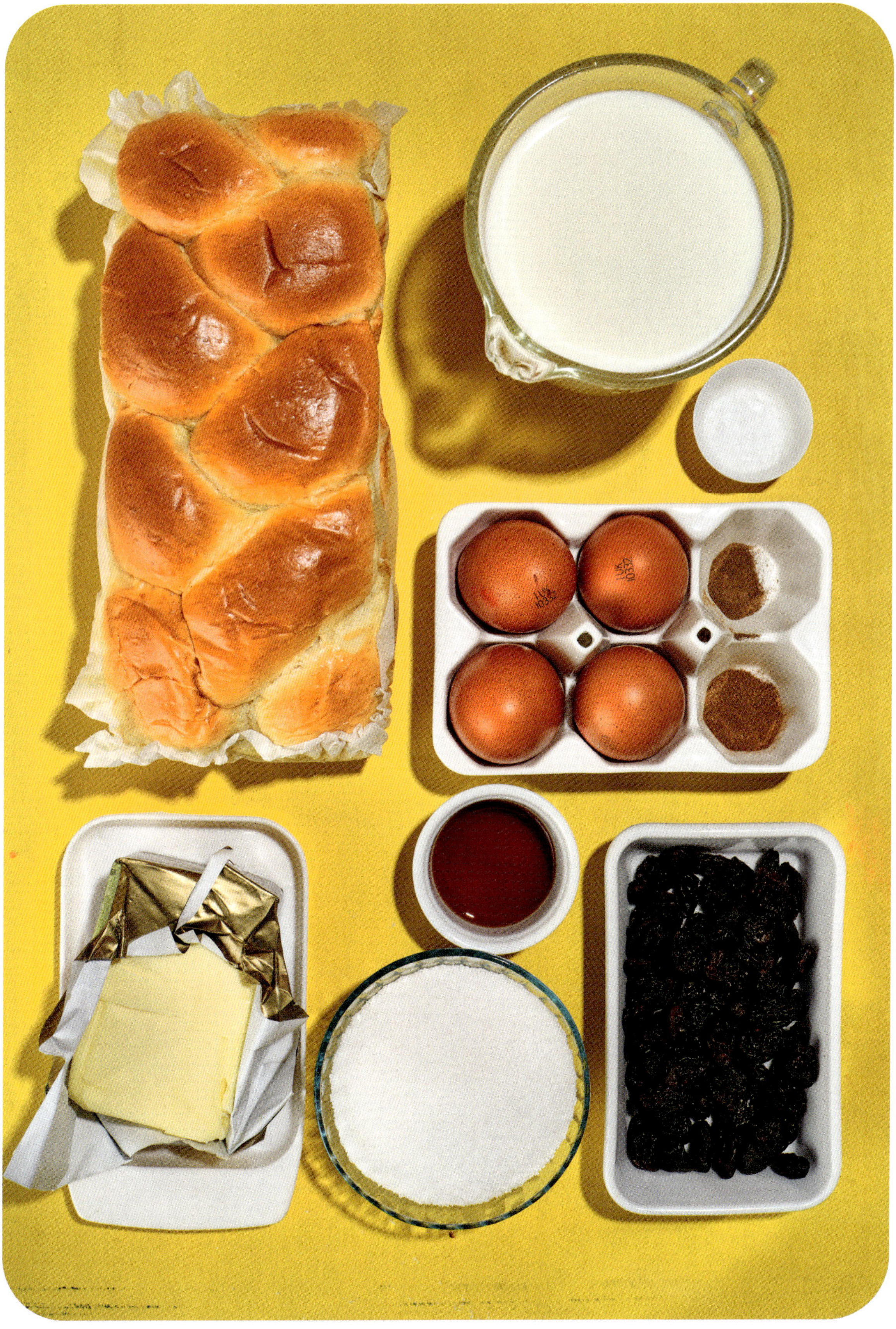

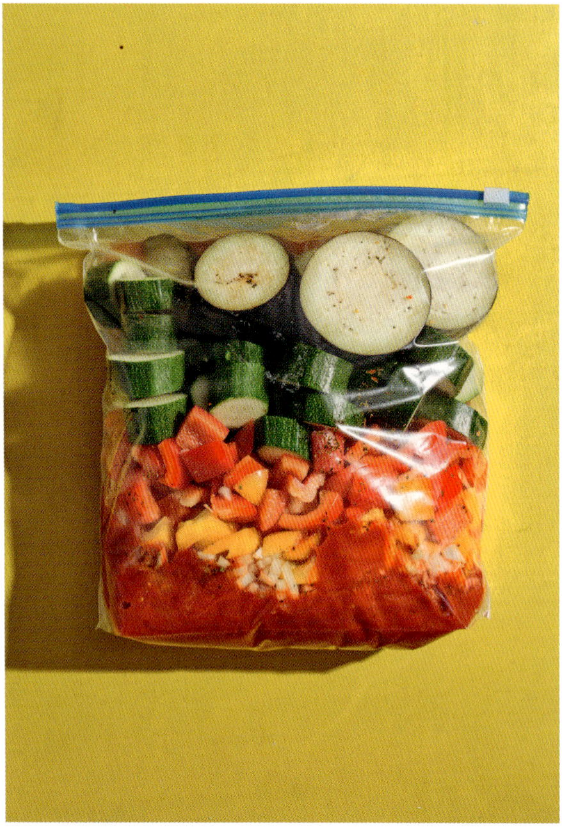
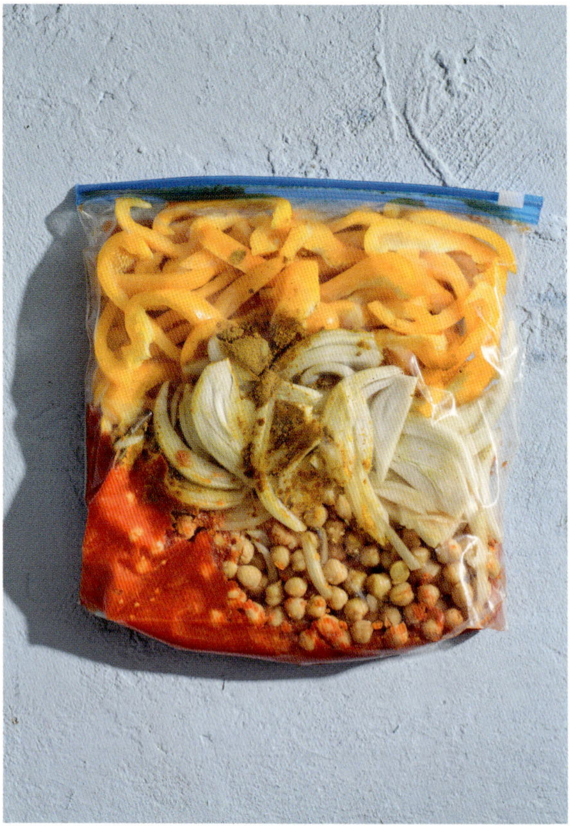
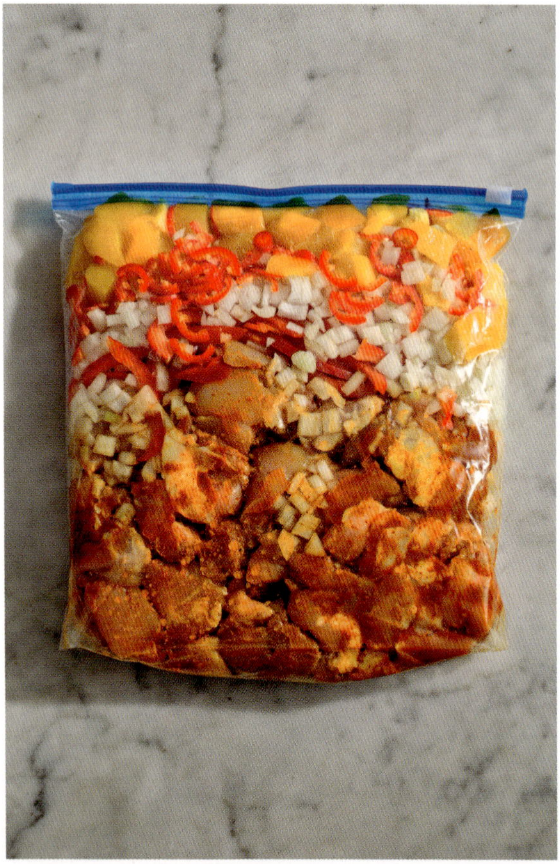
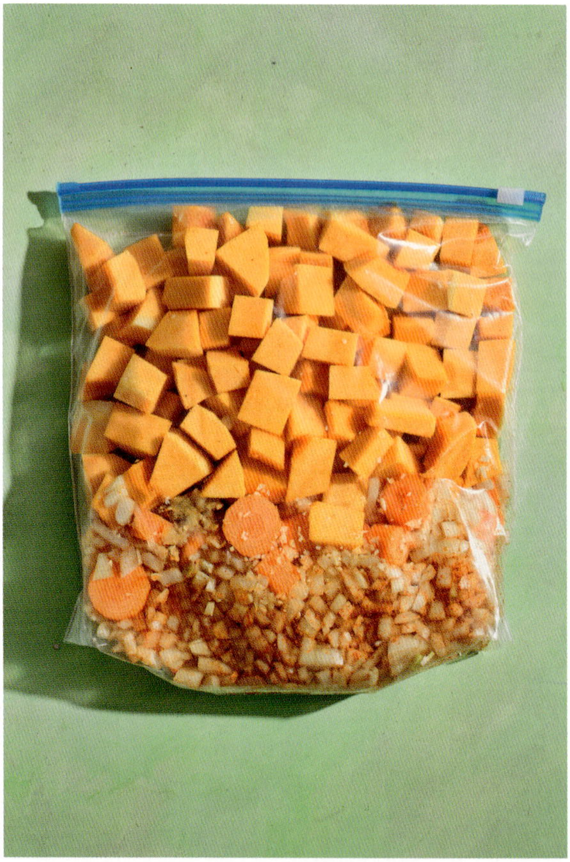

Index

A
apples: apple & honey drumsticks 59
  apple crumble 187
  caramel apple crispy 190
  cinnamon baked apples 191
  walnut apples 186
aubergines (eggplant): ratatouille 173
  vegan Bolognese 174

B
bacon: cheeseburger soup 131
  chicken & bacon pot 61
  chicken, bacon & potato stew 88
Balti, chicken 122
BBQ chicken 75
beans: campfire stew 93
  chicken burritos 36
  corn chicken chilli 68
  Italian vegetable soup 141
  Mexican beef taco shells 56
  Roy's mince & beans 30
  sausage stew 46
  shepherd's pie 42
  spinach & pumpkin chilli 176
  taco soup 134
  vegetarian chilli 166
beef: beef & coconut curry 126
  beef & red pepper curry 105
  beef & vegetable soup 150
  beef casserole with dumplings 32
  beef goulash 48
  beef ragu 80
  cheeseburger soup 131
  lasagna soup 149
  Lily's cottage pie 92
  Mexican beef taco shells 56
  Mongolian-style beef 66
  Roy's mince & beans 30
  sloppy Joes 55
  spaghetti Bolognese 50
  Spanish beef 62–3
  spicy beef 69
  spicy shredded beef 58
  taco soup 134
berry cobbler, mixed 192
blueberry jam 184
Bolognese sauce 50
  vegan Bolognese 174
bread: BBQ chicken 75
  pulled pork 70
  sloppy Joes 55
brioche: bread & butter pudding 194
broccoli: broccoli casserole 175
  cheese & broccoli soup 138
buffalo chicken pasta 72
burritos, chicken 36
butter chicken 100

C
campfire stew 93
caramel apple crispy 190
cashews: Kung Pao chicken 114
casseroles and stews: beef casserole with dumplings 32
  broccoli casserole 175
  butternut squash & courgette casserole 180
  campfire stew 93
  chicken, bacon & potato stew 88
  chicken casserole 31
  sausage stew 46
  see also hotpots; tagine
cauliflower: cauliflower soup 151
  potato & cauliflower hash 171
  tofu tikka masala 161
  vegan Bolognese 174
cheese: buffalo chicken pasta 72

INDEX

cauliflower soup 151
cheese & broccoli soup 138
cheeseburger soup 131
chicken enchiladas 41
lasagna soup 149
sloppy Joes 55
see also ricotta cheese
cheeseburger soup 131
chicken: apple & honey drumsticks 59
   BBQ chicken 75
   buffalo chicken pasta 72
   butter chicken 100
   chicken & bacon pot 61
   chicken & leek faux pie 76
   chicken & potato curry 109
   chicken, bacon & potato stew 88
   chicken Balti 122
   chicken burritos 36
   chicken casserole 31
   chicken chasseur 84
   chicken enchiladas 41
   chicken fajitas 28
   chicken noodle soup 146
   chicken tikka masala 120
   Chinese chicken curry 111
   corn chicken chilli 68
   jerk chicken 78-9
   Kung Pao chicken 114
   mango chicken curry 103
   orange chicken 98
   spicy chicken curry 125
   spicy honey chicken 108
   sticky chicken 106
   Thai red curry 110
   Thai yellow curry 112

chickpeas: sweet potato curry 158
   vegan chickpea curry 162
chilli: corn chicken chilli 68
   spinach & pumpkin chilli 176
   vegetarian chilli 166
Chinese chicken curry 111
cider: slow-cooked pork & cider hotpot 90
cinnamon baked apples 191
cobbler, mixed berry 192
coconut milk: beef & coconut curry 126
   butter chicken 100
   chicken & potato curry 109
   mango chicken curry 103
   pineapple & duck curry 86-7
   red pepper & sweet potato soup 132
   red tofu & green bean curry 168
   sweet potato curry 158
   Thai red curry 110
   Thai yellow curry 112
   tofu tikka masala 161
   vegan chickpea curry 162
cottage pie, Lily's 92
courgettes (zucchini): butternut squash & courgette casserole 180
   ratatouille 173
   turkey curry 124
cream cheese: buffalo chicken pasta 72

crumbles: apple crumble 187
   maple pear crumble 188
curry: beef & coconut curry 126
   beef & red pepper curry 105
   butter chicken 100
   chicken & potato curry 109
   chicken Balti 122
   chicken tikka masala 120
   Chinese chicken curry 111
   Kung Pao chicken 114
   lamb curry 118
   lamb vindaloo 117
   mango chicken curry 103
   orange chicken 98
   pineapple & duck curry 86-7
   pork loin curry 104
   pork vindaloo 116
   red tofu & green bean curry 168
   spicy chicken curry 125
   spicy honey chicken 108
   sticky chicken 106
   sweet potato curry 158
   Thai red curry 110
   Thai yellow curry 112
   tofu tikka masala 161
   turkey curry 124
   vegan chickpea curry 162
   vegetable curry 160
   vegetable korma 167

INDEX

D
defrosting food 15
duck: pineapple & duck curry 86–7
    shredded hoisin duck 39
dumplings, beef casserole with 32

E
enchiladas, chicken 41
equipment 10

F
fajitas: chicken fajitas 28
    vegetable fajitas 178
freezing food 14

G
gammon: campfire stew 93
    split pea & ham soup 142
goulash, beef 48
grab bags 12, 18–23
green beans: red tofu & green bean curry 168

H
ham: split pea & ham soup 142
hash, potato & cauliflower 171
herby tomato sauce 34
hoisin duck, shredded 39
honey: apple & honey drumsticks 59
    spicy honey chicken 108
hotpots: lamb hotpot 94
    slow-cooked pork & cider hotpot 90

I
Italian vegetable soup 141

J
jam: blueberry jam 184
    strawberry jam 185
jerk chicken 78–9

K
korma, vegetable 167
Kung Pao chicken 114

L
lamb: lamb curry 118
    lamb hotpot 94
    lamb vindaloo 117
    shepherd's pie 42
lasagna: lasagna soup 149
    veggie lasagna 170
leeks: chicken & leek faux pie 76
    leek & potato soup 155
Lily's cottage pie 92

M
mango chicken curry 103
maple syrup: maple mustard turkey 82
    maple pear crumble 188
meal plans 24–5
meatballs: meatballs with herby tomato sauce 34
    vegetarian meatballs 179
Mexican beef taco shells 56
Mongolian-style beef 66
mulligatawny soup 144
mushrooms: chicken chasseur 84
    vegetable fajitas 178
    veggie lasagna 170
mustard: maple mustard turkey 82

N
noodles: chicken noodle soup 146

O
oats: caramel apple crispy 190
orange chicken 98

P
pasta: beef ragu 80
    buffalo chicken pasta 72
    Italian vegetable soup 141
    lasagna soup 149
    spaghetti Bolognese 50
    vegan Bolognese 174
    veggie lasagna 170
pears: maple pear crumble 188
peppers: beef & coconut curry 126
    beef & red pepper curry 105
    beef goulash 48
    campfire stew 93

INDEX

chicken Balti 122
chicken burritos 36
chicken fajitas 28
Kung Pao chicken 114
ratatouille 173
red pepper & sweet potato soup 132
sausage & pepper soup 137
smoky pork loins 44-5
split pea & ham soup 142
Thai red curry 110
Thai yellow curry 112
turkey curry 124
vegan chickpea curry 162
vegetable fajitas 178
vegetarian chilli 166
pies: chicken & leek faux pie 76
   Lily's cottage pie 92
   shepherd's pie 42
pineapple & duck curry 86-7
pork: campfire stew 93
   meatballs with herby tomato sauce 34
   pork loin curry 104
   pork shoulder soup 154
   pork vindaloo 116
   pulled pork 70
   slow-cooked pork & cider hotpot 90
   smoky pork loins 44-5
   split pea & ham soup 142
   teriyaki pork loins 52-3
potatoes: beef goulash 48
   cheeseburger soup 131
   chicken & potato curry 109
   chicken, bacon & potato stew 88

lamb hotpot 94
leek & potato soup 155
Lily's cottage pie 92
maple mustard turkey 82
pork shoulder soup 154
potato & cauliflower hash 171
shepherd's pie 42
slow-cooked pork & cider hotpot 90
Spanish beef 62-3
puff pastry: chicken & leek faux pie 76
pulled pork 70
pumpkin: spinach & pumpkin chilli 176

R
ragu, beef 80
ratatouille 173
rice: mulligatawny soup 144
ricotta cheese: veggie lasagna 170
Roy's mince & beans 30

S
salsa: chicken burritos 36
   chicken enchiladas 41
   corn chicken chilli 68
sausages: sausage & pepper soup 137
   sausage stew 46
shepherd's pie 42
shopping lists 18-23
sloppy Joes 55
smoky pork loins 44-5
soups: beef & vegetable soup 150

butternut squash soup 152
cauliflower soup 151
cheese & broccoli soup 138
cheeseburger soup 131
chicken noodle soup 146
Italian vegetable soup 141
lasagna soup 149
leek & potato soup 155
mulligatawny soup 144
pork shoulder soup 154
red pepper & sweet potato soup 132
rich tomato soup 136
sausage & pepper soup 137
split pea & ham soup 142
taco soup 134
spaghetti Bolognese 50
Spanish beef 62-3
spicy beef 69
spicy chicken curry 125
spicy honey chicken 108
spicy shredded beef 58
spinach & pumpkin chilli 176
split pea & ham soup 142
squash: butternut squash & courgette casserole 180
   butternut squash soup 152
   Thai yellow curry 112
stews see casseroles and stews
sticky chicken 106
strawberry jam 185
sultanas (golden raisins): cinnamon baked apples 191

INDEX

swede: mulligatawny soup 144
sweet potatoes: red pepper & sweet potato soup 132
   sweet potato curry 158
sweetcorn: corn chicken chilli 68
   Mexican beef taco shells 56
   taco soup 134

T

taco seasoning: taco soup 134
taco shells, Mexican beef 56
tagine, vegetable 164
teriyaki pork loins 52–3
Thai red curry 110
Thai yellow curry 112
tikka masala: chicken tikka masala 120
   tofu tikka masala 161
tofu: red tofu & green bean curry 168
   tofu tikka masala 161
tomatoes: campfire stew 93
   chicken Balti 122
   herby tomato sauce 34
   Italian vegetable soup 141
   lamb vindaloo 117
   lasagna soup 149
   ratatouille 173
   rich tomato soup 136
   spaghetti Bolognese 50
   Spanish beef 62–3
   spinach & pumpkin chilli 176
   taco soup 134
   turkey curry 124
   vegan Bolognese 174
   vegetable fajitas 178
   vegetarian chilli 166
   vegetarian meatballs 179
   veggie lasagna 170
tortilla wraps: chicken burritos 36
   chicken enchiladas 41
   chicken fajitas 28
   vegetable fajitas 178
turkey: maple mustard turkey 82
   turkey curry 124
turnips: mulligatawny soup 144

V

vegetables: beef & vegetable soup 150
   Italian vegetable soup 141
   vegetable curry 160
   vegetable fajitas 178
   vegetable korma 167
   vegetable tagine 164
   veggie lasagna 170
vindaloo: lamb vindaloo 117
   pork vindaloo 116

W

walnut apples 186

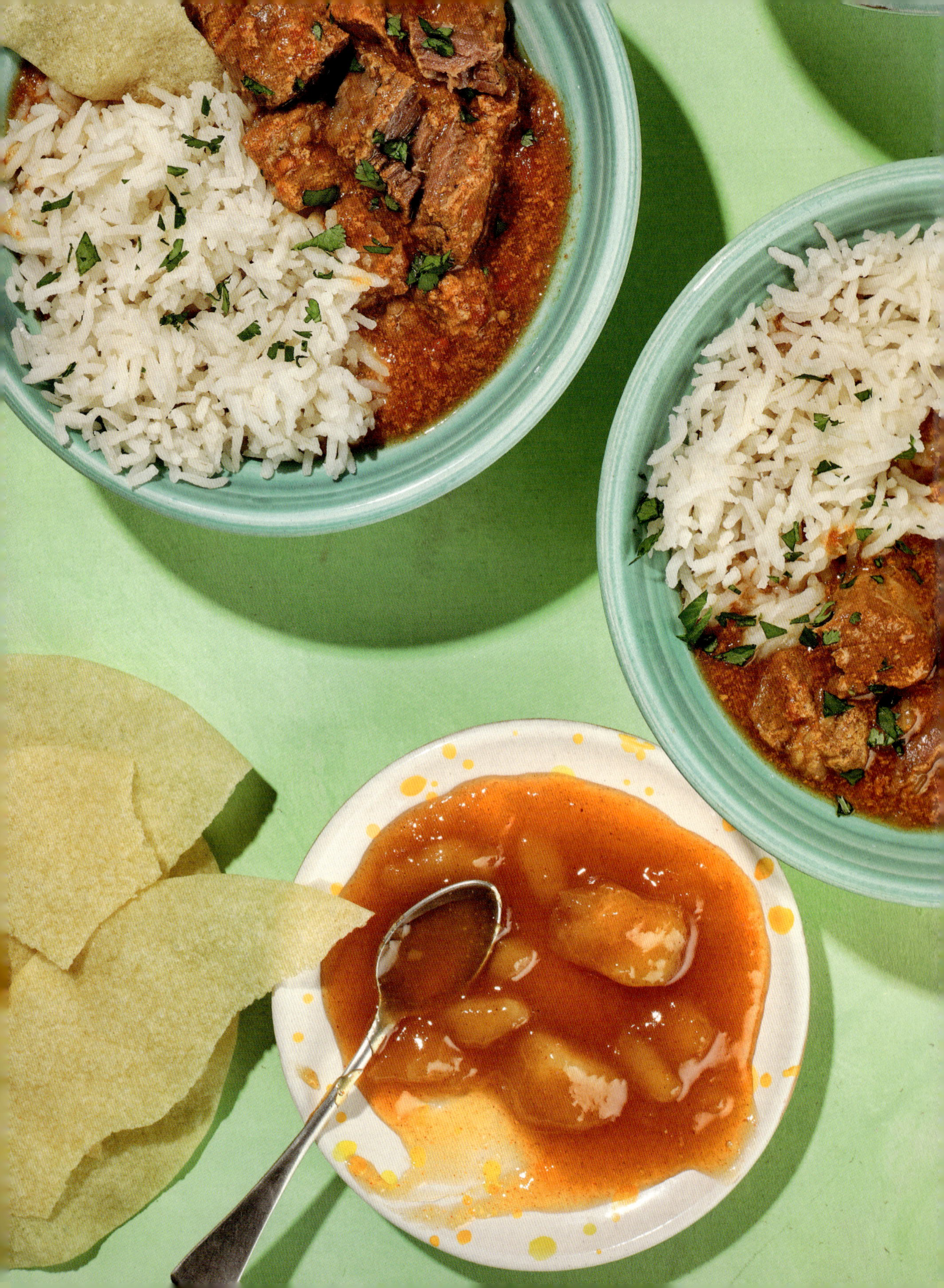

Supplier Information

SLOW COOKERS

Lakeland
www.lakeland.co.uk

Currys
www.currys.co.uk

Donaghy Bros
www.donaghybros.co.uk

Asda
www.asda.com

Tesco
www.tesco.com

Sainsburys
www.sainsburys.co.uk

REUSABLE BAGS

Lakeland
www.lakeland.co.uk

NomNom Kids
www.nomnomkids.co.uk

Amazon
www.amazon.co.uk
www.amazon.com

Dunelm
www.dunelm.com

The Range
www.therange.co.uk

GRAB BAG HOLDERS
(Also known as Freezer Bag or Food Storage Holders)

Amazon
www.amazon.co.uk
www.amazon.com

TikTok Shop
www.tiktok.com/shop

Walmart
www.walmart.com

About the Author

Abeygale Burne became fascinated with her slow cooker not long after having the last of her 3 children twelve years ago. She discovered the joy of a quick prep in the morning and then having a delicious home-cooked, hot meal ready at night, when things would always be a bit hectic.

She started posting slow cooker videos on TikTok in October 2023. The first one went viral, hitting 1.2 million views; from then not only did her love of the slow cooker grow, but so did her following.

Abeygale has amassed well over 350,000 followers on TikTok, and regularly achieves views of over 2 million a week and over 105 million in the last year alone.

Abeygale lives in Ely, Cambridgeshire with her husband David and their 3 children: Jayden, Lily and Sebastian. They are also proud parents to their beloved bulldog, Reginald.

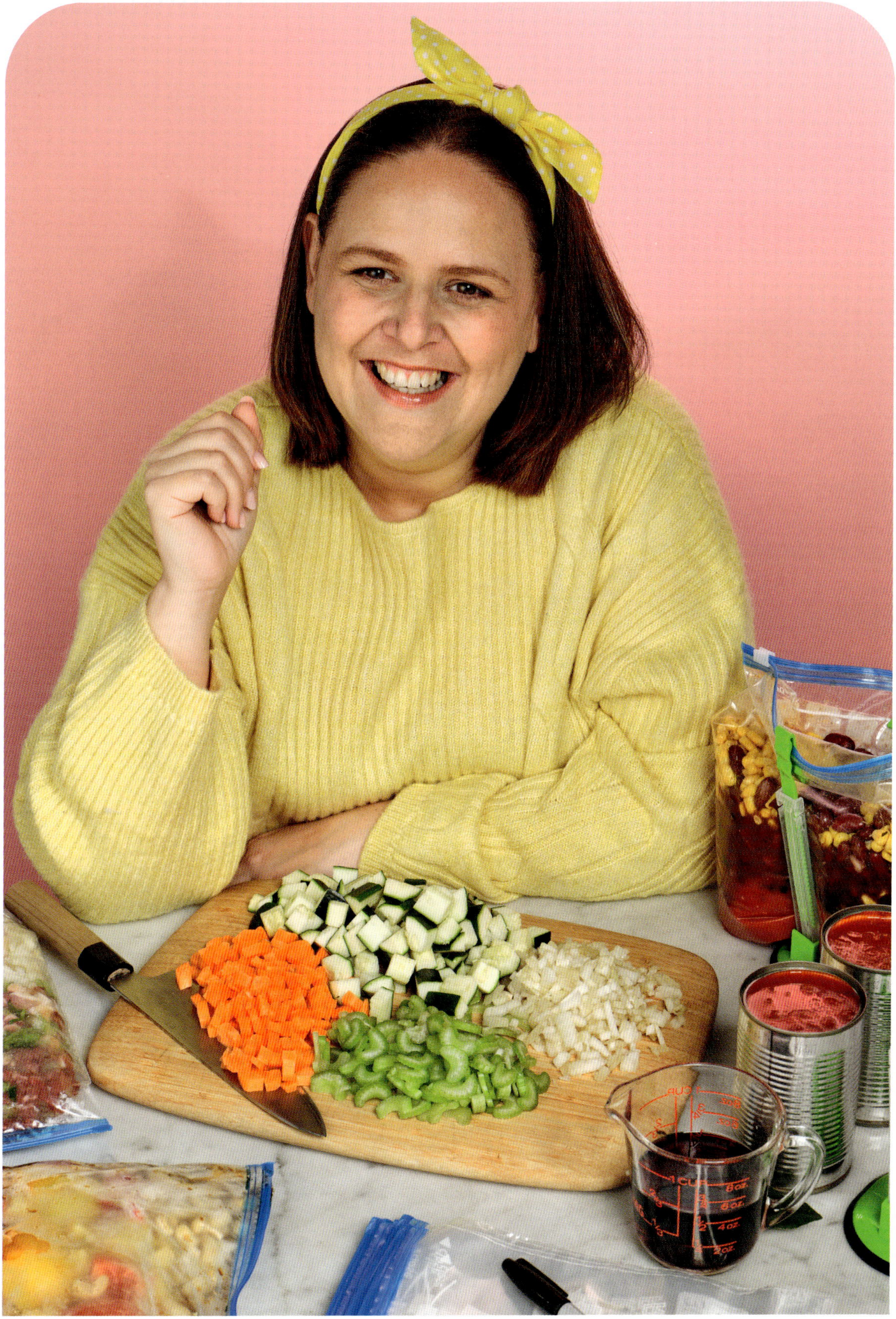

Thank You & Acknowledgements

This book wouldn't of been possible without my fabulous publisher, Jessica Axe at White Lion Publishing.

When Jessica reached out about the possibility of working on a cookbook together, never in a million years did I think the end product would be half as amazing as it is.

I've been encouraged and supported throughout the entire process and trust me it's been a long process! We've been working on this book for over a year and there have been the most inspirational team of ladies behind it, led by Jessica.

Nicky Hill the superstar editor, who just knows everything about everything, Rebecca Woods our copyeditor who again, knows so much and has been such a valuable resource.

The Team at Sidey Studios, led by the remarkable Saskia and Jo, for the quite frankly amazing amount of work in preparing the meals for photography, and the photography itself.
I managed to head to the studio for one of the photography days, with my mum in tow, and we were blown away by the care and time taken to make our book happen.

I say 'our' because this book isn't just mine. Its everyone's that worked on the project, I'm just lucky enough that they asked me to write the recipes.

I want to thank everyone that follows me on TikTok; without you this wouldn't have happened. To everyone that's ever left a nice comment on one of my videos, thank you.

A huge thank you to my mum, Liz and my sister, Adrienne for their unwavering support and patience as I bombarded them with updates, recipes ideas and self-doubt. We are a rock-solid team and that's all because my mum is an absolute powerhouse. She got that from my Grandma Lyn, who would have been this book's biggest cheerleader.

A massive thank you to my kids, Jayden, Lily and Sebastian. They are my chief taste testers and I thank them for trying recipes that didn't make this book… and for being the best kids a mum could ever want.

Finally, thank you to David. Twenty years together and he's supported my dreams and goals since day one. He's worked a normal, proper job all this time so I can pursue the things I love, and I don't think you'd find a better partner.

Quarto

First published in 2025 by White Lion Publishing
an imprint of The Quarto Group.
One Triptych Place, London, SE1 9SH,
United Kingdom
T (0)20 7700 9000
www.Quarto.com

EEA Representation, WTS Tax d.o.o., Žanova ulica 3, 4000 Kranj, Slovenia
www.wts-tax.si

Text © 2025 Abeygale Burne
Photographs © 2025 Jo Sidey
Design © 2025 Quarto Publishing plc

Abeygale Burne has asserted her moral right to be identified as the Author of this Work in accordance with the Copyright Designs and Patents Act 1988.

All rights reserved. No part of this book may be reproduced or utilised in any form or by any means, electronic or mechanical, including photocopying, recording or by any information storage and retrieval system, without permission in writing from White Lion Publishing.

Every effort has been made to trace the copyright holders of material quoted in this book. If application is made in writing to the publisher, any omissions will be included in future editions.

A catalogue record for this book is available from the British Library.

ISBN 978-1-8360-0641-1

Ebook ISBN 978-1-8360-0642-8

10 9 8 7 6 5 4 3 2 1

Design by maru studio G.K.

Publisher: Jessica Axe
Senior Editor: Nicky Hill
Senior Designer: Renata Latipova
Senior Production Controller: Rohana Yusof
Photographer: Jo Sidey
Food Stylist: Saskia Sidey
Photographer's Assistant: Chloe Akers
Food Stylist's Assistant: Caitlin MacDonald
Prop Stylist: Christina Mackenzie

Printed in Guangdong, China TT/Nov/2025

MIX
Paper | Supporting responsible forestry
FSC
www.fsc.org
FSC® C016973